CAST BY MEANS OF FIGURES

C A S T   B Y   M E A N S

Amherst

OF FIGURES

Herman Melville's

Rhetorical Development

BRYAN C. SHORT

The University of Massachusetts Press

Copyright © 1992 by
The University of Massachusetts Press
All rights reserved
Printed in the United States of America
LC 92-8104
ISBN 0-87023-812-4
Designed by David Ford
Printed and bound by Thomson-Shore
Library of Congress Cataloging-in-Publication Data

Short, Bryan Collier, 1942–
    Cast by means of figures : Herman Melville's rhetorical
development / Bryan C. Short.
        p.   cm.
    Includes bibliographical references and index.
    ISBN 0–87023–812–4 (alk. paper)
    1. Melville, Herman. 1819–1891—Technique.   2. Narration
(Rhetoric)   3. Fiction—Technique.   I. Title.
PS2388.T4S46   1992
813'.3—dc20   92–8104
                                                   CIP

British Library Cataloguing in Publication data are available.

For Frances

Contents

Acknowledgments

Like a postmodern text, the debts incurred by this book have no clear boundary. They reach back to my father, the late Dr. Raymond W. Short, and include all those who have helped along the way.

Topgallant thanks go to Harold Bloom for sponsoring and guiding the fellowship which gave this book its initial shape and to Sharon Crowley for tutoring me in the history of rhetoric.

Of those who have read and commented on the manuscript, special mention goes to Edgar Dryden for his insight into Melville's imaginative presence and to James Bartell for flogging my prose toward lucidity. Others whose consultation has been helpful include Richard Brodhead, Bill Burke, James Duban, Lis Møller, Lowry Nelson, Jr., Helle Porsdam, Douglas Robillard, Jan Swearingen, Yoshiko Tomishima, and Donald Yannella.

My colleagues at Northern Arizona University form a community of scholars to whose support and inspiration I am deeply indebted. I am grateful also to Alfred Weber and others at the University of Tübingen, Germany, for sharing ideas during my 1987 stay and to the faculties of the Universities of Copenhagen, Erlangen, Freiburg, Kassel, Marburg, and Munich for the opportunity to present and discuss parts of this book. The faculties of English and Comparative Literature at Yale University have made my time there valuable beyond my ability to judge. My students have kept me alive and honest.

Crucial to my research has been summer support from the Northern Arizona University Organized Research Committee and sabbatical and released time provided by the offices of the Vice President for Academic Affairs, Dean of Arts and Sciences, and English Department Chair. A short-term fellowship at the Newberry Library and a postdoctoral fellowship at Yale University enabled early stages of the project. The staffs of the Newberry, Sterling (Yale), and Cline (NAU) libraries have been continually gracious and helpful, as have Senior Editor Clark Dougan and the staff of the University of Massachusetts Press.

Among those who have offered friendship and kindness along the way, special thanks go to those whose extended or repeated hospitality made the peripatetic life of a researcher possible: Nicole and Eberhard Büser, Claude de Cherisey, Karen Dolby, Bob George, John Herkless, Mary Lou and Bruce Joslyn, Lis Møller and Søren Bruhm, Nancy Paxton, Georgianne Rogers, Agnes Short, Carol and Bob Swendsen, and Gisela and Alfred Weber.

Finally, at the inmost leaf of the bulb, my thanks to Ray and Lisa, who give meaning to it all, and to Frances, to whom this book is dedicated in honor of our twenty-fifth wedding anniversary, for everything.

CAST BY MEANS OF FIGURES

1

Manifest: "Cast by Means of Figures"

For the magic of it lay in the interpretation of dreams, and their application to the foreseeing of future events; so that all preparatory measures might be taken beforehand; which would be exceedingly convenient, and satisfactory every way, if true. The problems were to be cast by means of figures, in some perplexed and difficult way, which, however, was facilitated by a set of tables in the end of the pamphlet.
—Melville, *Redburn*

This book addresses two audiences: students of Herman Melville and students of literary and rhetorical theory. To the former it offers a fresh look at the development of Melville's fiction. It begins by assessing the decisive influence which the immensely popular eighteenth-century literary rhetoric of Hugh Blair had on Melville's creative beginnings. It traces his struggle, ultimately successful, to supplant Blair's neoclassicism with a high Romantic rhetoric in line with his emerging itch for "that play of freedom & invention accorded only to the Romancer & poet" (*Letters* 70). It describes, in the fiction after *Moby-Dick,* the growth of a post-Romantic rhetoric conditioned by Melville's strong-minded reaction to the aesthetic underpinnings of his earlier work.[1] In carrying out these tasks, I have employed the accepted tools of critical biography—factual evidence, some of it familiar and some of it less so, sources, letters, and close readings of the fiction—with an eye to producing a description of Melville's development that is not just innovative but compelling from the perspective of traditional humanistic criticism.[2]

The need, in performing the tasks outlined above, for an elaborate theoretical framework derives from Melville's own cast of mind. His aesthetic, insofar as he thinks about it—and he thinks about it all the time—combines high self-consciousness with breathtaking rhetorical sensitivity and a passion for dialectical oppositions and departures. In uncovering the keys to Melville's development, the present study describes a creative process that reacts incessantly, consciously, and dramatically to its own rhetoric, to its sense of the capacity, limits, and patterns of its literary techniques. To complicate matters further, Melville has a photographic memory for his aesthetic experiments. Nothing tried is lost. Images, figures, strategies, tonalities, and structural principles get carried along, revised, commented on, combined, turned upside-down, elabo-

3

rated, and reapplied in a process which often leaves them clotted with multiple layers of rhetorical significance. Melville describes his process of growth, in an 1849 letter to Evert Duyckinck, in fitting terms.

> Would that a man could do something & then say—It is finished.—not that one thing only, but all others—that he has reached his uttermost, & can never exceed it. But live & push—tho' we put one leg forward ten miles—its no reason the other must lag behind—no, *that* must again distance the other—& so we go till we get the cramp & die. (*Letters* 83)

The gathering rhetorical complexity, responsible for Melville's sense in 1851 of having exhausted conventional literary techniques and reached "the inmost leaf of the bulb" (*Letters* 130), drives him not into silence but on to bolder departures. On the one hand, like Tommo in *Typee,* he abhors "a right-about retrograde movement—a systematic going over of the already trodden ground" (*T* 54), and on the other hand, he remains obsessively in touch with the accumulating burden of his creative past.[3] Because of his tolerance for multiplicity, his self-consciousness, and his combined rhetorical and dialectical thinking, Melville's development cannot be accurately described in conventional terms. Yet, to the extent that I rely on theory, my analysis mirrors Melville's own theoretical reflections; and to the extent that I mix classical, neoclassic, Romantic, and postmodern rhetorical terms in my descriptive vocabulary, Melville's eclecticism keeps pace. His works reveal him to be a master of the rhetorical tradition, conceptually and in practice, and show him to have derived for himself a theoretical framework that literary criticism has only recently become capable of appreciating.

Both the complexities and the dialectical movements of Melville's work stem from an approach to literary creativity which is more rhetorical than philosophical.[4] Melville's writings reveal everywhere an abiding love of words, their forms and combinations, functions and inner workings, persuasiveness and authority. He is fascinated by the power of discourse, including its ability to shape and actualize the identity of its author. In rejecting his early role as a "man who lived among the cannibals" (*Letters* 130) in order to construe himself as a true artist, he embraces a sense of self whose authority depends on language.[5] As Charles Feidelson asserts, "From first to last, he presents himself as an artist, and a conscious artist. It is in this character that he seizes our attention" (163).

Both because and in spite of his commitment to conscious literary artistry, Melville comes to realize that words imprison what they manifest and that they cannot be trusted to represent life straightforwardly. As a result, his art shows an increasing involvement with figurative language as a determinant not simply of style but of underlying structural and representational strategies as well. His personal identification with the authority—persuasiveness—of extraliteral language becomes so profound that the quest for the figurative underpinnings of literary authority becomes for him the "great art of telling the truth" which he announces in his 1850 essay "Hawthorne and His Mosses." Melville's metaphysics may answer to Hawthorne's 1856 assertion that "he can neither believe, nor be comfortable in his unbelief" (Leyda, *Log* II, 529), but exactly the opposite view characterizes his rhetoric: he develops such unshakable faith in his voice, in the authority of his literary language, that his art bobs to the surface, like Queequeg's coffin, in one bold experiment after another, even when his surrounding life seems cloaked in depression.[6]

The rhetorical nature of Melville's aesthetic renders his development fundamentally independent of external events. The progress of his work is characterized by dramatic and abrupt technical departures which cannot persuasively be attributed to social or psychological influences. To understand his growth is to understand the internal dialectic of his writings. This dialectic takes into account such events as his reading of Emerson and his friendship with Hawthorne and with the German scholar George Adler, but it is never driven by them. Melville's voice follows paths which have only a tenuous relation to his nonliterary life. How his investment in literary rhetoric sustains and renews his creativity in the teeth of both physical and metaphysical woes is the central question which this study seeks to answer. Because critical biography traditionally accepts the influence of life on art, and because it traditionally sees the latter in thematic or formal rather than rhetorical terms, the task of describing the development of an art immune to external events and yet alive to shifts in authorial perspective requires a carefully elaborated theoretical framework.

From the beginning, in a manner in tune with both his rhetorical education and his cast of mind, Melville invests his literary authority in the power of tropes.[7] I show in my first chapter that the rhetoric with which Melville grew up recognizes tropes as figurative stylistic devices that go beyond artifice to reflect the inherent organizational logic of discourse. As Melville's art becomes more Romantic, the impact of tropes on both style and structure gives them increasing power over the voice—and thus the creative selfhood, subjectivity, or intentionality—of the author. Melville's thinking about basic issues of truth and creativity turns more and more from the philosophical to the tropological; he solves successive crises of artistic faith not by avowing new concepts but instead by putting into play new tropes. As particular tropes gain global influence within works or groups of works, they reveal their limitations as sources of rhetorical persuasiveness and thus as strategies for the ordering of experience. Melville is always painfully aware of his shortcomings—of the problems which his works bypass and the satisfactions which they fail to tender. As he becomes familiar with particular sets of rhetorical strategies, he becomes impatient with them and begins to seek alternatives.

Typically, Melville's growing impatience reveals itself in his putting key tropes under increased pressure: he exaggerates them and applies them more and more broadly until they crack under the strain, at which point he abandons them precipitously for new strategies that have been coalescing, in dialectical opposition, at the edges of his work. His new rhetorical strategies tend to emerge first in the tantalizing digressions, asides, subplots, minor themes, and seemingly gratuitous descriptive passages for which he is famous. Melville is capable of launching a dramatic new tropological program in the middle of a novel and then pursuing its implications with the zeal of Captain Ahab. Such departures strain the coherence of *Mardi, Moby-Dick,* and *Pierre,* even though they produce rushes of literary energy which both further his development and produce memorable fictional worlds.

Cast by Means of Figures carefully follows Melville's art through the dialectical leaps which it takes and the tropological environments which it evolves from its beginnings up to 1857, the year when he abandons prose entirely. In clarifying the forward movement of his work, I have turned attention away from the often brilliant ways in which he holds his books together against the tide of rhetorical change—his modes of closure and resolution; I have sought out and concentrated on the places where rhetorical crisis and innovation come to the fore. Thus, *Omoo, White-Jacket,* and Melville's magazine fiction receive briefer coverage than the other novels, and except for a brief "Pisgah view" of *Billy Budd,* the study ends with *The Confidence-Man.* Melville's second and fifth novels, for all their intrinsic interest, are simpler and more straightforward than the great, rhetorically conflicted works to which they point—*Mardi* and *Moby-Dick.* The rhetoric of the short fiction is less experimental than that of his longer works; and after 1857 Melville's turn to verse introduces a developmental logic complicated by poetic as well as rhetorical forms.

In highlighting the tropological departures which drive Melville's aesthetic forward, I place the story of his development above those of his various works. In this respect, I ally myself with a position taken by Paul Brodtkorb, Jr., in *Ishmael's White World:* "We are positing a second fictional narrator called 'Melville' whom we do not need unless, in good faith, we have tried and failed to account for the apparently Melvillean voice in terms of 'Ishmael'" (8). *Cast by Means of Figures* posits a narrative voice which we, in good faith, "need" because it shows significantly different qualities when viewed developmentally than it does in the compass of any of the novels alone. The study seconds Warner Berthoff's experience of encountering this "larger" Melville: particular works "come to seem to a degree incidental. We grow aware of something further, of a continuous imaginative presence and energy sustaining these particulars and positively generating them, of a distinct and original signature suggestive of some whole new apprehension, and corresponding organization, of things" (5).

The perspectives of Brodtkorb and Berthoff touch on a key question of literary biography: does the "continuous imaginative presence" represented justify itself "in good faith" by providing a better illumination of an author's works, or does it tell a tale that transcends the boundaries of the works? In the case of a rhetorical study like the present one, the question is complicated by the fact that the salient evidence is intrinsic to the works themselves. In the context of the present study, asking the question of biography is tantamount to asking what is meant by Melville's "development"—that is, what special aesthetic insights a chronological, intertextual study can claim to offer. In a broader theoretical context, asking such a question seems to me to be tantamount to asking the question of the author, made famous by Michel Foucault under the rubric of the "author-function." Foucault asks us to consider just what we gain or lose in placing a text or set of texts in the "possession" of an author, given that various schools of modern criticism view the author as a myth which is irrelevant to the value of a work for its readers.

To outline a theoretical answer to the question of what is gained by studying Melville's rhetorical development instead of simply studying the rhetoric of his works, I will begin with a brief revisit to Foucault's well-known formulation. I intend to argue that the author is still a viable notion, even in the "postmodern condition"; that from a rhetorical perspective the difference between an author and an author-function—between the author *of* a work and the author *in* a work (Brodtkorb's "second fictional narrator")—ceases to be troubling; that consideration of large-scale (intertextual) patterns of authorial development yields an otherwise unavailable wisdom; that the insights which a developmental perspective provides prove essential to an understanding of the exemplary literary power of Melville's works. To read a great experimental literature without an appropriately sophisticated notion of its author is like listening to a symphony with one ear: the fact that it is possible does not excuse cutting off an ear. In the act of illuminating Melville, *Cast by Means of Figures* also exemplifies a solution to the problematic status which critical biography enjoys in a new-critical, archetypal, structuralist, poststructuralist, or new-historicist environment—an environment in which an author's development lacks theoretical rationale.

At this point the present study turns to its second audience—students more interested in an example of applied literary and rhetorical theory than in a careful description of Melville's development. I hope, of course, that the two audiences come together in a joint-stock company liberally rewarded by the intellectual and artistic genius of Melville's rhetoric. It would be conventional to assume that this will happen, but the difficulty of the task justifies not blithely doing so: Melville is such a complex and well-studied author that it is impossible to argue for a radical rereading of his works and creative process without carefully marshaling a considerable amount of detail; the theoretical issues underlying "rhetorical biography," however, are themselves significant and technical. Each aspect of the enterprise validates the other, but each also has its own validity. Melvilleans will find plenty of interest in *Cast by Means of Figures,* even if they reject its rhetorical approach; students of theory will find plenty of interest in its tropology, even if unfamiliar with nineteenth-century American literature.

The unwillingness of the present study to gloss over the difficulty of integrating its two audiences relates to a weakness in the contemporary practice of theoretical criticism. Too often promising approaches are put forth either without application or in conjunction with essays that treat selected major works in isolation from accumulated scholarship concerning the authors of those works. Too often studies of individual authors include theoretical introductions which, however stimulating, do little more than rethematize the results of traditional analytical methods. As a result, the impact on practical criticism of poststructuralist theory, for all its radical pretensions, has often been superficial. It is against this background that the goal of *Cast by Means of Figures*—to describe Herman Melville's development in a way which dovetails literary biography with rhetorical theory—seems to warrant an extra measure of self-consciousness in its address to its double audience.[8]

The idea of the author is important even in textually oriented theories because its functions impinge in contexts where no "real" or known author exists: our belief that a text has an author, even if anonymous, limits the ways in which we look at or interpret it. Michel Foucault, as mentioned before, has defined the question of the author in modern criticism by postulating an author-function, which, he asserts, "results from a complex operation whose purpose is to construct the rational entity we call an author" (127). The author-function has much to do with how we authenticate, evaluate, interpret, and respond to all sorts of texts—religious, scientific, and legal as well as literary. To talk of a work in terms of its author has less to do with pinning down the facts of its historical and psychological circumstances (authors, after all, are also subject to conflicting interpretations) than it has to do with subjecting the use we make of the work and the way we analyze it to socially determined rules. These rules can as easily hinder as promote understanding of a text's full range of ideas, effects, and implications.[9]

In a critical biography, the author-function imposes two principles on the reading of works of literature: chronology and development. A critical biography asks that one read the works of an author as related to each other to define a "continuous imaginative presence" which changes over time. A problem arises, however, in the way what is contained within the works is related to what is thought to go on outside them in the author's "life." From a retrospective critical point of view, an author's life is simply a different set of texts—letters, journals, accounts of events, records—from his or her literary creations. Traditional critical biography asks that these texts be read differently from the texts that are judged to be "works." This distinction, sensible as it is, institutionalizes arbitrary judgments as to what is important and what is not. In Melville's case, letters contain important aesthetic or fictional formulations, and sometimes their rhetoric is as highly and consciously literary as his fictional narratives; secondhand accounts, such as those of Hawthorne and of Melville's wife, Elizabeth, make interpretive pronouncements that have become generally accepted as significant; the works themselves contain much that is thought to be autobiographical. From a rhetorical (as well as a common-sense) perspective, the distinction between what is art and what is not dissolves into a set of critical conventions.[10]

A second problem with critical biography comes in the way authorial development is plotted. Because of the powerful mandate to dovetail the development of an author's life with that of the author's works in some meaningful way, the works are generally subjected to a pattern of evolution which makes sense in external terms. Conventionally accepted life patterns—growth and decline, the crisis produced by trauma or success, the repeated or catastrophic return of the repressed—get imposed on the careers of artists. Such patterns have replaced classical fate and Christian wheel of fortune in determining the underlying plot of much modern biography. Even where they are sedulously avoided, underlying rules for the relation of intrinsic to extrinsic data limit alternative chronological and causal patterns.

The present study, in describing Melville's rhetorical development, both changes the rules and expands the horizons of critical biography without subverting the basic chronological wisdom of the genre. As a rhetorical biography, it analyzes tropological structures which cut across the boundary between Melville's works and the documents of his life. Events like his discovery of his literary talent, political engagements, reading, friendships, familial relationships, and career moves, as documented by letters, journals, public rhetoric, and the accounts of others, play and jostle often on equal footing with formulations inhabiting his fictional prose. The study depends far more heavily on works than on life because of the more numerous and telling instances of rhetorical experimentation and departure that the former provide.

Perhaps more important than permitting greater flexibility in the handling of documents, rhetorical biography permits Melville's development to be seen as a dialectical process. Because people, no matter how much they employ dialectical thought, by and large do not live demonstrably dialectical lives, instances of dialectical biography are rare. Even where a life is as highly conflicted as Melville's has been seen to be by such critics as Lawrence Thompson, William B. Stein, Michael Paul Rogin, and others, the movements of departure and synthesis are not rigorously traced. I do not mean to assert that all art and all artists progress dialectically, but Melville's clearly dialectical development may be one of many chronological patterns to which the conventions of biography blind us.[11] Rhetoric can play a powerfully revisionary role in freeing critical biography from conceptually limiting life-art analogies.[12]

The dialectical and tropological rhetoric of *Cast by Means of Figures,* as the Coda at the end of the volume explains, invokes the poetic theory of Harold Bloom, albeit drastically altered and in key ways contradicted. Once Melville begins to see himself as a novelist and trust in the power of his literary rhetoric, he goes to war with an intellectual past dominated by the rhetoric of Hugh Blair. From then on, although he appropriates and engages the writing of Hawthorne, Emerson, and many others, he continues in intimate, contentious transaction with himself. That ongoing transaction, dialectically structured and tropologically manifested, constitutes the "continuous imaginative presence and energy" which we sense behind his works. Rhetorically speaking, that transaction constitutes his voice. Everything of philosophical and experiential significance which bears on Melville's growth ultimately gets cast by means of the "perplexed and difficult" figures underlying the persuasive power and flexibility of his literary voice. For Melville the author, to say is to be, and to change one's form of saying is to be alive, to have a future. Any biography of Melville which attempts to understand the movements of his art will end by being a biography of his voice.

Melville's rhetoric forces us beyond the philosophical and experiential content of his works in order to gain an understanding of his extraordinarily commanding, flexible, and complex voice. Classical rhetoric would term the voice of Melville's works—his underlying "imaginative presence"—their *ethos.*[13] Ethos is the self-presentation of the rhetor in a discourse, singled out by Aristotle's *Rhetoric* as "the most potent of all the means to persuasion" (9). What one gains by studying the interrelations among and rhetorical development of a set of texts by a single author is a picture of their unifying ethos. Ethos, in turn, underlies *ethical* arguments. The ethos of a discourse calls up the human presence of the author as authority, as someone worthy of attention. Ethos, as James S. and Tita French Baumlin demonstrate, assumes a sharing of values and a healing transaction between rhetor and audience. In strictly defined rhetorical terms, what I have been calling rhetorical biography is really ethical biography, the "life-writing" of a vocal presence, or ethos, in transaction with its world.

Melville's ethos, if we accept its impatience and its tolerance for complexity, involves us as few others do in the ethics of linguistic creativity—the drama of a voice self-consciously plumbing the depths of its own stunning authority and frustrating limitations, a voice constantly stretching itself in order to convey both aspects of literary creativity more truthfully and to brighten the light that they cast on a wide range of human concerns. This is the signal gift which Melville's development gives to us. Whether that gift comes from Melville as author or from Melville as author-function is undecidable from an ethical standpoint, since his voice, his rhetoric, remains the same in either case.

Cast by Means of Figures, then, describes the ethos of Melville's work as it changes to reflect dialectical shifts in its tropological structure. From a traditional biographical perspective, the maturing ethos of Melville's work reflects his uniquely penetrating and courageous aesthetic consciousness. From a theoretical perspective, it exemplifies the way in which an author-function can be defined, and its operation described, in tropological terms. From a rhetorical standpoint, both perspectives lead to the same ethical results, since each posits the same authority; the difference between them is itself theoretical rather than practical. If, as I have argued elsewhere, rhetoric and literary criticism are sister arts, then the unseemly balance of audiences which the present study maintains should not be theoretically troubling.[14] Melville's example brings them together.

The final trust of the present study, then, is that a rhetorical criticism that acknowledges its roots in the analysis of persuasive discourse has a place among both traditional and postmodern perspectives. Whether one imagines oneself uncovering the real mind of a real writer or merely the free play of ideological and textual patterns, one serves the authority, the ethics, of literature. This trust gives the present study some of the color of phenomenological criticism as practiced by Gaston Bachelard, Georges Poulet, some of Roland Barthes, Paul de Man, and J. Hillis Miller, but that color ultimately derives from Melville's (and other nineteenth-century writers like him) understanding of literary rhetoric as a theater within which life's deepest processes can act out their stirring dramas of conflict and discovery.

2

"Dumb and deaf": Melville's Youth

She was dumb! Great God, she was dumb! DUMB AND DEAF!
—Melville, "Fragments from a Writing Desk"

Speech is the great instrument by which man becomes beneficial to man:
and it is to the intercourse and transmission of thought, by means of
speech, that we are chiefly indebted for the improvement of thought itself.
—Hugh Blair, *Lectures on Rhetoric and Belles Lettres*

"The material world," continued Dupin, "abounds with very strict
analogies to the immaterial; and thus some color of truth has been given
to the rhetorical dogma, that metaphor, or simile, may be made to
strengthen an argument, as well as to embellish a description."
—Edgar Allan Poe, "The Purloined Letter"

The rhetorical theory of his time, specifically that of the immensely popular eighteenth-century Scottish professor and cleric Hugh Blair,
shaped Melville's formative experience of literary composition.[1] More than any
other single influence, it defined the aesthetic to which he turned, and against
which he struggled, when he set pen to paper in 1844 to begin work on *Typee*.
Blair underlies Melville's views regarding the sources of persuasive authority,
his efforts to achieve a satisfying ethos—a voice or authorial image in which he
could believe—and his understanding of figurative language as a key to "the
improvement of thought itself."

Melville's education, scant and shadowy as it seems, gives ample space to
Blair's rhetoric.[2] Melville attended New York Male High School, starting at the
age of six, from 1825 until 1829. Evidence exists of his presence, along with his
brother Gansevoort's, at Columbia Grammar School in 1829 and possibly into
the spring term of 1830 (Runden 1). After his family left New York, he attended
Albany Academy in 1830–31, Albany Classical School in 1835, and Albany Academy again in 1836–37; he finished his formal education with a course in engi-
neering and surveying at Lansingburgh Academy in 1838–39. Although Melville
seems to have pursued a classical curriculum only during his brief stay at the
Classical School and subsequent two terms at Albany Academy, and thus cannot be credited with a formal rhetorical education, he would still have encountered the work of Blair in numerous contexts.[3]

A direct contact with Blair can be traced to large selections from his published sermons appearing in Melville's copy of Lindley Murray's *English Reader*, used as a textbook at the Albany Academy (Gilman 55, Sealts, *Melville's Reading* 201). Blair's moderate Protestant moralizing and belletristic critical judgments take center stage in Murray's anthology. However, in *White-Jacket*, Melville refers to "Blair's Lectures" as "a fine treatise on rhetoric" (*WJ* 168), and he entitles an anonymous 1847 *Yankee Doodle* satire "A Short Patent Sermon: According to Blair, the Rhetorician" (*PT* 443, 786). Even though Donald Yannella's attribution of the latter piece to Melville cannot be absolutely proven, its title shows Blair's stature to be a commonplace among those for and with whom Melville wrote during the early years of his professional career.

Hugh Blair's spectacularly popular 1783 *Lectures on Rhetoric and Belles Lettres* found fertile soil in the young scholar. A letter from Melville's father to his brother Peter Gansevoort brags that the eight-year-old "proved the best Speaker in the introductory Department" at New York Male High School (Gilman 28). Although family letters slight Herman's intellectual accomplishments compared with those of his older brother, Gansevoort, he spent much of his New York school days mentoring less advanced boys, a dubious blessing of the "Lancastrian" system practiced at the school (Titus 5–6). The duties of mentoring in the subjects which Melville studied, among them grammar, writing, and speaking (*Letters* 4), would have necessitated some familiarity with Blair, at least in the simplified form in which the famous rhetorician's precepts trickled down into the lower levels of nineteenth-century American education.[4]

In 1828, Gansevoort Melville finished the curriculum at New York Male High School and began higher studies. When the family moved to Albany, he was placed in a classical and Herman in a preparatory curriculum, circumstances appropriate to their four-year age difference. Melville's relationship with his brother, who preceded him into the formal debates organized by the Albany Young Men's Association, arranged both his 1839 voyage to Liverpool and the English publication of *Typee*, and enjoyed considerable success as a political orator in the mid-1840s (Rogin 52ff.), again bespeaks a rhetorical education beyond the selections in Murray's reader. By the time Herman transferred his interest from the debating group of the Young Men's Association to the Ciceronian Debating Society and then to the Philo Logos Society in 1837, he was confident enough in his rhetoric to carry the squabbles of the latter organization into the pages of the *Albany Microscope*. These fulsome exercises, along with the two "Fragments from a Writing Desk" published in the *Democratic Press and Lansingburgh Advertiser* in May 1839, paint a vivid portrait of a youthful writer flushed with the rhetorical excesses of his day.

In Blair's *Lectures* the students of Melville's generation encountered a text of extraordinary cultural authority. Hugh Blair (1718–1800) had preached from the most prestigious pulpit in Scotland, the High Church at St. Giles, occupied the first Regius Professorship of Rhetoric and Belles Lettres at the University of Edinburgh, helped found the *Edinburgh Review,* edited the works of Shakespeare, supervised publication of the first comprehensive British edition of the English poets, and enjoyed the friendship of David Hume, Adam Smith, Alexander Carlyle, James Boswell, and other famous Enlightenment intellectuals (Golden and Corbett 24–25). His lectures combine the classical theory of Aristotle, Cicero, and Quintilian with principles drawn from Lockean empiricism, associationist psychology, and Scottish common-sense philosophy. They include numerous capsule commentaries on authors from Homer to Addison; they offer cogent advice on many aspects of oral and written discourse, from grammar to eloquence; and they provide crystalline and informed wisdom on such current topics as genius, the sublime, and the history of language. It is hard to imagine a document better suited to the educational aspirations and cultural prejudices of the young American republic.

Hugh Blair's *Lectures,* for all their down-to-earth pedantry, culminates and formalizes a rhetorical revolution which had been brewing since the seventeenth century. Classical rhetoric assumes that the points upon which an argument can rest must be drawn from the existing wisdom of the culture. Aristotle's interest in the rhetorical canon of invention and in the "topics" on which an argument can rest shows his concern for developing methods whereby existing ideas, attitudes, and responses can be canvassed, organized, and analyzed for their suitability to rhetorical applications. Rhetorical argument—enthymeme—for Aristotle closely parallels the dialectic of philosophy. Mind, society, and language work together in the common project of determining the arguments—*logoi*—on which social action can be based. Sharon Crowley concludes that "in a fundamental sense, knowledge did not exist outside of language for classical rhetoricians" (3).

In the scientific and empiricist intellectual climate of the seventeenth and eighteenth centuries, the discipline of formulating *logoi* loses its classical integrity.[5] Logic and rhetoric separate under the pressure of various faculty psychologies. Invention, the formulation of arguments, becomes the province of reason. Discourse becomes a tool for persuasive representation of what reason has produced. Thus Blair asserts:

> Invention, is, without doubt, the most material, and the ground-work of the rest. But, with respect to this, I am afraid it is beyond the power of art to give any real assistance. Art cannot go so far, as to supply a Speaker with arguments on every cause, and every subject; though it may be of considerable use in assisting him to arrange, and express those, which his knowledge of the subject has discovered.

For it is one thing to discover the reasons that are most proper to convince men, and another, to manage these reasons with most advantage. The latter is all that Rhetoric can pretend to. (II, 399)

Rhetoric in Blair and the other British theorists attempted to compensate for the loss of classical invention by embracing an epistemology—what James A. Berlin calls a "noetic field" (2)—drawing from the empiricist and associationist psychology of the day. Rhetoric became located "solidly within the sphere of sensory experience," and "proofs now amounted to imitating the experiential process by which people acquire knowledge" (Crowley 23–24). The rhetor "would be able to tell or write only what she knew from her examination of, and meditation on, the world around her. Thus it was incumbent on her to be observant, to gather sensations and produce ideas, to study, to think" (Crowley 32). "What is truly solid and persuasive," Blair concludes, comes "from a thorough knowledge of the subject, and profound meditation on it" (II, 401).

The fragmentation of the classical unity of knowledge and language in Blair has a side effect of the highest importance to Melville. Seeking to extend the importance of rhetoric beyond the technical study of elocution, which was also becoming increasingly popular at the time, Blair allies rhetoric with the faculty of taste and its development through the activity of criticism. In both precept and example, Blair's is a literary rhetoric aimed more at the appreciation and analysis of literature than the production of oratory. It promotes a model of self-cultivation by which the improvement of taste and the exercise of critical judgment train and enhance supposedly a priori mental functions.

The exercise of taste and of sound criticism, is in truth one of the most improving employments of the understanding. To apply the principles of good sense to composition and discourse; to examine what is beautiful, and why it is so; to employ ourselves in distinguishing accurately between the specious and the solid, between affected and natural ornament, must certainly improve us not a little in the most valuable part of all philosophy, the philosophy of human nature. For such disquisitions are very intimately connected with the knowledge of ourselves. (I, 12)

Blair's rhetoric comprises a theory of reading as much as writing. We know that Gansevoort "took the trouble to write out careful criticisms of whatever he read" (Gilman 72), and that often-expensive forays to bookstore and library accompany the onset of new projects throughout Herman's life. Writing, for Melville as well as for Blair, is always an intertextual venture involving a self-conscious reaction to as well as the generation of discourse. Literary creation reacts back on the thought or experience behind it. If its authority rests on an ability to represent "the experiential process by which people acquire knowledge," reading and writing take center stage in that "process." Like the tattooing which threatens Tommo in *Typee,* the exercise of literary rhetoric becomes "so beautifying an operation" (*T* 219) whose surface markings have the power to shape and change underlying levels of human identity. Incipient in Blair is a model of the reflexive ethos which takes center stage in Melville's works during the late 1840s.

Hugh Blair's treatment of figurative language also determines Melville's practice. Blair speaks incessantly in behalf of a simple style and the cardinal qualities of "perspicuity and precision" (I, 231–57). He goes so far as to assert that "the Sublime is a species of writing which depends less than any other on the artificial embellishments of rhetoric" (I, 72). Yet when he begins his discussion of figurative language, he associates it with key persuasive qualities that get short shrift elsewhere in his lectures: "Figures, in general, may be described to be that Language, which is prompted either by the imagination, or by the passions" (I, 346). Furthermore, like the Romantic theory which follows him, Blair gives figuration the job of making up for the "barrenness" of languages for which, in their primitive state, vocabulary lags behind experience (I, 354). This latter power anticipates the twentieth-century phenomenology of Paul Ricoeur, which asserts that metaphor "brings an unknown referential field toward language" (*Rule* 299). Through figures, in the tradition which Melville inhabits, new knowledge crystallizes.

Blair's association of figurative language with the passions and the imagination has a profound impact on Melville when he declares his third book, *Mardi,* to be "a *real* romance" characterized by "that play of freedom & invention accorded only to the Romancer & poet" (*Letters* 70). To stir the passions and imagination of the audience, he writes a more figured prose. Melville's belief in the powers of literary rhetoric, as manifested in numerous passages from the letters of the late 1840s, directly reflects a set of ideas which Blair summarizes in what for him is an uncharacteristically purple passage.

> What I have now explained, concerning the use and effects of Figures, naturally leads us to reflect on the wonderful power of Language; and, indeed, we cannot reflect on it without the highest admiration. What a fine vehicle is it now become for all the conceptions of the human mind; even for the most subtile and delicate workings of the imagination! . . . it gives colouring and relievo [*sic*], even to the most abstract conceptions. In the Figures which it uses, it sets mirrors before us, where we may behold objects, a second time, in their likeness. It entertains us, as with a succession of the most splendid pictures; disposes, in the most artificial manner, of the light and shade, for viewing every thing to the best advantage; in fine, from being a rude and imperfect interpreter of men's wants and necessities, it has now passed into an instrument of the most delicate and refined luxury. (I, 364–65)

In spite of his neoclassic predilection for stylistic clarity, Blair associates figures intimately with representation, with the ability of language to mirror reality. The act of "mirroring," however, gives "objects" the tincture and chiaroscuro favored by the refined and even luxurious sensibility which persuasive writing addresses. Tropes, it seems, reach both outward and inward in characterizing language which achieves a successful (i.e. persuasive) transaction between mind and world. It is not surprising, then, that Melville later turns to them when he begins to explore and expand the limits of a self-consciousness embracing both the "likeness" of the world and the "delicate workings of the imagination."

Even the specific technical terms of Blair's discussion of figurative language lead directly into Melville's practice. Blair, in good associationist form, states that all tropes "are founded on the relation which one object bears to another; in virtue of which, the name of the one can be substituted instead of the name of the other" (I, 367). In listing the types of relations on which figuration depends, Blair distributes them among the four tropes of metonymy (cause and effect, container and contained, sign and thing signified), metalepsis (antecedent and consequent), synecdoche (whole and part), and metaphor (similitude and resemblance) (367–71). The first two lectures which follow Blair's introduction to figurative language cover metaphor and allegory (lecture 15) and hyperbole, personification, and apostrophe (lecture 16). Thus, the tropes central to Melville's first three novels all appear in the first volume of the 1785 (2d corrected) edition of Blair.[6] Whether Melville in the 1840s wrote with this work in hand or consciously in mind, or simply responded to a combination of memory and literary atmosphere (as evidenced by Dupin's Blair-like "rhetorical dogma" in Poe's 1844 tale "The Purloined Letter") cannot be absolutely decided; the similarity between Blair's discussion of tropes and Melville's employment of them remains striking in either case.

The letters which Melville published in the *Albany Microscope* in 1838— dealing with a quarrel over leadership of the Philo Logos Society—reveal the problems faced by the nineteen-year-old debater in trying to follow Blair's rhetorical program.[7] Blair's insistence on perspicuity—clarity—on the one hand and high literariness on the other produces a painful combination of bluntness and artifice. As if concerned that his points might be missed, Melville belabors and repeats them; in attempting to enhance the vividness of his voice, he lurches from pedantic exposition to petulant metaphor.

> It has not been, I can assure you, without reluctance that I have been drawn into any public disputation with one of your stamp, but a regard for my own reputation impelled me to expose the malevolence of your intentions; my only motive

being then removed, I cheerfully bid a long good night to any further newspaper controversy with you, and subscribe myself,

> Very respectfully
> Your obedient servant
> PHILOLOGEAN.

N.B. Your incoherent ravings may be continued if you choose; they remind me of the croakings of a Vulture when disappointed of its prey. (Gilman 258)

Both the pedantry and the exaggerated tropes of Melville's letters represent his desire to create an authoritative voice through the manipulation of style rather than concept. In line with Blair's rhetoric, Melville's youthful writings are exercises in the embellishment of given material; for all their energy, they are heavily clichéd. It is easy to see why Melville's South Sea adventures and the yarns of his shipmates, in redressing Blair's lack of a theory of invention by giving him a seemingly inexhaustible (especially if augmented by judicious reading) range of compelling topics, and in providing an attractive alternative to Blair's genteel ethos, enabled the start of his literary career. It is also easy to see why he had a difficult time leaving his authoritative—because experienced—nautical persona behind. His early training associates rhetorical persuasiveness with the superficial aspects of voice, with an ethos not generated out of oneself but adapted from existing, socially sanctioned models. Unlikely as it seems, America's great Romantic novelist, in his first published fiction, "Fragments from a Writing Desk, No. 1," avows himself an unabashed acolyte of Lord Chesterfield (*PT* 191).

At the beginning of the fourth *Albany Microscope* Letter, Melville catalogs many of the principles central to Blair.

> Without venturing to criticise the elegance of your composition, the absurd vagaries of your imagination, or impeaching the taste you have displayed in the abundance, variety and novelty of your scopes [tropes] and figures, or calling into question the accuracy of your mode of Latinising English substantive[s], I shall without further delay, proceed to consider the merits of your late most fanciful performance. And I cannot but sincerely deplore the rashness with which you have published a production evidently composed in the heat and turmoil of passion, and which must remain without the sanction of your cooler judgment, and the approval of your otherwise respectable understanding. (Gilman 255)

The passage invokes a panoply of late eighteenth-century conventions: elegance, imagination, taste, the liberal and innovative use of tropes, grammatical accuracy, and passion moderated by judgment for the sake of understanding. Melville has utter command over the theoretical lineaments of Blair's rhetoric. What fails him is a means of breaking the stranglehold which Blair's gentility, without a balancing theory of invention, has on the ethos of persuasive language. In the two "Fragments from a Writing Desk" which Melville publishes in the *Democratic Press, and Lansingburgh Advertiser* the following year, he takes a halting but crucial step toward freedom. For his later career, that step is, like the sea to Ishmael, not without meaning.

Melville's "Fragments from a Writing Desk" are saved from banality by their eroticism. Although he marshals all of the descriptive conventions of Blair's rhetoric in order to keep their erotic focus under the thumb of a decorous, rhetorical ethos, he fails. The sublimated sexual energy of the passages overflows the boundaries of neoclassic taste in a riot of visual images and figures which directly prefigures scenes in *Typee* of Fayaway bathing, sailing, and smoking and Kory-Kory striking a light, Isabel's guitar music in *Pierre,* and a host of other instances and passages throughout Melville's works. Since the "Fragments from a Writing Desk" still adhere to Blair's strictures, the effect of their transgressive zeal is absurd, bemusing, and ultimately distressing, but it sets the stage for the first of Melville's dialectical rhetorical departures.

The first fragment begins with a Chesterfieldian celebration of self-confidence, supposedly written in a letter by a Lansingburgh blade to his former mentor. After describing the favor which his savoir faire and demeanor gain with the ladies of the town, the narrator launches into a celebration of their beauties, which occupies most of the piece. What begins as an act of fictional *ethopoeia,* or self-fashioning, turns into an updated exercise in the blazon, conventional Elizabethan catalog of feminine physical charms. Melville's rhetoric exaggerates Blair's imaginative and passionate use of tropes to the point of absurdity, and the result is a rush of hyperbolic good humor which takes over and transforms the narrator's voice.

> And then her eyes! they open their dark, rich orbs upon you like the full noon of heaven, and blaze into your very soul the fires of day! Like the offerings laid upon the sacrificial altars of the Hebrew, when in an instant the divine spark falling from the propitiated God kindled them in flames; so, a single glance from that oriental eye as quickly fires your soul, and leaves your bosom in a perfect conflagration! Odds Cupids and Darts! with one broad sweep of vision in a crowded ball-room, that splendid creature would lay around her like the two-handed sword of Minotti, hearts on hearts, piled round in semicircles! (*PT* 195)

When Melville begins to have fun with the sheer, outrageous figurative texture of his description, his later voice—the voice which begins *Typee* by enthusiastically describing all the foods the ship's crew lacks—breaks through. His exuberance becomes funny, and he discovers what will remain one of his most characteristic rhetorical modes—a high-spirited inner apostrophe or self-directed expostulation, a kind of antic soliloquy which lays to waste argumentative or narrative decorum and yet which permits Brodtkorb's "second fictional narrator" to bloom. In the second fragment, the narrator finds himself outdistanced by his mysterious "conductress."

> This last failure was too much. I stopped short, and stamping the ground in ungovernable rage, gave vent to my chagrin in a volley of exclamations: in which perhaps, if narrowly inspected, might have been detected two or three expressions which savored somewhat of the jolly days of the jolly cavaliers. But if a man was ever excusable for swearing; surely, the circumstances of the case were palliative of the crime. What! to be thwarted by a woman? Peradventure, baffled by a girl? Confusion! It was too bad! To be outgeneraled, routed, defeated, by a mere rib of the earth? It was not to be borne! I thought I should never survive the inexpressible mortification of the moment; and in the heighth of my despair, I bethought me of putting a romantic end to my existence upon the very spot which had witnessed my discomfiture. (*PT* 198–99)

Melville's narrator decides not to commit suicide, lacking any "means of accomplishing my heroic purpose, except the vulgar and inelegant one, of braining myself against the stone wall which traversed the road." The moment passes, and the fragment resumes its arabesque adventure.

Melville drives his second fragment forward without resolving its conflict between outer erotic mystery and inner burlesque. Its high-spirited incongruity of voice and energetic enjoyment of language overshadow its incessant clichés; like the novels of Charles Brockden Brown or Poe's tales of the grotesque, it transcends its own preposterousness and keeps the reader's curiosity piqued. Because the fragmented decorum of the sketch seems likely to conclude on a note of either Romance or spoof, its strangely shrill ending comes as a surprise. Melville is unsure of what to do with his newfound rhetorical power, and more important, he seems distressed by its transgressive energy. He closes the tale with a sweeping tropological gesture which, perhaps unwittingly, constitutes the first dialectical departure of his rhetoric.[8]

Melville's second fragment establishes an opposition between external and internal, Romantic description and burlesque reflection. The rhetorical problem which it poses is how to get the two together, how to integrate both in an authoritative voice, without destroying the decorum implied by either. Specifically, the problem is that of irony. The self-conscious humor of Melville's "inner voice" threatens to ironize the entire fragment, turn it into parody; irony characterizes an emerging rhetorical ethos marked by both good will and imaginative energy; yet irony has no place in Blair's tropology—it is the one figure important to Melville's beginnings which Blair does not treat directly. If his literary voice is born out of the rhetoric of Blair, it is conceived in irony.

The grotesque conclusion of Melville's second fragment illustrates the violence with which irony penetrates his neoclassic rhetorical armor. Having been mysteriously and picturesquely led by his alluring "conductress" into the sequestered presence of an exotic odalisque, the narrator finds himself overcome by a transport of mad and passionate love. He cries out for a response, for verbal proof that the ardent looks of the "sweet Divinity" betoken her like passion for him. At that moment, the truth of her physical condition floods in on his consciousness, and the parodic irony of his inner voice gives way to horrified recoil against the very eroticism which has given the tale its life.

> I cried "Speak! Tell me, thou cruel! Does thy heart send forth vital fluid like my own? Am I loved,—even wildly, madly as I love?" She was silent; gracious God! what horrible apprehension crossed my soul?—Frantic with the thought, I held her from me, and looking in her face, I met the same impassioned gaze; her lips moved—my senses ached with the intensity with which I listened,—all was still,— they uttered no sound; I flung her from me, even though she clung to my vesture, and with a wild cry of agony I burst from the apartment!—She was dumb! Great God, she was dumb! DUMB AND DEAF! (*PT* 204)

The end of the fragment, in its hyperbolic insistence on the horror of speechlessness, tropes the entire rhetorical situation of the sketch. Without verbal communication, inner and outer worlds, sensation and consciousness, cannot meet, and without such a meeting, eroticism is thwarted. Melville seems to be extending Blair's proposition that "speech is the great instrument by which man becomes beneficial to man" into the arena of Romanticized sexuality. What worse can be imagined, the fragment asks, than a default of language? Without consummated linguistic intercourse, allure collapses into revulsion. Melville seems to be troping the failure of his rhetoric to achieve an authoritative or persuasive treatment of the erotic matter to which his imagination is drawn. In this light, his retreat into the linguistically and sexually muted world of nautical adventure makes sense.

Yet in the light of Melville's later triumph as a writer, the intrusive allegorical gesture which ends the fragment also makes sense. Its horror of speechlessness makes it clear that the sketch, its eroticism as well as its irony, exists only and entirely in rhetoric, that what lies at the end of its twisted and Romantic paths is not the promise of sensual gratification but the promise of an imaginative gratification which demands verbal participation. Put another way, the descriptive as well as the burlesque world of the tale proves itself, in the conclusion, to be internal, the stuff of mirrors, colors, lights, and shadows, and the opposition between inner and outer reduces to an opposition between two modes of self-consciousness, each accompanied by its corresponding vocal register. In true dialectical fashion, the ending of Melville's second fragment synthesizes its conflicting rhetorical environments not by compromising them but by leaping to a different plane of awareness. For an instant, literary language, in its radical figurality and dialectical progress, holds sway over the truths of mind and body and glimpses a means of moving toward what Blair's rhetoric asks but cannot offer to the young writer—"the improvement of thought itself" as manifested in a program of rhetorical invention that is not dependent on prior social authority.

3

"The author at the time": *Typee*

There are some things related in the narrative which will be sure to appear strange, or perhaps entirely incomprehensible, to the reader; but they cannot appear more so to him than they did to the author at the time.

—Melville, *Typee*

*W*hen *Herman* Melville drew his pay from the frigate *United States* on October 14, 1844, and returned to Lansingburgh after almost four years at sea, he had little reason to anticipate other than a temporary landward interlude.[1] Only fifteen months had elapsed between the end of his 1839 merchant voyage to Liverpool and his departure for the Pacific on the whaler *Acushnet* in early 1841. That time had been taken up by an uninspiring semester as a schoolteacher and a futile job-hunting trip to Galena, Illinois, where his uncle Thomas Melville struggled to improve on painfully diminished circumstances. The exuberant newspaper letters and fragments of 1838 and 1839 belonged to a past left far behind. Thus, when Melville decided to use his sailor's wages to support himself in the effort of writing up his adventures, he had little to lose. He also had the distance, experience, and self-confidence which he needed to make good the dialectical departure from Hugh Blair's rhetoric hinted at in the ending of his second fragment. *Typee,* written that winter, tells the ensuing tale of Melville's self-discovery as a writer—a tale bound hand in glove with the emergence of a literary voice of breathtaking energy and confidence.[2] Never again will Melville refer to himself, in his letters, as anything but an author; never again will he doubt his ethos.

The rhetoric of *Typee*, as it manifests Melville's self-discovery and concurrent struggle with Blair, explains the contradictions which characterize the novel on the level of theme and narrative perspective. On the one hand, from the moment of its inception to the present, the truthfulness of *Typee* has been subject to intense controversy;[3] on the other hand, it has been accepted as an ethnographically and historically serious account of cross-cultural contact.[4] On the one hand, Tommo represents key aspects of Melville early life;[5] on the other hand, inconsistencies in his point of view suggest his distance from an "irrecoverable" and highly Romanticized past.[6] In searching for the grounds of a persuasive rhetoric, Melville builds *Typee* around the ironic vocal structures which had brought his "Fragments from a Writing Desk" to life. As before, irony challenges Blair's notion that "what is truly solid and persuasive" derives above all from "a thorough knowledge of the subject, and profound meditation on it" (II, 401); through irony, Melville undercuts the idea that his unique nautical experiences constitute his authority. He highlights a network of conflicts in theme, character, point of view, and plot which he then mediates through a dialectic that reinterprets and gives new force to figures—apostrophe, hyperbole, metonymy, metaphor, and metalepsis—prominent in Blair. *Typee* shows Melville half abandoning and half resuscitating the neoclassic rhetorical authority of his youth.

The eclectic rhetoric of *Typee* turns out to be unusually successful because it interrelates form and content in a way which is both persuasive—artistically and intellectually compelling—and creative. The voice of the novel gives Melville freedom from Blair's oppressive gentility and at the same time a high degree of self-conscious control. It allows his sensitivity and thoughtfulness, as well as his verbal enthusiasm, to shine through. It also exemplifies a composing process—a way of thinking about literary creation—which poses new questions as it solves old, inspires exploration of the powers of language, and uses achievement not as a stable source of satisfaction but as an incentive to further dialectical departure.[7]

The rhetorical coherence of *Typee* emerges out of ironic structures, which, first and foremost, color the viewpoint of its narrator, Tommo. Melville characterizes his adventurous persona as "the author at the time," yet "the author at the time" is a trope possible only through hindsight: Tommo is not an "author" "at the time" of his experiences; instead, Melville's rhetoric retrospectively imposes his own authority on the plot and incidents of the tale in order to permit Tommo, who has no clear nonnautical future, to thematize the birth of a postnautical literary identity. This process determines the particular, ironic blend of "unvarnished truth" (xiv) and Romantic fancy in the novel.

The preface of *Typee* documents Melville's inclination, held over from Blair, to attribute the persuasiveness of his text to the unique experiences of his salty past. "Sailors are the only class of men who now-a-days see anything like stirring adventure," it asserts; a tale which has excited the "warmest sympathies of the author's shipmates" can thus "scarcely fail to interest" ordinary readers (xiii). Melville, however, is already moving beyond Blair, and thus beyond his own status as "man who lived among cannibals," toward an authorial identity in line with his later (1848) praise of *Mardi* as a "*real* romance" "unsullied by the dull common places" of his first two novels (*Letters* 70). In leaving behind Blair's theory of rhetorical invention based on "a thorough knowledge of the subject," he tends more and more to trade "the unvarnished truth" (xiv) for what he comes to see as a firmer basis of literary authority, "that play of freedom & invention accorded only to the Romancer & poet." *Typee* holds out the claim of verisimilitude against Melville's rapidly surfacing tendency to deny the rhetorical significance of a past associated in his mind with seamanship rather than authorship. In abandoning the experience of "stirring adventure," he also abandons the genteel decorum of his *Albany Microscope* letters for the free and inventive rhetoric emergent in the "Fragments from a Writing Desk."

The conflict between experience and Romance, adventuresome past and literary present, underlies *Typee*'s basic narrative and thematic oppositions. On the one hand, by braving in a straightforward manner the perils and charms of Typee valley, Tommo effectively represents the background of experience against which Melville defines the "freedom and imagination" of Romance. This side of Tommo not only suits Blair's brand of literary rhetoric, it draws heavily on the most neoclassic of Melville's contemporary sources, Richard Henry Dana, Jr., author and narrator of *Two Years before the Mast* (1840), a book which made Melville feel, he later wrote to Dana, "tied & welded to you by a sort of Siamese link of affectionate sympathy" (*Letters* 106). On the other hand, unlike Dana, Tommo often gives his experiences a subjective coloring (nicely described by Edgar Dryden, *Melville's Thematics of Form* 38–46) which draws on an equally important source, Poe's *Narrative of A. Gordon Pym* (1838).[8] Both Tommo and Pym avow an exorbitant love of adventure, undergo figurative death and rebirth, confront the terrors of cannibalism, and register numerous sensations foreign to Dana's unflappable persona. *Pym* offers a perfect antidote to the neoclassicism of Blair, one in tune with the gothic decor and exaggerated narrative self-consciousness of Melville's second fragment.

The conflict in Tommo's narrative standpoint mirrors Melville's conflicting views of rhetorical authority. Dana's narrator submits calmly to his experiences; his responses add realism but not "freedom and invention" to *Two Years before the Mast*. At one point, lowered off a sheer cliff, he reports, "I could see nothing below me but the sea and rocks upon which it broke, and a few gulls flying in mid-air. I got down, in safety, pretty well covered with dirt; and for my pains was told, 'What a d——d fool you were to risk your life for half a dozen hides'" (169). His account conveys little sense of the imaginative coloring of events to which Melville aspires. Pym, in a similar situation, falls victim, like the narrators of "Fragments from a Writing Desk," to the shaping powers of his own unfettered thoughts.

> At length arrived that crisis of fancy, so fearful in all similar cases, the crisis in which we begin to anticipate the feelings with which we *shall* fall—to picture to ourselves the sickness, and dizziness, and the last struggle. . . . And now I found these fancies creating their own realities, . . . in the next my whole soul was

pervaded with *a longing to fall;* a desire, a yearning, a passion utterly uncontrolla-ble. (1170)

Pym's fancies do not simply color experience, they create "their own real-ities." As a result, Pym cannot trust himself; his horror of cannibalism, unlike Tommo's, is not of being eaten but of becoming a cannibal. Like Melville's fragments, his tale crosses the line between Romance and phantasmagoria, yet unlike them, his voice remains unleavened by irony.

In a similar circumstance to Dana and Pym—descending hand over hand into Typee valley on a network of hanging vines—Tommo controls his vertigo by shutting out the sensations on which his imagination, unlike Pym's, con-tinues to depend: "My brain grew dizzy with the idea of the frightful risk I had just run, and I involuntarily closed my eyes to shut out the view of the depth beneath me" (61). Tommo mediates between Dana's levelheaded submission to experience and Pym's susceptibility to imagination. He also balances the adven-turousness of the latter against the former's prim desire for home. However, where Dana fears time lost from his Boston future and Pym responds to myste-rious compulsions, Tommo rationalizes his bold actions in terms of a well-articulated fear of entrapment in the past: "There is scarcely anything when a man is in difficulties that he is more disposed to look on with abhorrence than a right-about retrograde movement—a systematic going over of the already trod-den ground; and especially if he has a love of adventure, such a course appears indescribably repulsive" (54). Tommo's anxiety vis-à-vis the past makes him a fitting vehicle for Melville's ambivalence toward the sources of his own literary authority. Tommo's adventurousness tropes Melville's search for persuasive-ness, for the grounds of a literary creativity that transcends experience; yet his mix of the characteristics of Dana and Pym keeps contrasting modes of rhetori-cal authority in suspension while Melville works out the exact terms of his powerful new voice.

Tommo's imaginative coloring of his experiences and concomitant fear of the past come to blur the line between native and civilized culture in *Typee,* and thus the entire thematic thrust of the novel. The threat of entrapment in Typee valley echoes the prior threat of an interminable sea voyage; indeed the basic nature of Tommo's responses is determined before he reaches land; the Edenic harmony of valley life repeats the essential experience of sailing for the Mar-quesas, an experience of natural harmony important to both the tale and to Melville's rhetorical development.

What a delightful, lazy, languid time we had whilst we were thus gliding along! . . . Every one seemed to be under the influence of some narcotic. Even the officers aft, whose duty required them never to be seated while keeping a deck watch, vainly endeavored to keep on their pins; and were obliged invariably to compromise the matter by leaning up against the bulwarks, and gazing abstractedly over the side. Reading was out of the question; take a book in your hand, and you were asleep in an instant.

. . . The sky presented a clear expanse of the most delicate blue. . . . The long, measured, dirge-like swell of the Pacific came rolling along, with its surface broken by little tiny waves, sparkling in the sunshine. Every now and then a shoal of flying fish, scared from the water under the bows, would leap into the air, and fall the next moment like a shower of silver into the sea. Then you would see the superb albicore, with his glittering sides, sailing aloft. . . . At times, some shapeless monster of the deep, floating on the surface, would, as we approached, sink slowly into the blue waters, and fade away from the sight. But the most impressive feature of the scene was the almost unbroken silence that reigned over sky and water. Scarcely a sound could be heard but the occasional breathing of the grampus, and the rippling at the cut-water. (9–10)

What finally entrances about the sea, its "most impressive feature," is exactly that quality which Melville as author must escape—its silence. The charms of the sea, in spite of its teeming life, are mute, and under its spell language is foreclosed; one hesitates to intrude on the quietude, and one cannot read without falling asleep. In order to break into voice, to imagine himself as having a source of authority beyond experience, Melville creates a mediate realm, Typee valley, where the charms of sensation, under the shaping influence of the imagination, engender a rhetoric that surpasses that of Blair and Dana without risking the excesses of Poe.

Typee valley, unlike the sea, offers little indigenous animal life, shows the scars of age-old paths and ruins, and is colored a pervasive green that betokens not timelessness but decay.[9] It lacks the transcendent yet silent natural charms of Tommo's earlier experiences. In order to cast the valley in a Romantic light, Tommo exaggerates groundless dangers: "In looking back to this period, and calling to remembrance the numberless proofs of kindness and respect which I received from the natives of the valley, I can scarcely understand how it was that, in the midst of so many consolatory circumstances, my mind should still have been consumed by the most dismal forebodings" (118). Without Tommo's "most dismal forebodings," the Edenic harmony of Typee valley would lose the Romantic coloring which keeps it from having the soporific effect of the sea. The world of Typee valley is presented ironically so as to provide a theater for the exercise of a heightened rhetoric designed to save Melville from muteness, the past, the neoclassic values of Blair. The more pervasive the ironic substructure of *Typee* proves itself to be, the stronger the rhetoric becomes that Melville puts into play to mediate its oppositions. Irony grounds the dialectical departure hinted at in the second of the "Fragments from a Writing Desk" by provoking Melville's leap, through the use of Blair's major tropes, into a much more figurative rhetoric.[10]

The history and society of the Typees reveal additional ironic structures. Although Tommo imagines that the Typees are largely innocent of contact with whites, Melville makes it clear that it is their elaborately sophisticated response to European culture which preserves them from it; they remain constantly alert to the movements of the French in Nukuheva Bay, and they cultivate their xenophobia carefully. Typee life is characterized not by natural innocence but rather by numerous systems of articulation and differentiation—by talk and taboo—which Tommo only superficially acknowledges. While ignoring the historicity of Typee circumstances in order to present them as innocent children of nature, Tommo takes the further step of imposing a Romance history on them. Their charm is enhanced by the doom which hangs over them; they are the last unsullied tribe; Hawaii, Tahiti, and even Nukuheva have fallen into corruption. Typee timelessness and peace live in a fragile, fleeting moment poised between an endless natural past and an imminent, hopeless future. Tommo views corruption as an absolute state of being; he imposes on the culture of the islanders an imaginary gulf between innocence and degradation. Intensely aware of and indignant over results, he remains blind to processes, to his own corrupting influence.[11] Typee society is charmed because it is timeless, and timeless because Tommo "closes his eyes" to change and causality during his stay—as if "involuntary" to "shut out the view" of the cultural movements in which he participates.[12]

The pattern of ironic relationships informing Tommo's responses, the state of nature and life in Typee valley, and the sense of history in the work can be summarized as follows: a situation which lends experiential authority to Tommo's narrative turns out to be self-contradictory; Tommo imposes on his perceptions a series of imaginary gaps—between past and present, art and experience, sea and valley, civilization and primitivism, corruption and innocence—which clear space for "freedom and invention" by stressing the artificiality, the essential literariness, of the narrative situation. Tommo's growth into wisdom, his "progressive unfolding of the self,"[13] turns out to be a ruse of fiction ultimately dependent on the persuasiveness of Melville's voice. By sustaining the thematic oppositions in *Typee* and by drastically ironizing Tommo's perceptions, Melville justifies the overriding dialectical power which his rhetoric accrues in the novel, and thus the freedom of his own authorial identity.

What Tommo seeks to escape from is Melville's own entrapment in a mute and impotent past; his escape can never be realized because its enactment figures Melville's emergence into authorship, and that emergence leaves Tommo the sailor behind. Tommo cannot grow because, ironically, he tropes the need for growth on Melville's part; he is not "the author at the time" because "the author at the time" is a purely imaginative construct holding together conflicting perspectives that come to make sense—achieve persuasiveness—only on the basis of self-conscious rhetorical manipulation. Tommo achieves no satisfactory growth or resolution in terms given by his experiences or by his narrative point of view. Resolution in *Typee* comes, and comes powerfully, through dialectical departure on the level of Melville's self-discovery—the level of ethos.

Tommo's surprise at the happiness of Typee valley life mirrors Melville's surprise at finding himself suddenly wielding the authority of a masterful rhetoric. To be in charge of such creative power makes its earlier lack equally surprising. A phenomenological gap opens between Melville's vocal and voiceless selves, a gulf which inspires his sense of wonder and delight in being a writer. *Typee* images the preliterary self of its author as a regression which can only be spoken figuratively and dialectically, an authority in words emerging out of that which is prior to words (the sea), an image of growth possible only if, like the figures on Keats's urn, willfully and gracefully frozen in a rhetoric involved, above all, with its own self-consciousness. *Typee* expresses both ironic fragmentation—the impossible, mute past of the sailor—and dialectical achievement—the miracle of a found voice. In order for the novel to work, Melville both has to push his prose to unanticipated levels of rhetoricity and has to learn fast how to read himself and his intentions. Just how self-conscious he is in both efforts is indicated by the textual history of the work.

Typee was published first in London and almost simultaneously in New York. Between the American copyright date of March 17, 1846, and August of that year, Melville prepared a second American edition, incorporating Toby's story and making numerous excisions. Melville's letters suggest the excisions to have been made in response to his American publisher's objections over antimissionary sentiment and certain "sea freedoms" in the first edition (*Letters* 39). However, several factors suggest that the excisions reflect Melville's own growing authorial identity. First, Melville's letters express the opinion that the excisions give the book "a unity . . . which it wanted before" (*Letters* 39). Second, many of the removed passages bear only minimally on the publisher's ostensible objections. Third, comparison of the original and excised editions with Melville's sources and manuscript pages show a continuous trend of development toward the "play of freedom and invention" which Melville wrote of in regard to *Mardi*. Finally, Melville made no move to restore any of the excised material in later editions during his lifetime.

Melville's excisions have the effect of simplifying both the language and the world of *Typee* and of giving freer play to his emerging rhetoric.[14] In many of the excised passages, Melville speaks with an aggressive wit backed up by hindsight, the citing of sources, or historical data not immediately relevant to Tommo's adventures. These passages are often strong and delightful, and modern readers tend to prefer the first edition, but they draw attention away from Tommo's half-innocence and the essential contradictions in his situation. Interestingly, Melville's manuscript pages show the first edition to benefit from corresponding "purifications of style," excision of numerous colorful metaphors and allusions, and softening of tone. Many readers will undoubtedly prefer them to the first edition.

Melville's excisions weigh particularly heavily on the first four chapters of *Typee,* which are reduced by about half in the second American edition. The first chapter loses its famous "Oh! ye state-room sailors" passage and two humorous incidents—the natives' curious disrobing of a missionary's wife and the embarrassment of the French over the public display of "her own sweet form" by Mowanna's consort. The history of French occupation of the islands in chapter 3 vanishes entirely. Chapter 4 loses a disquisition on the brutalization of the natives by European violence, a description of Tior, and a meditation on the relative happiness of native and civilized humankind. With the excisions disappears all reference to the genuine, historical world of the islands and the aggressive play of Melville's satire—directed in turn against genteel voyagers, the French, missionaries, civilization, and the childish immodesty of the natives. Between the two editions, the beginning of the novel changes from a rhapsodic history, narrated in a neoclassic voice almost Voltairean in its witty superiority of tone, to a much more unified account of supposedly personal experiences. The story of Tommo's arrival at Nukuheva, immediate escape, life among the Typees, and rescue by the *Julia* leaves little time for his learning about the French presence in the islands so prominent in the removed material. Excision of the incident involving Mowanna's consort cancels a humorous treatment of the theme of tattooing in conflict with its later figurative importance in the novel. Removal of the "state-room sailors" passage dispels an early belligerence out of tune with Tommo's personality in the rest of the work; as Melville comes to rest his faith in literature rather than adventure, he becomes less inclined to berate his readers' lubberliness.

Melville's excisions deemphasize the historical world within which the narrative takes place, leaving a stronger sense of the timelessness and innocence of Typee life. As T. Walter Herbert concludes, "Revisions of *Typee* had the effect of rendering the work more 'romantic'" (189). They blur the neoclassic bite of Melville's contrasts between civilization and savagery and the corresponding moralistic indignation of the narrative voice. The second American edition permits Tommo's experiences to speak more on their own terms; comparisons between European and Typee emerge from the context of happenings in the tale rather than seeming laid on ex post facto. The narrative voice of the second American edition is left to seek the meaning of observed events without reference to a library of sources. A similar effect can be attributed to the omission in the first edition of a number of biblical, classical, and literary allusions, and a degree of humorous elaboration, notable, for example, in the description of Kory-Kory's speech at the end of chapter 14, which enliven Melville's manuscript. As Melville moves from manuscript to printed text, excisions significantly outnumber additions, a further indication of his sharpening focus. In numerous places, he softens his references to the Typees, referring to them, for example, as men rather than savages.

The key distinction between *Typee* and earlier treatments of native life in the Marquesas such as those of Stewart, Porter, Langsdorff, and Ellis is the degree of intimacy with the islanders which it establishes.[15] The history of Melville's text demonstrates his growing willingness to Romanticize the natives and bring Tommo into closer contact with them. As the dual effects of romance and intimacy become more pronounced, the contradictory nature of Tommo's responses and the inappropriateness of a neoclassic rhetoric become highlighted. Tommo's contact with the Typees produces a weight of descriptive detail which makes his tale realistic yet which also undercuts the ethnocentric rationalism characteristic of the earlier travel narratives. The problematic structure of Tommo's involvement, amplified by successive versions of the text, displays Melville's increasingly confident departure from the models available to him—a departure which justifies and is justified in turn by his new rhetorical program.

Tommo's intimacy with the Romanticized native world of *Typee* depends on the timelessness of valley life. The uncertain temporality of Tommo's experiences is a fact which Melville finds important enough to justify in the preface. No Robinson Crusoe, Tommo counts the days only when he expects Toby to return with help. The obverse side of Tommo's attenuated time-sense is the heightened spatialization of experience in which he participates. Spatialization, as Joseph Frank defines it,[16] helps define the special rhetoric of *Typee*. The timelessness of Tommo's life, once Toby leaves and his leg begins to heal, brings to a halt the progress of the narrative from Tommo's entry into the head of the valley toward his ultimate escape by sea at its far end. It also puts out of play his sense of the causal processes by which the Typees adjust to European encroachment, his own included. In rhetorical terms, it signals a move from a metaphoric to a metonymic perspective,[17] from a system of logical comparisons to one of associations justified by contiguity within a uniform, static field. As Tommo loses his compulsion to escape, he wanders the valley, inescapably enfolded in a closed, undifferentiated space, "nothing but a labyrinth of footpaths twisting and turning among the thickets without end" (194); and yet he continually encounters new sources of wonder—ruins, idols, natural phenomena, structures, activities—included with little regard to the forward movement of plot.

Tommo's entrapment within a timeless, regressive,[18] metonymic world focuses attention on the visual quality of his experiences—their incongruousness, beauty, or shock value—apart from their meaning in relation to rationalized cultural values and correspondingly "perspicuous" (to use Blair's term) metaphors. This focus is clear, for example, in Melville's handling of the theme of tattooing. Scholars have pointed out that the Typees are tattooed with marks of their own status and that Tommo must avoid being inscribed with a native identity envisioned, like the bars etched across Kory-Kory's face, as a prison (Stern 59). Yet Tommo is willing to have his arms tattooed, an act which would signal, in the same metaphoric terms, acceptance of the identity of a sailor— equally threatening to Melville's authorial selfhood. Tommo must remain free from tattoos, from metaphoric determination, because the unspecified nature of his identity is crucial to the figurative freedom of *Typee*. Tattooing, like literary rhetoric, is "so beautifying an operation" (219) which has the ability to fix the essential identity of something by working on its surface.

Melville does not achieve rhetorical authority by giving *Typee* the powerful narrative drive of *Mardi* or *Moby-Dick;* instead he takes individual scenes and events and colors them in a way which stresses the imaginative vividness of his voice. The central sections of the novel present a series of visual tableaux which could be reordered without loss. Tommo himself often becomes one of the figures within such a tableau, as when he reclines among bathing "nymphs," sails on the lake with Fayaway, or dresses for a native gala. Tommo's relationship with the natives is presented in the same visual, spatialized, metonymic terms as the world of the valley. A description of valley music can lead by association into an account of Tommo delighting the Typees by singing a sea chanty; a sense of kinship with Marheyo is built up out of bits of description of the native's happy, aimless movements near the mat where Tommo lies. Tommo's intimacy with the natives is predominantly picturesque; that picturesque intimacy comes across as profound because Melville's rhetoric imbues it with the intensity of feeling accompanying the discovery of his voice.

Melville's rhetoric draws extraordinary power from its use, for basic expository purposes, of tropes associated by Blair with the passionate or imaginative colors of literary language. His highly figurative style suggests defensiveness vis-à-vis the pure, mute nature of experience, but it ultimately becomes the vehicle for a rapacious linguistic appropriation of physical facts. Unlike Poe, who turns inward, Melville fills his book with realistic detail held together metonymically but colored by a brand of hyperbole which annexes sensation to voice. The beginning of the novel, as it remains in the second American edition, offers a prime example:

> Six months at sea! Yes, reader, as I live, six months out of sight of land; cruising after the sperm-whale beneath the scorching sun of the Line, and tossed on the billows of the wide-rolling Pacific—the sky above, the sea around, and nothing else! Weeks and weeks ago our fresh provisions were all exhausted. There is not a sweet potatoe left; not a single yam. Those glorious bunches of bananas which once decorated our stern and quarter-deck have, alas, disappeared! and the delicious oranges which hung suspended from our tops and stays—they too, are gone! Yes, they are all departed, and there is nothing left us but salt-horse and sea-biscuit.
>
> Oh! for a refreshing glimpse of one blade of grass—for a snuff at the fragrance of a handful of loamy earth! Is there nothing fresh around us? Is there no green thing to be seen? Yes, the inside of our bulwarks is painted green; but what a vile and sickly hue it is, as if nothing bearing even the semblance of verdure could flourish this weary way from land. Even the bark that once clung to the wood we use for fuel has been gnawed off and devoured by the captain's pig; and so long ago, too, that the pig himself has in turn been devoured. (3–4)

Rarely has a novel opened with such an exuberant rhapsody on the subject of unavailable delights. The passage, rather than paining the reader with a vision of the privation experienced on the voyage, eulogizes the richness of fare associated with the South Seas. It overwhelms the reader with the pure joy of describing. Hyperbole has the effect of drawing attention to the telling rather than the message; it suggests the imaginative vigor of a mind capable of marshalling any amount of detail, of spinning a chain of metonymically related signifiers which might stretch on indefinitely, no matter what the limits of actual experience.

In the opening passage of *Typee,* the privation experienced by sailors is troped by an imaginary sensual world, a world of gustatory relish, that goes beyond rhetorical hyperbole to preempt the thematics of feasting in the valley. Melville's humorous longing for the sacrifice of Pedro, the captain's rooster, as both Michael Clark (219) and Neal Tolchin (47) have noted, combined with the reference to "heathenish rites and human sacrifice" (5), introduces the theme of cannibalism as a metonymic by-product of his exuberant rush of images. Before we know it, Melville's narrative voice has proleptically touched on many of the issues central to Tommo's later responses to the natives. That they will prove to be just like the sailors, like Tommo himself, and cannibalize their prisoner out of hunger or pure enthusiastic self-awareness is a possibility, despite his own tabooed status, which Tommo never dispels from his mind. The reader looks ironically on Tommo's fears because their content has been foreshadowed and preempted by Melville's delight in voicing the entire, metonymic range of imaginative possibilities associated with the South Seas.

The beginning of *Typee* displays an additional rhetorical technique, which I will call promiscuous apostrophe. It is a perfect example of Melville's adopting a figure from Blair and then exaggerating it and broadening its application beyond recognition. Blair discusses the address, by apostrophe, of both absent persons and inanimate objects, but he discourages the latter because the personification which it implies requires a greater effort on the part of the reader's imagination (I, 424). Melville throws caution to the wind. He begins by addressing the reader directly, fades into soliloquy, and in subsequent paragraphs addresses the rooster, another sailor, and the "poor old ship" itself. The impression created is of a voice ready to fix on any imaginable auditor. The world of *Typee* gets personified and made immediate in the process. Even when he is not employing direct address, Melville's voice lends its topics an air of intimacy between author and reader. Melville's dissertations on the difference between primitive and civilized life almost always have a synthetic quality which, under the pennant of voicing—the placing of the fictional world in a close relation to the act of its articulation—bridges the gaps and overcomes the ironies which they touch on. Frequently the gaps bridged are temporal; what was "so long ago" is made current or projected into a near future, as when he says to the ship: "But courage, old lass, I hope to see thee soon within a biscuit's toss of the merry land" (4).

The synthetic nature of Melville's rhetoric is clear in the famous passage in which Kory-Kory lights a fire. Melville signals the start of his tableau by announcing in an apostrophe to the reader that, because the act "was entirely different from what I had ever seen," he will describe it. He then shifts to the present tense, as if, in spite of his generalizations, he were addressing a scene taking place in front of him. As Kory-Kory speeds up and Melville's figures become more vivid, concrete, and hyperbolic, phrases like "amazing rapidity" and "this is the critical stage of the operation" maintain the fiction of a present auditor in the description. In the final sentences, Melville's vocal force comes to rest in two strong metaphors, the second of which has been anticipated earlier in the passage.

> His hands still retain their hold of the smaller stick, which is pressed convulsively against the further end of the channel among the fine powder there accumulated, as if he had just pierced through and through some little viper that was wriggling and struggling to escape from his clutches. The next moment a delicate wreath of smoke curls spirally into the air, the heap of dusty particles glows with fire, and Kory-Kory almost breathless, dismounts from his steed. (111)

The point is not that the metaphoric structure of the passage makes it an allegory of masturbation—an interpretation reinforced by its intimate tone but complicated by the existence of additional comparisons between Kory-Kory and both a locomotive and a steamship which appear in Melville's manuscript pages. The image of the viper is so unusual, indeed catachrestic, and yet visually pointed, that it breaks down the metaphoric structure of references on which the native-civilized comparisons which follow the passage depend. Because of the violence of the viper image, the physical impact of the passage refuses to rest within the confines of irony. In the manuscript, Melville ends his subsequent suggestion for a "college of vestals" to keep valley fires lit with a rather abstract sentence making it clear that the "special difficulties" mentioned in conjunction with this scheme refer to the lack of virgins among native women. In revising, he decides to give the subject a more serious and pointed treatment: at stake, he concludes, is the demand which the act makes on Kory-Kory's "good temper," "toil," and "anxiety"; a process undertaken for the purpose of lighting Tommo's pipe takes on a weight which would drive a "European artisan" "to his wits' end." The coloring given by the viper image is reflected, and the intimacy of visual detail in the passage prevents the use of a cooler, more condescending, more neoclassically witty tone.

In "Kory-Kory strikes a light à la Typee," Melville begins with a paragraph of colorful, present-tense description in which an unusual image creates a swerve in tone and reference; he prevents the passage from being read in terms of logical, metaphoric references by placing the figure of the "viper" too close to that of the "steed" for the two to be reconciled. They throw each other into catachresis. Melville then moves to a paragraph of understated humor containing his suggestion for a "college of vestals"; finally he compares European with island life in a way which picks up the disconcerting note introduced earlier by the viper image. The entire passage not only mediates thematically between the two societies, its apostrophes integrate three distinct and characteristic time senses: present-tense immediate ("Kory-Kory goes to work quite leisurely"), retrospective reflection ("had I possessed a sufficient intimacy with the language to have conveyed my ideas upon the subject, I should certainly have suggested"), and generalized commentary ("what a striking evidence does this operation furnish").

Furthermore, Melville's rhetoric draws together, through punning metaphors, the "striking evidence" of his discussion of native and European obligations with the initiatory motive for the passage—"often he was obliged to strike a light for the occasion." The "intimacy with the language" which Tommo lacks in the second paragraph metonymically evokes the extraordinary physical intimacy of passages preceding "Kory-Kory strikes a light," in which Tommo's body is rubbed down with *aka* by native girls. The various aspects of the whole scene come together in an act of address where visual content, speaking voice, and assumed audience are made to intermix and cohere through the complex struc-ture of the locutionary act. Native and civilized culture are synthesized in Tommo's responses, but that synthesis takes place rhetorically through a dialec-tical departure to the level of voice; Melville's concatenated figures raise the passage above its content, above Tommo's reflective capacities, and into the realm of his ethos.

The dialectical power of Melville's voice in "Kory-Kory Strikes a Light à la Typee" critically involves the handling of time in the passage. Melville deliber-ately elides distinctions between the time of the event and the time of writing about it. The fact that the passage relates associatively (metonymically) to its context helps. It is presented as a contiguous part of the prior domestic scene, a natural prelude to Tommo's musings on family obligations. It has no determi-nate temporal position. The same use of rhetoric to shape the timeless time-sense of *Typee* appears in bolder outline in a key later passage.

> For hours and hours during the warmest part of the day I lay upon my mat, and while those around me were nearly all dozing away in careless ease, I remained awake, gloomily pondering over the fate which it appeared now idle for me to resist. When I thought of the loved friends who were thousands and thousands of miles from the savage island in which I was held a captive, when I reflected that my dreadful fate would for ever be concealed from them, and that with hope deferred they might continue to await my return long after my inanimate form had blended with the dust of the valley—I could not repress a shudder of anguish.
>
> How vividly is impressed upon my mind every minute feature of the scene which met my view during those long days of suffering and sorrow! . . .
>
> Just beyond the pi-pi, and disposed in a triangle before the entrance of the house, were three magnificent bread-fruit trees. At this moment I can recal[l] to my mind their slender shafts, and the graceful inequalities of their bark, on which my eye was accustomed to dwell day after day in the midst of my solitary mus-ings. It is strange how inanimate objects will twine themselves into our affections, especially in the hour of affliction. Even now, amidst all the bustle and stir of the proud and busy city in which I am dwelling, the image of those three trees seems to come as vividly before my eyes as if they were actually present, and I still feel the soothing quiet pleasure which I then had in watching hour after hour their topmost boughs waving gracefully in the breeze. (243–44)

This passage so clearly presages a host of others in Melville's later works—Redburn's memories of his model ship, Ishmael's commentary on the "Coun-terpane" experience, the memorable, damned tortoises of "The Encantadas"—that it deserves careful attention. It is the only passage in *Typee* where Tommo suggests either a past (loved friends) prior to his experiences on ship or the fu-ture circumstances of his life ("the proud and busy city in which I am dwelling"). It dramatically oversteps the temporal boundaries of the rest of the novel, but it does so in a way which rhetorically determines the novel's temporality.[19]

At the beginning of the passage, Tommo places himself in exactly the position which he imagines the Typees to be in—suspended between an endless innocent past and an endless, hopeless future. His anguish derives not from fear of approaching events, of which he has no sense, but rather from fear of silence—that his "dreadful fate would for ever be concealed." As with the novel itself, the gap between past and future is a theater for imaginatively articulated, picturesque experience: "How vividly is impressed upon my mind every minute feature of the scene which met my view during those long days of suffering and sorrow" (243). Here the present tense indicates the time of writing or reflection, and the whole experience is projected forward to a moment which replaces the original point of sensation: "At this moment I can recal[l]. . . ." This instant then opens out further into a sense of the process of the author's continuing life: "Even now, amidst all the bustle and stir . . . the image of those three trees seems to come as vividly before my eyes." The memory of images from Tommo's tale, in turn inspired by the memory of "loved friends," gives time and substance to Melville's authorial personality. The passage presents a moment of looking back which enables a looking forward, both perspectives outside the fictional bounds of the novel, both therefore aspects of voice rather than theme. The same temporal figure lies hidden behind the assertion "I can never forget . . ." which opens the description of the sea in the second chapter and which Melville repeats throughout *Typee*, for example in the final line of chapter 6 (40), twice in chapter 7 (45, 46), and three times in the final chapter (248 twice, 252). In this case, the moment of telling is eclipsed by a going back— remembering—which goes endlessly forward, never to be forgotten.

The backward and forward movement of time in *Typee* corresponds to the trope of metalepsis, defined by Blair as "founded on the relation between an antecedent and a consequent" (I, 369), central to the intertextual rhetoric of Harold Bloom as the master trope that permits a poem to imagine itself as engendering its own precursor.[20] In *Typee* it enables the existence of "the author at the time"—a consciousness embedded in the work and yet free to range beyond its boundaries, and thus beyond the limits of Tommo's figurative existence. As a locus for the imposition of metaleptic time on the novel, Tommo gives over his status as both narrator and character to Melville's "continuous imaginative presence." "The author at the time" is an author who appropriates time to voicing. Metalepsis tends to show up throughout Melville's first-person narratives wherever the substance of authorial identity, the relation between author and subject matter, and the imaginative generation of discourse are in question. It integrates theme and style, content and form, in a way which sets *Typee* apart from both its nonfiction sources and earlier sea novels from Defoe through Marryat; it is precisely the narrative function which Poe fails to control in attempting to get Pym's story told.

The power of Melville's rhetoric is cast by means of figures: metonymy, preemptive prolepsis, hyperbole, apostrophe, catachresis, and metalepsis. The ending of *Typee* resolves the novel's thematic and narrative contradictions—its irony—through the combined force of these figures and thereby realizes Melville's emergence from silence into his particular, compelling voice. The final chapter begins by canceling out the sense of timelessness in which Tommo is trapped; yet in returning Tommo to time, it also returns him to the threatening silence evoked in Melville's early description of the sea: "Nearly three weeks had elapsed since the second visit of Marnoo, and it must have been more than four months since I entered the valley, when one day about noon, and whilst everything was in profound silence . . ." (245). Melville establishes directly that Tommo's escape must come by a return to the sea, a sea which for the moment suspends its power to suffocate Tommo's sense of self.

> Having been prohibited from approaching the sea during the whole of my stay in the valley, I had always associated with it the idea of escape. Toby too—if indeed he had ever voluntary deserted me—must have effected his flight by the sea; and now that I was drawing near to it myself, I indulged in hopes which I had never felt before. (246)

"Hopes which I had never felt before" repeats the metalepsis responsible for the enabling timelessness of Typee valley—now attached to the idea of the sea. At issue is the ability, in escaping from the island, to avoid a relapse into the world of silence, muteness, which it supplanted. Tommo is, at this point, still trapped in the Typee world of metonymic stasis, and his progress toward the beach is thwarted by a throng of gesturing, talking, shouting, and arguing islanders. Finally, he communicates. His own "eloquence of gesture" prevails on the otherwise hostile Mow-Mow to permit him to struggle onward. Within the world of the Typees, Tommo can only gesture, not speak, and he exists under a pseudonym which indicates as much a lack of identity as a created one. Gesture must give way to real articulation, even if imposed by Melville, before flight is possible.

At this point, in a trope of the process by which the contradictory world of *Typee* provides a theater for Melville's rhetoric, the talk of the natives divides to open a space for Tommo's escape.

> To my surprise I was suffered to proceed alone, all the natives remaining in front of the house, and engaging in earnest conversation, which every moment became

more loud and vehement; and to my unspeakable delight I perceived that some difference of opinion had arisen between them; that two parties, in short, were formed, and consequently that in their divided counsels there was some chance of my deliverance. (248)

Immediately after this passage, Marheyo, with an expression that Tommo says he "shall never forget," articulates, on behalf of the mute Tommo, the space between the "divided counsels" of the natives by pronouncing the words "home" and "mother" to him. Marheyo's words give Tommo a past and a future; they signal the metaleptic action of Melville's controlling voice. Six lines later, Tommo nears the sea.

Never shall I forget the extacy I felt when I first heard the roar of the surf breaking upon the beach. Before long I saw the flashing billows themselves through the opening between the trees. Oh glorious sight and sound of ocean! with what rapture did I hail you as familiar friends. By this time the shouts of the crowd upon the beach were distinctly audible, and in the blended confusion of sounds I almost fancied I could distinguish the voices of my own countrymen. (248)

Marheyo's words give way to the noise of the surf and the voices on the beach: the babble of the arguing natives conflicts and blends with sounds which Tommo can understand. It is another experience which he can "never forget"; the metaleptic device which has informed the suspended time of the valley now relates Tommo the sea, which, in the guise of "familiar friends," echoes the "loved friends" of Tommo's musings in the valley. By recalling the figure of authorial time in *Typee,* the waves transcend their own threatening past. The "opening between the trees" yields in the next paragraph to "the open space between the groves and the sea" (249). Tommo's escape is staged in the in-between space of the beach, a figure which will retain its significance to Melville to the end of his life, in the "Pebbles" which complete *John Marr and Other Sailors.*

> But Orm from the schools to the beaches strays,
> And, finding a Conch hoar with time, he delays
>   And reverent lifts it to ear.
> That Voice, pitched in far monotone,
>   Shall it swerve? Shall it deviate ever?
>   (*Poems* 203)

Tommo, tossed between images of transcendence and suppression in time, fears that he has arrived "too late" to take advantage of the "divided counsels" of the natives and proceed to the beach, when again Melville imposes a mark of metaleptically enabling articulation—the sound of Tommo's "own name shouted out by a voice from the midst of the crowd" (249).

It is of course not "Tommo" which he hears, since Karakoee would not have known his native name.[21] The unrevealed word prompts Tommo to two crucial acts which relate him to a previously unavailable past—he recognizes and he remembers. A page later, as Tommo's escape is threatened by the "detestable word 'Roo-ne' " spoken by the natives, a second reference to Tommo's ability to remember leads to the exertion of all his strength in plunging toward Karakoee, who now stands "to the waist in the surf." Tommo's success is signaled by Fayaway, who is rendered "speechless" with sorrow and immediately described as "retired from the edge of the water." The other natives may follow Tommo "into the water," but the power of those who are key ingredients in the Romance world of Typee valley ends at the shore. Mow-Mow is the only recognizable native who swims after the boat, and his "ferocious expression" at being defeated is the final thing of which Tommo says "never shall I forget" (252).

The entry of the natives into the water in pursuit of Tommo elides, once and for all, the valley-sea distinction which Melville has maintained throughout *Typee.* He is able to give up his ironic trope because its crucial opposition is translated, in the final moments of the story, into a figurative contrast central to Melville's later works—to be afloat rather than immersed. The natives seek to overturn Tommo's boat; to be swamped in the sea is the last threat of residence in Typee valley. It is Melville's trope of the allegiance which sea and valley share in figuring the danger of the past, of experience, and of silence to the emergence of an authorial identity dependent on rhetoric rather than "the unvarnished truth." The natives, unaccountably more formidable in the water than on land, usher into Melville's fiction the fear of drowning associated with the end of *Mardi,* White Jacket's plunge, and the tragedy of Pip in *Moby-Dick.* Tommo can make good his escape only through a violent blow at Mow-Mow that repeats the wrenching emotional revulsion evident in his thrusting aside of Fayaway.

The emotional rejection by Tommo of his Typee past cancels his submission to the timelessness of the valley, but it returns him to the same circumstances which he escaped, through a similar negative act, at the start of the novel. The narrative circles back to the salty muteness and timelessness of life on board the *Dolly.* Although Tommo is given no future, Melville transforms him figuratively in one key way: "On reaching the 'Julia' I was lifted over the side, and my strange appearance and remarkable adventure occasioned the liveliest interest" (252–53). His phrase echoes the assertion of the preface that a tale which could "excite the warmest sympathies of the author's shipmates . . . could scarcely fail to interest those who are less familiar than the sailor with a life of adventure." The echoed language constitutes a final metaleptic trope by which the end and beginning of the book evoke each other and complete its narrative circle. The circle is closed not by Tommo's adventures but by the "interest" displayed by auditors in the accomplished tale. Melville's narrator may not prove himself to be "the author at the time" by giving up his nautical life, but he has a new source of authority among his "shipmates."

Melville's transformed narrative persona never takes substantial shape; for him to do so would be to traduce the dialectical leap into rhetoric which frees Melville's voice from the authority of the past. On one level, then, nothing has been solved; Tommo faces one more in an unending series of sea voyages. On another level, everything has been solved, for Tommo's circular experience occasions and expresses Melville's experience of and identity with the power of an emerging literary voice. The tale does not end with the completion of its narrative circle either on the thematic level with Tommo's escape or on the narrative level with his newfound ability to arouse the interest of his shipmates; instead it projects itself outward into an appendix which tells of the cession of the island to Lord Paulet, a sequel which tells the story of Toby, another sequel—*Omoo*—and the subsequent seagoing novels which form the backbone of Melville's literary career. Never does Melville's faith in the power of rhetoric leave him; his self-discovery in *Typee* carries the force of a conversion, an inconceivable but undeniable election whose meaning may be obscure but whose substance cannot be doubted. *Typee* is the first in a series of instances where literary voice and salvation interweave to determine the ethos of Melville's fiction, and it initiates a corresponding sequence of figurative experiments which rapidly leave Blair's rhetoric behind. It is hard to imagine a first novel which does more to initiate the creative development of its author.

4

"No further connection": *Omoo*

The present narrative necessarily begins where "Typee" concludes, but
has no further connection with the latter work. All, therefore, necessary
for the reader to understand, who has not read "Typee," is given in a brief
introduction.

—Melville, *Omoo*

*O*moo consolidates Melville's self-discovery; it evidences little anxiety over the sources of literary authority, practically no irony, few contradictions in theme and narrative viewpoint, and hardly any of the rhetorical
fireworks which brought *Typee* to life. Confident in his independence from
Blair, Melville unself-consciously follows the master rhetorician's program of
perspicuity and truthfulness more closely than anywhere else. His submission
to the dictates of a "plain style" does not last long: *Omoo's* easy vigor yields
rapidly to the artifice of *Mardi,* justified by Melville's pronouncement of "incurable distaste" at his second novel's eschewal of rhetorical invention in favor of
"the dull common places" of a "narrative of *facts*" (*Letters* 70, spelling corrected). Yet in spite of Melville's negative reaction, *Omoo* displays the charms of
an authorship exhilarated by its achieved voice and, for a brief moment, at
peace with the burden of the past. Its breezy vividness defines Melville's "degree
zero" rhetoric—a mode of straightforward narration, authoritative in neoclassic terms yet shorn of Chesterfieldian gentility, to which he later reverts
between tropological experiments.

Melville's retreat from the highly figured prose of *Typee* into a perspicuous
tale authorized by the experiences which it represents is not as simple as his
judgment makes it seem. In order to claim "no further connection" with its
predecessor, *Omoo* puts into play a rhetorical departure of its own, signaled by
a narrative viewpoint associated with articulation rather than muteness. As
"Typee"—the name which his new shipmates give him—the narrator of *Omoo*
is identified with his own interest-arousing tale. A proven storyteller, he no
longer fears, as did Tommo, that the temporal vagueness of his story will
undermine its persuasiveness.

No journal was kept by the author during his wanderings in the South Seas; so
that, in preparing the ensuing chapters for the press, precision with respect to
dates would have been impossible; and every occurrence has been put down from

simple recollection. The frequency, however, with which these incidents have been verbally related, has tended to stamp them upon the memory. (xiv)

"Simple recollection"—Melville's counterpart to the "thorough knowledge of the subject" insisted on by Blair—is legitimated by frequent recounting. In *Omoo*, Melville does not push his narrative into intimacy with a spatialized, metonymic romance-world in order to produce a theater for convincing articulation. Instead, articulation grounds the concreteness of the world presented: the tale is true because repeated telling has fixed its details in the author's mind; what is persuasive is the story told, not the story lived.

Having gained a voice, an ethos, Melville uses it to appropriate the sources of threatening authority from which he sought escape in *Typee*. To be a sailor now means to be a storyteller, to speak out of the experience of one's own speaking. This stance permits Melville to protect himself from Blair's gentility—associated in his mind with the authority of his older brother, Gansevoort[1]—while following Blair's precepts. For the space of one novel, author, narrator, and audience coexist in a rational harmony, and voice, experience, and the sea draw naturally on each other's power. Within a year of its completion, Melville, now the oldest male in his immediate family, has married the daughter of a prominent Boston lawyer, set up as the head of an extended New York household, and joined the literary circle of the wealthy brothers George and Evert Duyckinck. His adolescent self-confidence has returned at full flood, and he has taken on all the trappings of maturity, sophistication, and responsibility denied by his itinerant youth.

In order to access Blair's power, Melville turns the Chesterfieldian dandy who narrates "Fragments from a Writing Desk" into the adventurer "Typee." If influence-anxiety, as defined by Harold Bloom, demands a willful misreading or misprision of the precursor, no better starting point can be imagined than to have the voice of the Regius Professor of eighteenth-century Edinburgh taken up by a footless American beachcomber. The disregard of laws and conventions and the sheer, adolescent fecklessness which give *Omoo* its thematic and narrative drive correspond to its rhetorical focus. "Typee" displays "no further connection" not just with the complexities of Tommo's voice and stance but with the earnestness and tension which characterize both Blair and Melville's key American sources, Poe and Dana.

In departing from *Typee*, *Omoo* teaches Melville how dramatically his ethos can impose underlying structural principles on the thematic as well as stylistic order of his fiction. *Omoo* everywhere shows the imprint of a shift from the enabling irony of *Typee* to a synecdochic rhetoric which will not reveal its troubling implications or prompt a further dialectical reaction until *Mardi*.[2]

Synedcoche—substitution of a part for the whole—is the modus operandi of literature which represents its protagonist as "everyman" or describes local conditions as a microcosm of the world.[3] The rhetoric of *Omoo* is synecdochic insofar as it presents its narrative as exemplary of a general and noncontroversial act of voicing. It assumes that author, narrator, shipmates, and audience inhabit a speech community characterized by shared "interest" rather than differences of background and opinion. One can speak for all. Because of this general, neoclassic trust, the persuasiveness of the tale seems to emerge from its events rather than from the idiosyncratic verbal genius of its author, and these events themselves take on synecdochic value. The "mutiny" which "Typee" finds himself mixed up in tropes both Melville's own emergence from and appropriation of Blair and the general state of affairs introduced into island culture by colonial (military and religious) powers. In each case, rebellion against arbitrary rules ushers in neither punishment nor a new set of rules but a lawlessness in which people are abandoned to their own impulses. For the sailors, arrest leads to the undisciplined life of the Calabooza Beretanee, from which they wander away after the *Julia* sails. For Melville, freedom from the balanced threat of silence and vocal assertiveness in *Typee* leaves him without clear rhetorical imperatives, without the tools for sustaining his momentary escape from an anxious past. For the islanders, the utterly arbitrary adoption of Christian ("mickonaree") values occasions more vanity and self-justification than it does moral progress.[4]

The synecdochic substructure of *Omoo*'s rhetoric turns its narrative into a series of piquant fables—lessons in human nature illuminated by the experiences of the narrator and his companion, Doctor Long Ghost: the slackness of consular discipline, for example, has everything to do with coercing the sailors back into usefulness rather than punishing them; the vaunted hospitality of the natives is balanced by thievery and deception; the value of the two wanderers to their potato-farming employers owes more to their culture and companionship than to their labor; the flirtatiousness of the native girls is trammeled by their pride; paradise is rendered unpleasant by mosquitoes; the largess of nature and the needs of the population exist in a delicate balance; even in diminished circumstances, Pomaree's court—viewed by the adventurers as a curiosity and an opportunity for further freeloading—does not tolerate a breach of etiquette. The overriding rhetorical confidence and lack of tension in *Omoo* permit its synecdochic parables to pass by without inducing the gnarled cross-cultural comparisons that weigh heavily on *Typee*.

In establishing its lack of "further connection" with Melville's first novel, *Omoo* reverses many of the former work's key figures, beginning with those having to do with linguistic competence. Books, rather than putting "Typee" to sleep, become "an invaluable resource" which he reads "through again and again"—even to a treatise on yellow fever and a file of Sidney newspapers (36). "Typee" writes and becomes known as the writer of the famous "round robin" voicing to the English consul the grievances of the *Julia*'s crew, amusingly penned on a leaf from "A History of the most Atrocious and Bloody Piracies" in ink mixed by "a fellow of a literary turn" (74). The narrator's identity is reinforced by the "passport" which he gets the farmer Zeke to write on his behalf (250). Toward the end of the tale, his knowledge of the Marquesan dialect—a clear distinction between him and Tommo—gains him entree into the residence of Queen Pomaree (307). The found voice of *Omoo* permits none of the concern over imperfect, foreclosed, or impossible communication that was such an issue in *Typee.*

Even tattooing wears a different face in *Omoo*. Although "Typee" is initially horrified by the decorated visage of Lem Hardy, he comes to realize that Hardy's tattoos have given him a selfhood impossible in the white world.

> "Friends," indeed, he had none. He told me his history. Thrown upon the world a foundling, his paternal origin was as much a mystery to him as the genealogy of Odin; and, scorned by every body, he fled the parish workhouse when a boy, and lanched upon the sea. He had followed it for several years, a dog before the mast, and now he had thrown it up forever.
>
> And for the most part, it is just this sort of men—so many of whom are found among sailors—uncared for by a single soul, without ties, reckless, and impatient of the restraints of civilization, who are occasionally found quite at home upon the savage islands of the Pacific. And, glancing at their hard lot in their own country, what marvel at their choice? (28)

Hardy does not merely gain an identity, he becomes a legendary patron of the art which he represents. His support at "the time of tattooing" is not simply remembered but rendered into enduring song. He experiences not the prison which being tattooed promises a white man in *Typee* but an expanded selfhood and a place in the native version of literary history.

The synecdochic appeal which distinguishes the world of *Omoo* from that of *Typee* touches even Melville's most important trope of self-discovery, the "interest" which Tommo evokes at both the beginning and the end of the earlier novel. Of the inhabitants of Tahiti, Melville reports, "in truth, every thing about them was calculated to awaken the liveliest interest" (66). Before the *Julia* reaches the island, the sea prompts a like response: "The uncertainty hanging over our destination at this time, and the fact that we were abroad upon waters comparatively little traversed, lent an interest to this portion of the cruise which I shall never forget" (35). Not only are island life and sea rendered equal by the repeated assertion, in the only instance in *Omoo* which employs the phrase "I shall never forget," it is the "interest" lent to experience rather than experience itself which is memorable; thus, the metaleptic figure of *Typee* is firmly lodged within rather than outside the envelope of the narrated story—validated by the "interest" which signals persuasiveness and rhetorical authority. A circumstance which cannot be forgotten has presumably become so through the "frequency with which these incidents have been verbally related"; there is no sense of an authorial voice in conflict with past muteness or future wonder; voice identifies itself with its subject matter in a way which fills up the temporal horizon of the narrative act. Metaleptic time gives way to a synecdochic time in which the moment of telling represents all articulated moments, equal parts of a repeated tale which appropriates sea, native life, and past to an ethos free from anxiety and the resulting machinery of self-justification.

The synecdochic temporality of *Omoo* emerges clearly in the only other place in the novel where Melville appears to call on his old metaleptic figure. On examining a beached and decaying whaling ship off Papeetee harbor, he exclaims:

> What were my emotions, when I saw upon her stern the name of a small town on the river Hudson! She was from the noble stream on whose banks I was born; in whose waters I had a hundred times bathed. In an instant, palm-trees and elms—canoes and skiffs—church spires and bamboos—all mingled in one vision of the present and the past. (102)

Rather than swinging from prior past to unforeseen future in order to evoke a "preposterous" temporal order, the passage collapses time into an aggrandized narrative moment. In *Typee*, past and future slide into and intrude on each other, but they do not blend into "one vision of the present and the past" which is the product of "an instant." The synecdochic rhetoric of *Omoo* gives the point of telling within the story the ability to trope the authority associated with its writing, with Melville's discovery of his voice. As a result, nowhere do we feel less inclined to repeat Brodtkorb's search for a "second fictional narrator" whose voice transcends that of "Typee" as the author's does Tommo's in *Typee*.

By appropriating the past into a synecdochic narrative moment, *Omoo* escapes the past-present dialectic central to Melville's rhetorical self-discovery in *Typee*. Without that conflict—without Tommo's fear of silence—the sea loses its threatening force, becoming instead an occasion for narrative "interest." "Typee," at the end of his beachcombing adventures, avows that "like all sailors ashore, I at last pined for the billows" (312). Yet in carrying over his program of "no further connection" to its treatment of the sea, Melville's synecdochic rhetoric begins to reveal a disquieting side, a set of implications which look directly ahead to *Mardi*. The figurative nature of Melville's treatment of the sea in *Omoo* is the first instance in his career where the seeds of a cataclysmic rhetorical departure germinate in an environment which they will ultimately deny and destroy. Nothing about the sea in *Omoo* traduces the seamless vocal confidence of the novel, but by its end Melville's rhetoric can no longer rest its case on that confidence. As so often in his career, it is the sea—as trope and as source of tropes—which gives Melville the unsettling impetus to further growth.

When "Typee" is hauled on board the *Julia,* an experience yearned for in the valley—meeting an old friend—carries the weight of insecurity: "Years had rolled by, many a league of ocean had been traversed, and we were thrown together under circumstances which almost made me doubt my own existence" (6). "Safe aboard of a ship," the narrator experiences Tommo's old malaise: "With home and friends once more in prospect, I nevertheless felt weighed down by a melancholy that could not be shaken off" (7). His depression derives from the thought of "leaving" his former "captives" "forever." It produces a radical sense of dislocation: "My recent adventures had all the strangeness of a dream; and I could scarcely believe that the same sun now setting over a waste of waters, had that very morning risen above the mountains and peered in upon me as I lay on my mat in Typee" (7). Having "no further connection" with his recent past unsettles "Typee's" sense of selfhood.

"Typee" is saved from depression by the sea, which soon shows a different face than that of a threatening "waste of waters." The next day, "there was a fine breeze; and, notwithstanding my bad night's rest, the cool, fresh air of a morning at sea was so bracing, that, as soon as I breathed it, my spirits rose at once" (8). For the first time, Melville affirms the curative powers of the ocean, a figure which runs throughout his later work, from Ishmael's use of it to redress the "damp, drizzly November" in his soul to the conclusion of *John Marr and Other Sailors,* published near the end of his life.

> Healed of my hurt, I laud the inhuman Sea—
> Yea, bless the Angels Four that there convene;
> For healed I am even by their pitiless breath
> Distilled in wholesome dew named rosmarine.
> (*Poems* 204)

What Melville does not realize in *Omoo* is that the act of healing carries its own, redemptive relationship with the past and that that relationship contradicts the synecdochic temporality which permits the novel to claim "no further connection" with *Typee.* Although "Typee" continues to regard the sea positively, the figurative structures which attend it in the novel retain an unsettling complexity, exemplified by Melville's first fictional account of an ocean burial.

Twenty days out from Nukuheva, the crew of the *Julia* dispenses with the remains of two of their number who have succumbed to disease.

> These two men both perished from the proverbial indiscretions of seamen, heightened by circumstances apparent; but had either of them been ashore under proper treatment, he would, in all human probability, have recovered.
>
> Behold here the fate of a sailor! They give him the last toss, and no one asks whose child he was.
>
> For the rest of that night there was no more sleep. Many stayed on deck until broad morning, relating to each other those marvelous tales of the sea which the occasion was calculated to call forth. Little as I believed in such things, I could not listen to some of these stories unaffected. (45–46)

In the beginning of *Typee*, the sea breeds silence and sleepiness. Now the threat is compensated by language, wakefulness, and emotion. At its most dire, the sea gives rise to a verbal art characterized by imaginative freedom. Yet the cost of that freedom is the experience of parting, of "no further connection" with the deceased, and of the disconnectedness and rootlessness of the sailor's life, poignantly summarized in the line "no one asks whose child he was." *Omoo*, as we will see, is a novel of partings whose cumulative effect undercuts its breezy rhetoric.

Melville's experience of the sea as a locus of imaginative articulation—"marvelous tales"—inspires one of the very few passages in the novel given over to "that play of freedom and invention" lurking behind his dissatisfaction with Blair.

> Within, nestled the still, blue lagoon. No living thing was seen, and, for aught we knew, we might have been the first mortals who had ever beheld the spot. The thought was quickening to the fancy; nor could I help dreaming of the endless grottoes and galleries, far below the reach of the mariner's lead.
>
> And what strange shapes were lurking there! Think of those arch creatures, the mermaids, chasing each other in and out of the coral cells, and catching their long hair in the coral twigs! (64)

The passage prefigures in miniature the motivational structure of the beginning of *Moby-Dick*: a love of the unknown pricks the narrator's imagination, which then finds its object in the sea. For the first time, Melville's mind is carried below the surface in a flight of fancy which contradicts the imagery of threatened drowning called up at the end of *Typee*. Self-confidence momentarily permits the easy domestication of two of his most portentous motifs—dreaming and immersion. The dangerous sea of his first novel has become the object of light fancy. Yet this is accomplished through a radical, synecdochic cancellation of the past—"no further connection." The partings of *Omoo* are absolute, unredeemed and unredeemable; they traduce the motivational structure of

Melville's rhetoric, based on reaction to and dialectical transformation (*aufhebung*), but not denial, of the past. As the frenzied rhetoric of *Mardi* will prove, the tropological program of *Omoo* ultimately makes him "doubt [his] own existence."

Omoo contains roughly a dozen final partings, marked by such expressions as "I was leaving them forever" (7); "he had now thrown it up forever" (28); "they give him the last toss" (46); "what eventually became of him, we never heard" (148); "nothing more have I ever heard of her" (149); "there would now be a serene sadness in thinking over the scene—since we never saw them again" (199); "very sad at parting with them" (268); "when the parties separating, never more expect to meet" (270); and "I have never seen or heard of him since" (316). In each case the guilt or pain of the occasion is anesthetized by the novel's rhetorical unwillingness to account for the past. The synecdochic moment is all as the narrative rushes forward into an undifferentiated future. "Typee" ends up in exactly the situation which Tommo dreads—with nothing behind to fear and thus nowhere to head except out into the "wide Pacific," the ineluctable fate of a sailor pining for the billows.

The penultimate parting in *Omoo* modifies the pattern of "no further connection" which dominates the novel. Just before an emotionless and final goodbye to Doctor Long Ghost, "Typee" drinks "a parting shell" with his last native host, Po-Po, and his family. "To remember her by," the "warm-hearted Arfretee, her grief unbounded," presents him with "a roll of fine matting, and another of tappa." "Typee" comments, "these gifts placed in my hammock, I afterward found very agreeable in the warm latitudes to which we were bound; nor did they fail to awaken most grateful remembrances" (315–16). In the context of *Omoo*, Arfretee's gesture has minimal significance, but in the context of Melville's "continuous imaginative presence," it functions as a redemptive repetition of Tommo's abrupt parting with Fayaway, punctuated by his throwing a roll of cloth to her. Furthermore, it gives rise to a larger repetition by introducing at the end of the novel the theme of memory, which, in the guise of "simple recollection" and the effect of repeated verbalization ("to stamp them upon the memory"), took center stage in its preface. *Omoo* circles back on memory as *Typee* does on the "interest" of Tommo's shipmates. The ending of Melville's second novel establishes an ethical "connection" with that of his first, in spite of his seemingly unwavering commitment to its synecdochic rhetorical program. Synecdoche, in the larger theater of Melville's developing ethos, gives way to a metaphoric similarity between the two works, which in turn evokes the irony (as "Typee," through a figurative reversal, tropes Fayaway) central to the earlier work's conflicted yet lively temporal relationships.

What the ending of *Omoo* reveals is that the novel's seamless, synecdochic rhetoric and easy appropriation of Blair are too good to be true. Melville cannot live with such free, verbal authority. The attempt fails because the sea cannot give up its threatening power in the way the novel would like it to. The sea, for Melville, always tropes the past, and the past is always for him the endlessly fertile yet inarticulate, inchoate, and anxiety-producing substrate of his artistic identity. Without escape from the sea, from his authority-less youth as a "dog before the mast," Melville cannot write himself into being; yet without the sea, writing has no motive. The sea, in Melville's art, demands redemption, a movement of active self-awareness which takes responsibility, figuratively, for the past in all its both expressed and inexpressible pain. This is the hard lesson which Redburn and Ishmael must learn; this is why Pierre, just before his suicide, returns to the sea.

The fancy, the easy flightiness, with which *Omoo* attempts to deal with the sea leaves Melville with an "incurable distaste," in spite of the novel's exuberance and charm. Both the delights of *Omoo*'s straightforward rhetorical persuasiveness and Melville's negative reaction underlie his gathering quest to become familiar with the denizens of a world formed in fright, to base his dialectic on and force his rhetoric to take strength from the appalling power of blackness. Newly exuberant in the exercise of his talent and his social authority, Melville defers to his next novel, *Mardi*, his reaction against a synecdochic rhetoric capable of domesticating and dismasting the sources of human anguish that it will become one of the chief marks of his greatness to confront honestly, as well as with brilliance.

5

"The drawn soul of genius": *Mardi*

We mortals ourselves spring all naked and scabbardless into the world.
Yet, rather, are we scabbards to our souls. And the drawn soul of genius is
more glittering than the drawn cimeter of Saladin.
—Melville, *Mardi*

In March of 1848, just as the English edition of *Omoo* was
about to appear, Melville announced to his publisher, John Murray, that his
next novel would be a departure: "A *real* romance of mine is no Typee or Omoo,
& is made of different stuff altogether." Feeling "irked, cramped & fettered by
plodding along with dull common places," he vowed "to plume my pinions for
a flight" (*Letters* 70). After *Mardi* appeared, a review in the *New York Daily
Tribune* of May 10, 1849, judged that it "aims at a much higher mark and fails to
reach it" (Leyda *Log* I, 303), and Melville, in July, explained to his new British
publisher, Richard Bentley (Murray had rejected the manuscript because of its
fictional nature), that, despite hostile reviews, " 'Mardi,' in its higher purposes,
has not been written in vain" (*Letters* 86). From the beginning, the novel
represented an expanded and risky venture for the fledgling writer.

Modern criticism reasserts both *Mardi*'s departure from its predecessors and
the negative judgments of contemporary reviewers;[1] the novel is forgiven its
"gaucheries" because it represents "the first bold stroke of Melville's greatest
work."[2] Yet in spite of obvious sense and almost universal currency, this judgment ignores the extent to which *Mardi* grows directly out of the synecdochic
rhetoric of *Omoo*. In his third novel, Melville, rather than setting an entirely
new course, exaggerates his reaction against the enabling irony of *Typee* and his
quest for the grounds of a declaration of independence ("no further connection") from the past. This exaggeration in turn reveals implications of his
tropological program which *Omoo* had passed over. It is more accurate to say
that the real departure for Melville as an author comes not between *Omoo* and
Mardi but within the latter novel, a view which helps to explain its glaring
structural inconsistencies.[3]

Synecdochic rhetoric, in *Omoo*, permits the *narrative* voice to appropriate
the terms of *authorial* self-discovery; freed from the metaleptic temporality of
Typee, the moment of telling absorbs the processes by which it came into being
as a persuasive act: the rhetoric of *Omoo*, in grounding itself on "the frequency

with which these incidents have been verbally related" and on its assertion of "no further connection" with *Typee,* denies the authority of its past, represented by the escape-narrative of its predecessor. In the exuberant, helter-skelter enjoyment of his voice, Melville gives his second novel over to a narrator construed without the irony which gave his initial work its authorial presence. Rather than basing its persuasiveness on a complex and suspenseful encounter between protagonist and setting, *Omoo* bills itself as a "simple recollection" or set of "most grateful remembrances" of its hero's wanderings. Having no past to account for, it moves from event to event without anxiety as to its narrator's future; its tale, after all, has been told many times before. Its protagonist is directionless—he yearns only for the "billows"—and its events do not establish or aggrandize its authorial ethos.

Mardi picks up where *Omoo* leaves off in shifting the theater of its action from suspenseful events and historical encounters to memory, the mind. Michael Davitt Bell follows Feidelson and others in associating the shift with a form of Romance in which "the imagination clearly undermined conventional conceptions of reality" (146). Dryden sees in *Mardi* "an almost unbearable tension between the freedom of the inner world and the restrictions of the outer" (56). Brodhead concludes that Melville "comes to see that its true action is not his characters' adventures but his own creative process: that the real object of its quest is nothing his characters seek but the mental world he himself discloses through the act of creating his book" ("Creating the Creative" 39). The synecdochic rhetoric carried over from *Omoo* to *Mardi* leads to internalization, a phenomenon common in high Romantic literature.[4]

The internalized quest-romance which *Mardi*'s exaggerated, synecdochic rhetoric grounds in turn explains the bemusing plenitude of the novel. If its center of consciousness is to be associated with author rather than narrator, then anything on the author's mind may become grist for its mill, as Melville acknowledges in apologizing to Bentley for "the peculiar thoughts & fancies of a Yankee upon politics & other matters" as well as the "metaphysics" and "conic-sections" which throng the book. The "mental world" of *Mardi* reflects a "certain something unmanageable in us, that bids us to do this or that, and be done it must—hit or miss" (*Letters* 86). It displays a sprawling weight of detail which leaves it cloaked in what Elizabeth Melville, writing to Hope Shaw, calls its "fogs" (*Log* I, 302). Detached from the real islands of *Omoo*'s world, *Mardi* exercises a freedom which seemingly escapes rhetorical control.

The bagginess of *Mardi* teaches Melville an important lesson about synecdochic rhetoric—its tendency to reduce events, experiences, images, ideas, and formulations to mental bric-a-brac; within the solipsistic (to use Bloom's term) world of internalized quest-romance, since anything is possible, all things tend to become equal; the ironic relationships on which judgment depends in *Typee* reduce to metonymies, associations without objective justification. Mardi becomes an internal counterpart to the metonymic, spatialized, directionless world of Typee valley. In a similar manner, the literal nature and function of the novel's characters and actions become unstable. Taji is first and third person, pursuer pursued, guilty savior; Babbalanja at times duplicates the historical lore of Mohi and at other times the poetical flights of Yoomy, and he himself is duplicated by his own indwelling devil, Azzageddi; Taji's quest loses rather than gains focus as the complex presences of his companions are peeled off from it; Hautia must be escaped and confronted both, but nothing comes of either tactic; Yillah, for whom Taji yearns and quests, leads him to the foggiest of encounters with Hautia. The synecdochic world of *Mardi*, in all its spectacular freedom, undercuts the achieved rhetorical structures responsible for the clarity and focus of Melville's earlier authorial voice.

Mardi exemplifies Melville's process of development in the spectacular leeway he gives his rhetoric before reigning it in. He risks the coherence of the novel in order to explore the limits of synecdoche; for all that it risks, his exploration yields breathtaking insights into rhetorical processes themselves—into the literary structures on which the expression and communication of human meaning depend. In *Mardi* Melville's understanding of time and its relationships both to creativity—to authorial selfhood—and to death sharpens dramatically and finds expression even as the novel, viewed as a coherent work of literature, or "mental world," risks being swamped by its bloated rhetoric. Figurative representations of time and creativity in *Mardi* set the terms for Melville's engagement with the ideas of Emerson, which surface in his consciousness just after completion of the novel.[5] This engagement, which represents a significant commentary on the rhetorical underpinnings of Romanticism, then underlies the subsequent dialectical recoil against synecdochic rhetoric evident in *Redburn*. As an experiment in applied rhetoric, *Mardi* is not the least bit baggy.

In discussing Melville's treatment of time in *Mardi*, Dryden summarizes the essential case. As the book progresses, "the distinctions which the narrator has made between past and present gradually dissolve until *Mardi* becomes not only an account of past dreaming but an account of present dreaming as well" (*Melville's Thematics* 54). Both Taji's and the narrator's dream worlds "illustrate the truth of man's subjection to the tyranny of time" (57). Thus, the "narrative circularity" which "dovetails" Taji's and the narrator's levels of the work produces a "darker, more appalling vision" than the "good-natured cynicism of the verbose Ishmael" (58). The structure which Dryden describes results from the synecdochic order of the novel. Because Melville avoids the metaleptic resolution of *Typee*, Taji and narrator blend and overlap without producing an enabling interplay between physical experience and imaginative freedom. Yet the tone of *Mardi*, as Feidelson points out (175), is more comic than appalling. A novel in which the present expands synecdochically into the past and future cannot move pointedly toward either epiphany or apocalypse. Synecdoche distinguishes *Mardi*, in spite of its portentous ending, from mainstream, tragic forms of American Romance.[6]

The complexity of Melville's treatment of time in *Mardi* emerges in the first chapter of the novel.

> The days went slowly round and round, endless and uneventful as cycles in space. Time, and time-pieces! How many centuries did my hammock tell, as pendulum-like it swung to the ship's dull roll, and ticked the hours and ages. Sacred forever be the Arcturion's fore-hatch—alas! sea-moss is over it now—and rusty forever the bolts that held together that old sea hearth-stone, about which we so often lounged. Nevertheless, ye lost and leaden hours, I will rail at ye while life lasts. (5)

On the one hand, current time stands as a synecdoche for "ages" and "endless" cycles—a trope repeated throughout *Mardi* in such statements as "to ourselves, we all seem coeval with creation" (12); "all generations are blended" (12); "her fabulous past was her present" (158); "with Oro, the sun is co-eternal; and the same life that moves the moose, animates alike the sun and Oro. All are parts of One" (615). On the other hand, the present is belated, a "rail" at "lost and leaden hours" preempted by the past: "that which long endures full-fledged, must have long lain in the germ" (228); "it is Time, old midsummer Time, that has made the old world what it is" (271); "all Mardi's history—beginning, middle, and finis—was written out in capitals in the first page penned" (580–81). The future, in *Mardi*, is "sacred forever" but "rusty forever"—a projection of stasis, of "Time's endless tunnel" (230)—and "the eternity to come, is but a prolongation of time present" (576).

Time, in *Mardi*, expands out synecdochically from the present moment through a rhetorical process of "seeing that somehow all presence is at least part of a mutilated whole," to quote Bloom on the characteristic working of the trope (*Map* 98). The exhilarating but disturbing ("mutilated") nature of synecdochic time carries over into, and becomes clearer, in the context of the novel's discussions of art: "Our eyes are pleased with the redness of the rose, but another sense lives upon its fragrance. Its redness you must approach, to view: its invisible fragrance pervades the field. So, with the Koztanza. Its mere beauty is restricted to its form: its expanding soul, past Mardi does embalm" (597). Synecdochic rhetoric in *Mardi* compensates for the "mutilated" status of the whole which it represents—"forever rusty" or "embalmed"—by promising the freedom of unlimited expansion, unrestricted beauty. The "whole" is "muti-lated" because its denial of metaleptic or ironic relationships calls to mind not merely the imaginative freedom of art (and its correspondingly baggy mental world) but, as we will see, death. At this point, the rhetorical world carried over from *Omoo* begins to reveal the full measure of its distressing complexity.

Numerous pronouncements on death in *Mardi* repeat Babbalanja's percep-tion that "we die, because we live. But none the less does Babbalanja quake. And if he flies not, 'tis because he stands the center of a circle; its every point a leveled dart; and every bow, bent back" (587). Experience, in *Mardi,* is circular not in the progressive sense of *Typee* but because the soul "finds eternities before and behind" (230), and "backward or forward, eternity is the same" (237). Time in the novel reduces to "cycles" which are "endless" and "uneventful." Like the image of the Koztanza as a rose, it translates into spatial terms, troped by the meaningless, hypnotic oscillations of Taji's hammock. Life evokes death in its synecdochic temporal stasis.

All of Mardi participates in the figurative pattern evident in Melville's han-dling of time. The archipelago presents a spatialized, microcosmic world in which past, present, and future blend together in a proliferation of static, metonymically related images of human passivity or powerlessness. Both the fictional Taji and his narrative alter ego are not so much subject to the tyranny of time as disabled by its synecdochic expansiveness. Rather than genealogizing the author's voice—explaining how the story came to be—as *Typee* did, *Mardi* succumbs to a grotesque inflation of the fanciful but passive wanderings of *Omoo.* When the search for Yillah begins, as John Seelye notes, "the complex personality of the narrator is anatomized into a polysensuum" composed of the five peripatetic comrades, "yet all of the participants in the sea-borne sym-posium are but constituents of a larger subjective consciousness—the chartless voyager" (32). Taji's quest, in its chartlessness, takes on the synecdochic colors of time and art in the novel, turning the entire work into an exploration of the implications of Melville's break with the rhetoric of *Typee.*

The synecdochic vision of art's "expanding soul" in *Mardi* gives rise to a set of images of the creative process which profoundly influence Melville's develop-ment and reform his understanding of authorial ethos. For the first time, Melville begins to acknowledge the importance of the sea to his sense of artistic self. He is still optimistic about escape from the past, so the "endless sea" which faces Taji at the end of his quest is not yet the "expanding" horizon which drives Pip prophetically insane in *Moby-Dick.* Ishmael's sea, gazed into, will give back the "tormenting mild image" of the self, which is the "ungraspable phantom of life"; here, when Yillah looks into the sea, the narrator can believe that she "would fain have had me plunge into it with her, to rove through its depths"

(145). Both surface and deep (opened to the gaze in *Omoo*) promise unbounded exploration, "no limit but the limitless; no bottom but the bottomless" (460). Melville is as entranced with the synecdochic freedom of *Mardi* as he was with the irony of *Typee* or escape from the past in *Omoo*. In a central group of tropes of artistic creativity, he attempts to explain the relationship between this freedom and his own rhetorical self-image and authority.

At the point when *Mardi* abandons its first mode—Davis's "narrative beginning"—for its second, or "Romantic interlude," a chapter with the obvious title "Something under the Surface" describes the attack of a predator on a school of blithe and uncaring fish who have just sung Melville's first published poem. Melville's swordfish "chevalier," who travels "with spear ever in rest," charges the shoal, "transfixing the fish on his weapon" (151). Previous to this event, Melville has spelled out the figurative significance of his "dread fish of prey."

> A right valiant and jaunty Chevalier is our hero; going about with his long Toledo perpetually drawn. Rely upon it, he will fight you to the hilt, for his bony blade has never a scabbard. He himself sprang from it at birth; yea, at the very moment he leaped into the Battle of Life; as we mortals ourselves spring all naked and scabbardless into the world. Yet, rather, are we scabbards to our souls. And the drawn soul of genius is more glittering than the drawn cimeter of Saladin. But how many let their steel sleep, till it eat up the scabbard itself, and both corrode to rust-chips. (104)

"Something under the Surface" consciously and willfully tropes the relationship between Melville's developing sense of his popular audience—including those who want nonfictional, cannibal-island tales—and the "drawn soul of genius," which he had determined to ply in *Mardi*. The swordfish becomes a synecdoche for "we mortals ourselves" and for the dangerous creative life which we hide within the womblike scabbard of conventional thought. At this point, Melville offers a synecdochic trope of creativity as an answer to the "rust-chips" of progressive time. Later on, in the famous chapter "Dreams," he repeats and elaborates his figure.

> Dreams! Dreams! golden dreams: endless, and golden, as the flowery prairies, that stretch away from the Rio Sacramento, in whose waters Danae's shower was woven;—prairies like rounded eternities: jonquil leaves beaten out; and my dreams herd like buffaloes, browsing on to the horizon, and browsing on round the world; and among them, I dash with my lance, to spear one, ere they all flee. (366)

Amid a welter of synecdochic spatial and temporal imagery, the narrator recapitulates the attack of the swordfish in the earlier passage. A trope of aggressiveness against society now operates within the mind. The lovely expansiveness of the scene—the endless richness of the "mental world"—is unsettled by the suggestion that internal aggression is necessary lest its denizens "all flee" from one's lance. The "drawn soul of genius" has now become associated with the particular requirements of the author, who must attack his own limitless internal resources in order to keep sword and scabbard from corroding.

Melville acknowledges both his synecdoche and its potentially disturbing implications just shortly after the passage quoted above, in the surprising turn-around which ends the chapter. He asserts that "Ay: many, many souls are in me" (367) and that "with all the past and present pouring in me, I roll down my billow from afar" (368). If thwarted in his exercise of genius, he avows, defiantly, that "down unto death, whence I came, will I go, like Xenophon retreating on Greece, all Persia brandishing her spears in his rear" (368). "Dreams" concludes with an image of the possessed writer.

> My cheek blanches white while I write; I start at the scratch of my pen; my own mad brood of eagles devours me; fain would I unsay this audacity; but an iron-mailed hand clenches mine in a vice, and prints down every letter in my spite. Fain would I hurl off this Dionysius that rides me; my thoughts crush me down till I groan; in far fields I hear the song of the reaper, while I slave and faint in this cell. (368)

The final picture of the writer in "Dreams" adds to the initial imagery of the chapter a note of pain and defiance which brings to light its full disturbing power. This agonized defiance duplicates Taji's final gesture at the end of the novel. Melville imposes on the expansive imagery of freedom which gives shape to the novel an additional set of figurative values which begin to claim increasing force.

"Dreams" moves from aggressive, synecdochic images of creativity to images of possession; it predicts Babbalanja's comment that the wise Bardianna "spoke right out, going straight to the point like a javelin" (317) in asserting the universal bedevilment of humankind. Melville's tropes of creativity superimpose on the synecdochic "chartless voyage" of *Mardi* multiple instances of the classical topos of "daimonization," which Brodhead finds at the center of the works (including *Moby-Dick*) that Melville later writes under Hawthorne's influence (*School* 34–38) and which Robert Milder traces to Melville's reading of Goethe. As with his synecdoches, Melville's images of possession infiltrate *Mardi* throughout. The relationship between voyager and narrator becomes one of reciprocal possession; Yillah and Taji inhabit and daimonize each other's memories in a manner which looks, on the one hand, to the synecdochic denial of progressive time and, on the other hand, to the generation of fabulous tales, microscopic versions of the freely creative plenitude which "fogs" the novel;

indeed, the entire work is placed by Melville under the sign of the "certain something unmanageable in us" whose daimonic influence "bids us to do this or that, and be done it must."

Bloom associates possession, or "daimonization," with the trope of hyperbole and the corresponding Freudian defense mechanism of repression (*Map* 83ff.). The logic of Melville's tropes embraces these associations clearly, on a rhetorical or ethical rather than psychological level. Hyperbole, beginning with the list of imaginary comestibles which opens *Typee*, designates a use of language which, through exaggeration, calls attention to itself, to the possibilities of telling rather than to the situation reported. In a strong form, hyperbole can repress the underlying content of an utterance in the way, for example, that the exuberant and picturesque narratives of Melville's early novels occult the importance of the sea, as a trope of muteness, to his dialectic of self-actualization. In writing to his publisher about *Mardi*, Melville proposes possession by his own voice, by undeniable expressive needs, as the reason for the novel's bagginess. This is a logical outcome of synecdochic internalization, of finding oneself wandering in a mental world populated by a clamoring and ever-expanding plenitude of metonymically related subjects. Synecdoche, the assertion of "no further connection" with one's enabling past, results in a hyperbolic ethos, an authorial presence possessed by a free, self-authorizing, and repressive language.

What the synecdochic and hyperbolic rhetoric of *Mardi* represses is Melville's investment in the ironic and metaleptic structures of *Typee*, the tragic impossibility of his voice finally achieving freedom from the past. What is expelled from the rhetorical level of the novel returns thematically, as Babbalanja's discussion of Lombardo's "Koztanza" makes clear. In spite of Augusta Melville's equation of *Mardi* with the Koztanza (Leyda, *Log* I, 287), it is *Typee*, not Melville's work in progress, about which Babbalanja discourses. Deep within himself the writer Lombardo finds a simulacrum of Typee valley, locus of creative birth for Melville. It is "a serene, sunny, ravishing region; full of sweet scents, singing birds, wild plaints, roguish laughs, prophetic voices" (595). Again in typically expansive fashion, the hyperbolic world of the Mardian archipelago recuperates all of the key impulses—realistic, satiric, and romantic—of the found authorial voice of *Typee*, including the cross-cultural commentary deemphasized in excised versions. Melville's new voice retells and represents his old in a gesture, now global in the novel, comparable to the narrator's figuratively backward-looking acceptance of the gift of tappa from his native hostess at the point of final parting in *Omoo*.

In *Mardi* a dialectical opposition emerges between the thematic content of the novel—Taji's exploration of the archipelago and "voyage thither"—and its overriding rhetorical organization. The story of *Mardi* repeats and represents, in its sprawling but futile quest, the ironic and metaleptic modes of time and enablement discovered by the author of *Typee*. In contrast, the synecdochic structure of the novel, its internalized freedom, shows itself more and more static, deadly, threatening, and daimonic. In *Typee*, the voice of the novel struggles to find and identify with a source of authority which can escape from the dangerous muteness of the sea, of its own preliterate past. In *Mardi*, the large-scale shape of the tale, determined by the rhetorical program carried over from *Omoo*, takes on that disabling potential.

In *Typee*, metaleptic time redeems the narrator's ironically disabled or fragmented status and builds a bridge to and away from the threatening past represented by the sea. In *Mardi*, Melville's overarching commitment to freedom, to his synecdochic rhetorical experiment, dooms the processes of redemption to failure. Taji can never make up for the past, find Yillah, escape guilt, or stop fleeing; yet his lack of success results from the large-scale rhetorical structure of the work rather than from internal thematic logic. His narrative consciousness, his defiance of the conditions of the fiction within which he finds himself, continues to make sense. His rhetoric, after all, is that of Melville in *Typee;* he holds out for metaleptic redemption against all odds. When Hautia offers him the dream of a synecdochic present—"I will take thee, where thy Past shall be forgotten, where thou wilt soon learn to love the living, not the dead"— he responds, "Better to me, oh Hautia! all the bitterness of my buried dead than all the sweets of the life thou canst bestow; even, were it eternal" (651).

Taji, as a trope of Melville's found literary voice in *Typee*, refuses to understand that his novel, *Mardi*, will end. His metaleptic quest seems likely to expand, synecdochically, forever. He presents the interesting figure of a fictional character who sets out to transcend the boundaries of the work in which he exists. Yet he insists on challenging the limits of *Mardi* in thematic terms rather than in the rhetorical terms which, as narrator, he should control. As a result of this inside-out turn in Melville's rhetorical dialectics, Taji effectively gives up his status as narrator in order to attempt an impossible escape, in order to become a figure of freedom in the enabling ironic and metaleptic terms of Melville's earlier voice rather than the pervasive synecdochic terms of his internalized fictional environment.

Since the dialectic acted out by Taji in *Mardi* recapitulates thematically the terms of Melville's rhetorical self-discovery of *Typee*, the synecdochic structure which dooms Taji tropes its successful introjection and *Aufhebung* of its own past, now represented by the earlier novel. *Mardi* achieves a successful metaleptic rhetorical gesture in sticking to a synecdochic program of internalization that figures the threatening endlessness and muteness of the sea, which in turn troped the past in Melville's first work. Melville's ethos, in the sprawling yet rhetorically pointed bagginess of *Mardi,* takes on the tropological colors of its own impossible past, of his preliterary experiences. Were it incapable of appropriating its history, the terms of its own generation, *Mardi* would have nothing to celebrate except muteness; its very sense of freedom would be foreclosed; it would have no voice. The dialectical interplay between the synecdoche and hyperbole of *Mardi* and the metalepsis and irony of *Typee* makes the figures necessary to each other, reciprocally enabling, in Melville's developing ethos. By establishing, fictionally, the interplay between them, Melville internalizes the interplay between rhetorical freedom and the quest for redemption of the past. This is a "higher aim" of the last importance to the accelerating pace of his literary career.

The complex rhetorical triumph which takes place in *Mardi* leads Melville back to the sea and to a consideration of the extraordinary figurative weight which it carries in relation to his sense of authority and of his developing career. The sea, as Melville meditates on it in *Mardi,* carries over into a famous letter to Duyckinck, written shortly after he finished the novel, in which he locates himself in relation to Emerson, whom he had recently heard lecture for the first time. Melville's treatment of the sea in *Mardi* and subsequent pronouncements concerning Emerson fit together to form a coherent and concerted response to the tropology of the novel. This response composes one of the clearest and most profound chapters in the story of his development, and it enables us to understand the motivation and direction behind his next rhetorical departure.[7]

The sea inhabits Melville's comments on Emerson in terms of the famous image of the "deep dive" which it elaborates.

> Nay, I do not oscillate in Emerson's rainbow, but prefer rather to hang myself in mine own halter than swing in any other man's swing. Yet I think Emerson is more than a brilliant fellow. Be his stuff begged, borrowed, or stolen, or of his own domestic manufacture he is an uncommon man. . . . The truth is that we are all sons, grandsons, or nephews or great-nephews of those who go before us. No one is his own sire. . . . I love all men who *dive.* Any fish can swim near the surface, but it takes a great whale to go down stairs five miles or more; & if he dont attain the bottom, why, all the lead in Galena can't fashion the plumet that will. I'm not talking of Mr Emerson now—but of the whole corps of thought-divers, that have been diving & coming up again with bloodshot eyes since the world began. (*Letters* 78–79)

On the one hand, Melville seems to appropriate the "brilliance" of Emerson to the rhetorical formulations of *Mardi:* "better to sink in boundless deeps, than float on vulgar shoals" (557); "the ocean we would sound is unfathomable; and however much we add to our line, when it is out, we feel not the bottom"

(577). On the other hand, his letter expresses the concern that he not be accused of borrowing Emerson's views. The exact relation between the two depends on the image of the "dive," which appears, tellingly, in several places in *Mardi*. It is through the trope of "deep diving" that Melville chooses to explore his relationship with both the sea and Emerson's thought.

In Moldoldo, the Mardian travelers witness a funeral ceremony referred to as the "last, long plunge of the diver" (303). Later, Babbalanja says to Yoomy, "Though Yoomy soars, and Babbalanja dives, both meet at last" (438). At the end of the novel, Hautia implores Taji to "dive thou" in her cave, since "all these may be had for the diving; and Beauty, Health, Wealth, Long Life, and the Last Lost Hope of man" (651). When Taji returns empty-handed, she concludes, "Ah, Taji! for thee, bootless deep diving." Diving links the synecdochic "bottomless sea" of the novel with its temporal counterpart, evoked by the line "As thou sinkest, and sinkest for aye" in the Moldoldo burial song (304). Both are associated in the ceremony with death and thus prefigure the dire overtones of Taji's final flight.

In Hautia's cave, Taji spies "the Past and Yillah" side by side, but when he challenges Hautia, "All the Past smote all the Present in me" (652). Taji's diving remains trapped within the synecdochic structure of *Mardi*—limitless and thus bootless—and thus fails to redeem the past, return the novel to the metaleptic pattern of *Typee*. In diving after the image of Yillah in the vortex, Taji feels himself die and become, in another figurative reversal, his own "spirit's phantom's phantom" (653). The movement of metaleptic vocal authority which Taji's voyage tropes is frozen into an endless oscillation between past and present, life and death, quest and flight, depth and height, dark and sight, fate and will, and other figural pairs with which Melville plays throughout the novel: images of past authority remain paralyzed by the synecdochic and hyperbolic disablement imposed upon them by the larger structure of *Mardi*. The oscillation of key image-pairs, like the static, repetitive movements of Taji's hammock early on in the tale, evokes death. It is through the dialectical counteroperation of metalepsis and irony on the internalized, synecdochic world that death comes to figure the "mutilation" of the whole which that world represents.

Death has little bearing in *Typee*; the metaleptic and ironic voice of the story seeks escape instead from muteness, the past, and the sea. In *Omoo*, only the nautical burial of the two shipmates brings death into the picture, and in this case it becomes another trope of rootlessness, of "no further connection" with the past. Death plays a more central role in *Mardi*, but its impact is dispersed by the rhetorical structure of the work: Taji operates within the novel in the death-defying metaleptic and ironic terms of *Typee*, and the synecdochic, internalized world within which he roves permits death to exist only in the mode of endless expansion—the endlessness or bottomlessness of the sea, as the Mold-oldo burial makes clear. Melville locates death in the intersection of his two figural programs, and as such attaches it to the novel's images of diving. Thus, the trope of diving and, by later association, the philosophy of Emerson preside over the incorporation of death into the rhetoric of Melville's authorial voice—an incorporation which comes to full fruit in the magnificent and poignant figures of his next novel, *Redburn*.

Melville's letter to Duyckinck associates the philosophy of Emerson with the metaleptic enterprise of appropriating the past, including one's own origins: "I could readily see in Emerson, notwithstanding his merit, a gaping flaw. It was, the insinuation, that had he lived in those days when the world was made, he might have offered some valuable suggestions" (*Letters* 79). Emerson's pretense strikes Melville as "cracked right across the brow." His own formula for relating to the past has become antimetaleptic, for "no one is his own sire." By taking the "long plunge," Emerson dooms himself to failure; yet in doing so, he himself becomes a synecdoche for "the whole corps of thought-divers, that have been diving & coming up again with bloodshot eyes since the world began." Melville, newly aware of the problematic nature of a set of attitudes precisely troped by his novel, distances himself by invoking a metaphor for suicide: "to hang myself in mine own halter than swing in any other man's swing."

Melville's commentary on Emerson demonstrates how profoundly the deadly concatenation of contradictory figures—irony and metalepsis on the one hand and synecdoche and hyperbole on the other—has interrupted and complicated his understanding of the sources of vocal authority. Rather than escaping from the past, he asserts the necessity of being the "son" of the multi-tudinous progenitors who "go before us." It is no coincidence that the hero of Melville's next novel is his first to sail without an alias, to give his family name to his tale, and to seek an understanding of both his own childhood and his father. Yet in making the assertion which leads to *Redburn*, Melville figures himself as standing suicidally alone, ready to "hang myself in mine own halter," like Taji at the end of *Mardi* or Harry Bolton in the work to come.

The letter to Duyckinck, in the context of the "diving" imagery of *Mardi*, again typifies the dialectical manner in which Melville's rhetoric develops. He commits himself willfully to the synecdochic program of his novel, follows it into its hyperbolic implications, uses this framework to appropriate and review his earlier (ironic and metaleptic) rhetoric, and then gives expression to the deadly (death-invoking) nature of his concatenated figures. Each element of his tropological program is balanced by the others; he refuses to back off from any of them; his figures pressure and corrupt each other to the point that any assertion of authority would seem to be contradictory, impossible. He forces his art to an impasse, to the sort of catachresis which might easily produce a creative block. Yet in the five months following his letter to Duyckinck he finishes, incredibly, two additional novels, one of them—*Redburn*—a masterpiece.

What rescues Melville's voice and gives birth to his next rhetorical departure emerges directly out of his dramatic, suicidal pose of independence from Emerson. In declaring his freedom from Emerson's influence, he ends up, as the nautical figures transported from *Mardi* suggest, comparing himself to Emerson, a gesture of extraordinary confidence. Later in the same letter, in a gesture even more outrageous, he implicitly compares himself to Shakespeare.

> I would to God Shakespeare had lived later, & promenaded in Broadway. Not that I might have had the pleasure of leaving my card for him at the Astor, or made merry with him over a bowl of the fine Duyckinck punch; but that the muzzle which all men wore on their souls in the Elizabethan day, might not have intercepted Shakspers full articulations. For I hold it a verity, that even Shakespeare, was not a frank man to the uttermost. And, indeed, who in this intolerant Universe is, or can be? (*Letters* 79–80)

For the first time, Melville's rhetoric has become centrally and essentially metaphoric. Rather than emphasizing tropes in which one term appropriates, includes, preempts, or accounts for the other, he begins to make comparisons between distinct and separate entities—himself and Emerson, himself and Shakespeare. Metaphor, as *Redburn* will show, addresses the disabling ironic fragmentations embodied in Tommo and the world of *Typee* without superimposing figures of temporal redemption (metalepsis) or internal freedom (synecdoche), in which Melville can no longer entirely take stock.[8]

If there is an irony in the role which *Mardi* plays in Melville's development, it is that the work which evokes comparisons with Emerson leaves him further from Emerson's brand of Romanticism—overtly metaleptic and synecdochic—than before. Melville's new rhetorical understanding incorporates death—evidenced in his suicidal pose of independence—as a figure of difference, of unbridgeable gaps, of the limits of the power and freedom of literary language, of a past which must be understood in terms of figurative comparisons rather than processes of encompassment or redemption. Melville's fantasy of Shakespeare on Broadway involves less an attempt to redress the muteness of the past—to remove Shakespeare's "soul" from its "muzzle" as he has his own from its "scabbard" in *Mardi*—than a gesture of appreciation which metaphorically distinguishes Melville's genius from the values of the mob: "And do not think, my boy, that because I, impulsively broke forth in jubilations ⟨at discovering⟩ over Shakspeare, that, therefore, I am of the number of the *snobs* who burn their tuns of rancid fat at his shrine. No, I would stand afar off & alone, & burn some pure Palm oil, the product of some overtopping trunk" (*Letters* 79).

Nowhere before the letter to Duyckinck has Melville overtly discussed or implicitly compared himself to other writers and seen himself among their company in spite of his modernism, egoistic independence, and unique genius. Nowhere since the antic fantasy of head-bashing in the second of the "Fragments from a Writing Desk" has he described himself so exuberantly in terms of a suicidal gesture. His extraordinary leap of confidence, breezy superiority of tone, and new sense of accommodation with the past enable his ethos to encompass other circumstances than those gathering in the rhetoric of *Mardi.* Melville now has a son, Malcolm, born February 16, and a niece, Allan's daughter, born two days later. He is fast accruing all the social as well as literary authority which he had previously associated with Gansevoort and with the genteel posture of Blair's rhetoric. The "higher purposes" of his third novel do not, in any way, seem "in vain."

Viewed against the background of his social as well as literary life in early 1849, Melville's February 5 attendance of Emerson's lecture may have been fortuitous in other ways than occasioning his telling exchange of letters with Duyckinck. If Sealts is right, the Emerson lecture which Melville heard was "Natural Aristocracy" or "The Superlative in Manners and Literature," most likely the former (*Pursuing Melville* 258). In either case he would have been introduced to a line of thought which placed artistic genius at the top of the social order—exactly the sort of argument calculated to lay to rest any remaining anxiety in regards to his own circumstances as measured against the early example of Blair and Chesterfield. The author of *Mardi,* like that of the Koztanza, can declare himself to have "created the creative" in discovering, putting into play, and experimenting with a form of rhetorical invention—a figurative program—capable of transmuting its limited sources into an authorial ethos able to stand up to comparison with writers of genius occupying the highest rank of the literary and cultural order. For Melville to see himself in this light would, in turn, have been reinforced by the chauvinism of the *Yankee Doodle* and *Literary World* circles in which he moved.[9]

In chapter 2 of *Mardi,* "A Calm," Melville relates the entire range of rhetorical figures on which the novel depends with his experience of the sea, imbued with the overtones of death which will drive him to the metaphoric response indicated by the Duyckinck letter. This passage, like many throughout Melville's later works, plays off against his description, early in *Typee,* of sailing for the Marquesas Islands. As an example of both the expanded power and dramatically altered tropological structure of Melville's rhetoric, "A Calm" provides a good benchmark of the extent which he had developed in his four years as a novelist.

"A Calm" begins by evoking the metaleptic sense of self central to *Typee:*

"Certain nameless associations revived in me my old impressions upon first witnessing as a landsman this phenomenon of the sea. Those impressions may merit a page" (9). Melville disables the metaleptic nature of the experience by judging its origins to be "nameless" and by placing the entire scene within the narrator's mind—rather than interesting the reader or his shipmates, it interests himself. Correspondingly, the rhetorical apostrophe which helps enliven the beginning of *Typee* turns into soliloquy. The narrator refers to himself as "he" throughout the incident in order to present himself as a synecdoche for all who undergo the ordeal. The narrative self is all.

The narrator's disabled metaleptic memories only add to the distressing nature of the experience. He becomes conscious of his "utter helplessness" and the loss of "his glorious liberty of volition." He finds himself trapped in a static, timeless and spaceless, synecdochically expansive world: "And all this, and more than this, is a calm." He "shakes himself," "grows madly skeptical," feels "horrible doubts," and is "anxious concerning his soul." The all-embracing motionlessness makes him question his own life: "He is taken by surprise, never having dreamt of a state of existence where existence itself seems suspended. He shakes himself in his coat, to see whether it be empty or no."

In the midst of the deadly calm, the narrator becomes possessed by his own voice in the most striking example of "daimonic" hyperbole that will appear in Melville's writings until Isabel plays her guitar for Pierre.

> His voice begins to grow strange and portentous. He feels it in him like something swallowed too big for the esophagus. It keeps up a sort of involuntary interior humming in him, like a live beetle. His cranium is a dome full of reverberations. The hollows of his very bones are as whispering galleries. He is afraid to speak loud, lest he be stunned; like the man in the bass drum. (10)

"A Calm" pointedly reverses the rhetoric associated with articulation and muteness in *Typee*. In the earlier novel, the uniformity of the outside world breeds quiet and torpor. Here it produces an expanding internal din which daimonizes every corner of the body and threatens to explode into speech with stunning force. The sea provokes not muteness but a choking plenitude of internal reverberations. In *Typee* and *Omoo*, the external world, as in the figure of tattooing, marks and determines the inner; in *Mardi*, the inner voice feeds its own monstrous expansion until there is nothing left to do but "endure" it, of which the narrator exclaims, "Enough to attend to, Heaven knows." External quest gives way to internalized endurance. Having escaped from the past, one is grotesquely trapped within oneself.

The spectacular, unbearable rhetoric of "A Calm" exemplifies the unsettling power which Melville's ethos achieves in *Mardi*. Having demonstrated his authority, justified his literary identity, and asserted beyond all doubt his vocal freedom, Melville faces a new rhetorical challenge—the capacity of his voice to throttle—mutilate—its own creative representations. *Mardi*'s rhetoric is rescued from solipsism by sheer exuberance and by its unceasing drive toward better understanding of its tropological imperatives. Yet the only way which Melville can finally discover a way to escape from the entropic circle of his internalized quest is through the violent suicidal trope of the Duyckinck letter—a deep dive which is also, as Ishmael will understand, a figurative falling on the drawn sword of one's own genius. The risk of *Mardi*'s "higher purpose" gives rise dialectically to the even greater risk of direct, metaphoric confrontation with death, which will bring *Redburn* closer to the bone of a literary ethos which Melville is coming to see as inexorably linked to an irredeemable past.

"More names, than things": *Redburn*

But people seem to have a great love for names; for to know a great many
names seems to look like knowing a good many things; though I should
not be surprised, if there were a great many more names, than things in
the world.

—Melville, *Redburn*

If Mardi reflects a "mental world" stimulated by the intellectual passions of the literary life, *Redburn* embodies a different type of inspiration—an authorship engaged, in full maturity, with worldly circumstances. Where the former novel calls to mind Melville's diving into Burton, Browne, Spenser, and Rabelais, as well as La Motte Fouquet and other Romancers, the latter evokes his clamorous milieu: his growing family and household, brother Tom's youthful turn to the sea, global political unrest, famine, and pestilence, and the jingoistic violence of the Astor Place riots;[1] *Redburn* spills from Melville's pen at "almost maniacal" speed (E. H. Miller 175) during the early summer of 1849 in a New York City terrorized by cholera. Yet despite its rushed and distracted circumstances and Melville's characteristic scorn for a "little nursery tale" produced under pressure from "duns all round" (*Letters* 93, 95), his fourth book advances his rhetorical development as much as does any of its predecessors; *Redburn* critiques the dialectical interplay of tropes—synecdoche, hyperbole, irony, and metalepsis—central to *Mardi* and transforms the static, internalized voice into a source of active metaphoric power. Suspicious of "that play of freedom & invention accorded only to the Romancer & poet," it explores the figurative underpinnings of realistic fiction, and it makes final Melville's break with the genteel rhetorical authority of Hugh Blair.

The interplay of metaleptic and synecdochic structures central to *Mardi* and to Melville's comments on Emerson reappears in *Redburn* in a passage describing emigrants on Prince's Dock.

For who was our father and our mother? Or can we point to any Romulus and Remus for our founders? Our ancestry is lost in the universal paternity; and Caesar and Alfred, St. Paul and Luther, and Homer and Shakespeare are as much ours as Washington, who is as much the world's as our own. We are the heirs of all time, and with all nations we divide our inheritance. On this Western Hemisphere all tribes and people are forming into one federated whole; and there is a future which shall see the estranged children of Adam restored as to the old hearth-stone in Eden. (169)

"Universal paternity," an echo of the "whole corps of thought-divers" which Melville opposes to Emerson's metaleptic self-siring in his letter to Duyckinck, introduces the emigrants whose plight dominates the second half of *Redburn*.[2] Equal symbols of fate and hope—Harry and Carlo—the emigrants experience time in a manner that touches the central concerns of the novel: Redburn's own attempt to redeem an image of "paternity" embodied in his "inherited" guide-book; the failure of his friendship with the "estranged" Harry; his initiation into his own "future" as a sailor. The work takes place in and attempts to rationalize the period between childhood and maturity, and it constantly calls on a combined retrospective and prospective vision—a past and future—embodied in the theme of emigration, to find meaning in the circumstances which it maps.

Redburn's narrative accrues synecdochic authority as an indefinitely protracted "in-between" tale suggestive of the voyage of life out of childhood and toward death; yet from this perspective its figurative meaning cannot be plumbed unless its end points—which correspond to the duality of its narrative perspective—can be metaleptically reconciled, a task at which the book has been judged to fail.[3] Redburn remains literally and figuratively at sea to the end; correspondingly, the emigrants carry their particular personalities into the new world. What one has been or can become in *Redburn* lies encysted in what one currently is. Tropes of hope and fate remain suspended and unresolved. Wellingborough's adventures affirm neither synecdochic expansiveness and freedom nor metaleptic redemption and self-actualization. However one chooses to interpret this impasse, its implications for Melville's rhetoric cannot be overstated.[4] It sets the stage for the operation of genuine metaphoric structures—an ordered play of comparisons, sublimations, and logical relationships—which underlie the novel's wealth of realistic observation and define the terms of its confrontation with the overarching theme of death, which now takes center stage in Melville's art.

The space which the metaphoric voice of *Redburn* occupies is announced by the novel's peculiar subtitles. The title page advertises:

Redburn
His First Voyage
Being the Sailor-boy Confessions and Reminiscences of
the Son-of-a-Gentleman, in the Merchant Service

Dryden points out that "reminiscences" implies a continuity between narrating and experiencing "I" but that "confessions" necessitates a gap: one confesses only when one has somehow changed (*Melville's Thematics* 60). Yet confession promises forgiveness, a reconciliation of fragmented subjectivity through an act of self-revelation. To Dryden, the narrative act itself indicates Redburn's achieved self (67); to Durand, in contrast, the uncanny return of the repressed power of the father destabilizes the grounds of identity, an indication that the "original metaphor" on which selfhood depends has "lost its moorings" (53).

A third way of making sense of *Redburn*'s subtitles begins with their acknowledgment of a source of identity in between the maturity implied by the narrative act and the lost paternal or childhood origins responsible for Wellingborough's disabled sense of self. The tale recounted is that of a "first voyage," and its "confessions and reminiscences" are those of a "sailor-boy." The subtitles imply that both further voyages and subsequent, adult "confessions and reminiscences" have preceded its telling.[5] The narrator holds himself aloof not just from his adventures but from his act of narrating; he deliberately disables the metaleptic structures which, in *Typee*, identify narrator with author. In so doing, he stresses the specificity, the particular moment and embodied experience, rather than the exemplary (synecdochic) nature of Wellingborough's voice. If author, narrator, and character relate to each other, they do so metaphorically, by means of figures that generate meaningful comparisons and judgments without bridging the gaps which separate them, at times tragically, from each other. For the first time, Melville exercises a "continuous imaginative presence" which is not invested in appropriating the mute past to the power of a current authorial ethos.

The metaphoric rhetoric of *Redburn* inscribes the narrative within a provisional, "in-between," irredeemably double standpoint which becomes its central figure, a figure repeated in the twins, comparisons, and relationships which its hero encounters throughout. This standpoint—in the contradictory blend of fatalism and hope which pervades *Redburn*—opens the door to its new rhetorical focus. In no longer seeking to expand or redeem time, the novel releases the socially engaged side of Melville's imagination, uncomfortably present in the cultural contrasts of *Typee* and satiric allegories of *Mardi*. Of the various social and political issues which *Redburn* addresses, the most important for Melville's rhetorical development is its attack on the class system as represented by "old-world" models of gentility—an attack explicated in detail by Samson in *White Lies*. Gentility in *Redburn* brings Melville back into confrontation with Blair and with the intimidating authority of his own earliest training and circumstances.

Samson ties Melville's satiric attack on gentility in *Redburn* to his references to Adam Smith and to the name of Wellingborough's ship, *The Highlander*. These allusions indicate, in the context of Melville's concern for "estranged" emigrants, alertness to "the irony of a Scottish people impoverished and cast Ishmael-like our of their homeland by a Scottish philosophy" (101). Adam Smith would almost certainly have been associated in Melville's mind with the values of his contemporary, fellow rhetorician, and close friend Hugh Blair.[6] Redburn's discovery that to be "the Son-of-a-Gentleman" offers no protection in a world dominated by a harsh, laissez-faire social order tropes, metaphorically, Melville's own detachment from Blair. In the course of *Redburn*, the intimidating force of hereditary aristocracy begins to give way to a notion of Emersonian natural aristocracy, evident, for example, in the seamanship and commanding personality which Jackson will bequeath to Ahab, and to the melting-pot democracy which Melville's ships come to represent. Never again will he justify rhetorical experimentation in terms of conventionally defined "higher" purposes.

Melville's democratic angle of vision, metaphoric rhetoric, and escape from Blair's authority color his newfound understanding of the past, as evidenced in *Redburn*'s marvelous, troubling treatment of early childhood. From all three perspectives, one can no longer count on memory to provide the substance, Blair's "thorough knowledge of the subject, and profound meditation on it," on which a metaleptically redeemed identity can be grounded. Neither can one imagine that the literary act is a synecdoche for vocalization in general. Because a unique identity, voice, or ethos cannot be assumed to represent, except on the basis of specific metaphoric relationships, that of others, the past becomes not a source of authoritative experience but of persuasive, albeit neither redemptive nor microcosmic, tropes. Redburn looks into the past, and it is just as complex and conflicted as the present.

On the one hand, Redburn calls on "shadowy reminiscences" in order to explain how his "imaginations" of seagoing life were "wonderfully assisted" by prior impressions (4). On the other hand, he complains that "I had learned to think much and bitterly before my time; all my young mounting dreams of glory had left me" (10). In the chapter entitled "How Wellingborough Redburn's Taste for the Sea Was Born and Bred in Him," which envisions past and future as fated results of each other, yet which denies resolution, identity comes to reside in the glass ship which "more than any thing else, converted my vague dreamings and longings into a definite purpose" (7). The "secret sympathy" which Wellingborough admits for the ship's broken figurehead (9) establishes the role of metaphoric similarity in representing a selfhood neither damned by absent paternity nor redeemed by confession, an "Ishmael" (62) incurably vulnerable to the provisional richness of worldly experience.

Redburn's famous refusal to put the glass figurehead "on his legs again, till I get on my own" (9) repeats the key trope of disablement—lameness—crucial to

Tommo's entrapment in Typee valley. Tommo, however, is rescued, "put on his legs again," by the power of Melville's found voice. In the inverted rhetorical world of *Mardi,* voice becomes inward, daimonic, trapped inside the disabling expansiveness of the novel's synecdochic structure. Concomitantly, authority, in *Mardi,* becomes associated with "deep diving" into the internalized sea of the mind. In *Redburn,* the hero feels an "insane desire" to "pry open" or "be the death of" the glass ship in order to discover "something wonderful" hidden inside. Wellingborough associates this childhood impulse with tales of the "dive" after Captain Kidd's treasure (8). Later on, Harry Bolton's unspoken secret, his unrevealed inner self, will cripple his relationship to Redburn. In these and other cases throughout the novel, to be an "Ishmael" is to be alienated from the inner truth which puts one on one's legs and gives one an authoritative voice.

Redburn articulates a sense of identity without access to figures of either freedom or temporal redemption, without the rhetorical underpinnings of a persuasive, ethical wholeness. Wellingborough continually defines himself in relation to people and objects from which he is inexorably separated or disjoined: ships, relatives, officers, shipmates, beggars, books, settings, friends, emigrants. These metaphoric comparisons and imagined relationships accumulate to produce an ethos determined by sublimation, by the displacing of desire onto related but distinct objects, a process characteristic of metaphor.[7] As comparisons accumulate in *Redburn,* Melville's voice discovers in the modesty associated with Wellingborough's disabled sense of self an organ for the exploration of dimly felt yet coherent responses to the social world. These responses and the metaphors which express them come to reveal, in a new and penetrating manner, the presence of death in human affairs.

The metaleptic and synecdochic programs of the Melville's earlier works measure the authority of experience in terms of its contribution to a "self-siring," or microcosmic ethos; familiarity with the frightening denizens of the universe comes through rhetorical appropriation of the past or expansion of the moment of voicing; continuity of self and other is imposed. In turn, death hardly bears on *Typee* and *Omoo* and is a vague aspect of the "mental world" of *Mardi.* In *Redburn,* however, it marks both the disabling fate of selfhood and the essential condition of its articulation; it suggests that the job of literature is not to know but to establish figurative relations to the not-known. Persuasive meaning in a world of dead or dying friends, shipmates, paupers, emigrants, and relatives hinges on sympathy rather than identity; one does not share the fate of those to whom metaphoric processes compare one. Death lurks behind all meaningful differences in *Redburn,* unites inner and outer worlds, and becomes the sign of metaphor itself, of the unbridgeable gap between terms, on which ethos in an unredeemed world, depends. Ishmael's escape from death at the end of *Moby-Dick* will throw him back into the world of redemptive and microcosmic (metaleptic and synecdochic) voicing, but the drama of his salvation will depend for its tension on the underlying metaphoric understanding of death brought to the fore in *Redburn*.

Death marks both the beginning and the end of *Redburn*. In the first chapter, Wellingborough's sisters thwart his "insane desire to be the death of the glass ship" (8) which dominates his explanation of his "Taste for the Sea." The final chapter brings news of Harry's death, which the narrator contrasts to his own "chance to survive" (312). Like the ship, Harry hides "something wonderful" inside his charming exterior that will not submit to scrutiny. In both cases, the result of secrecy is distance, and in both cases the lesson of death—wished or real—is that meaning must be sought on the surface, in the recognition of differences which the futile desire for inward revelation cannot reduce. "Reminiscence," the process by which Redburn seeks meaning in the past, fails to tell him "how to account" for his "madness" (8); Harry aggrandizes his self-image by "spending funds of reminiscence not his own" (221). His lies, the gap between inner world and outward circumstances, consign him to a shipboard status of which Redburn concludes, "Better you had never been born" (255). The inability to "account" for himself leaves Wellingborough unredeemed, metaphorically comparable, in his own alienation, to his dead friend.

Nowhere does death reveal its metaphoric force more brutally than in the Launcelott's-Hey episode at the center of the Liverpool section of the book. On realizing that the starving paupers will die unaided, Redburn's first reaction imbues them with synecdochic significance.

> I stood looking down on them, while my whole soul swelled within me; and I asked myself, What right had any body in the wide world to smile and be glad, when sights like this were to be seen? It was enough to turn the heart to gall; and make a man-hater of a Howard. For who were these ghosts that I saw? Were they not human beings? A woman and two girls? With eyes, and lips, and ears like any queen? with hearts which, though they did not bound with blood, yet beat with a dull, dead ache that was their life. (181)

When he realizes that they are beyond help, he feels "an almost irresistible impulse to do them the last mercy, of in some way putting an end to their horrible lives" (183–84). His "irresistible impulse" to inflict death repeats the deadly "insane desire" of chapter 1, only now the act is motivated by sympathy for another rather than the quest for self-siring insight; it is metaphoric rather than metaleptic.

The Launcelott's-Hey chapter ends with Redburn's judgment, "Are we not like people sitting up with a corpse, and making merry in the house of the dead?" (184). Death marks the synecdochic "we" of his soliloquy; it haunts our pleasures, contradicts the salvation offered by our "creeds," paralyzes our redemptive gestures, undercuts our sense of self, renders us anonymous. The tattooing which fixes identity in Melville's earlier works in *Redburn* turns an unknown sailor into "his own head-stone" (178). All strategies for asserting a reconciled (redeemed) or exemplary (microcosmic) selfhood run up against death, the gap between ego and other, the doubleness of perspective instituted by the secret inwardness of truth.

The Launcelott's-Hey episode and Harry's doom prove the essential aloneness of humans, cut off, as they are, from the synecdochic evocation of a generalized destiny or verbal standpoint. The emigrants on ship reduce to a crowd of individuals having no determinate unity of fate or purpose. Likewise, the metaleptic strategies for relating past and present exemplified by Redburn's inherited guidebook also fail. Wellingborough recognizes that his father has "gone whither no son's search could find him" (155), and he learns that his father's past is also dead, that the book is "no more fit to guide me about the town, than the map of Pompeii" (157). Redburn's love for the old book, preserved and venerated for its green morocco cover, even if the descriptions inside evoke only "the past and forgotten" (143), makes it a parallel metaphor for the glass ship with its hidden secret. Like the bell-buoy which welcomes them to Europe, it is "fuller of dirges for the past, than of monitions for the future" (127). Redburn refuses to quote the old guidebook for fear of subjecting its "antiquities" to "be skipped and dishonored" (150). The dead world of inner voices in each case preserves its mute secret, now seen by Redburn as having a special, unbreachable sanctity. Melville's metaphoric voice replaces understanding with veneration as it replaces redemption with sympathy.

Redburn's refusal to quote his guidebook exemplifies a decorous silence in the face of death, the irredeemable past. When Jackson dies, the sailors never again mention him (296). The "animal combustion" of a dead shipmate drives all levity from the forecastle, and only the impious Jackson dares to "invoke the dead man" (246). Redburn learns that one's "behavior" when death "suddenly menaces him" is "the best index to his life and faith" (291), that one's job is to carry on past childhood pain, even though "never again can such blights be made good; they strike in too deep, and leave such a scar that the air of Paradise might not erase it" (11). On sailing out from the harbor, he resolves "not to look at the land any more" (36). The sailors suffering from their "terrific dissipation" ashore "breathe nothing about such things, but strive their best to appear all alive and hearty" (32). For the first time, Melville's fiction acknowledges the limits of vocalization, the inevitability of endurance, as in "The Calm" in *Mardi*, as a condition of human life; gone is the obsessive impatience and utter fear of muteness which characterize his earlier works. *Redburn* fleshes out the quality of life as lived in a calm, where "penitence" (confession) "avails not" (*M* 10). External decorum and acceptance of necessary silences replace the "awful" stillness and repressive, daimonizing voice of *Mardi*.

As in its predecessors, muteness in *Redburn* associates figuratively with the sea and with the imagination as a "deep dive" below the surface of its threatening "wastes." In an extraordinary reminiscence characteristic of Melville's most experimental rhetoric, Redburn ponders Harry's future maritime death.

> Poor Harry! a feeling of sadness, never to be comforted, comes over me, even now when I think of you. For this voyage that you went, but carried you part of the way to that ocean grave, which has buried you up with your secrets, and whither no mourning pilgrimage can be made.
>
> But why this gloom at the thought of the dead? And why should we not be glad? Is it, that we ever think of them as departed from all joy? Is it, that we believe that indeed they are dead? They revisit us not, the departed; their voices no more ring in the air; summer may come, but it is winter with them; and even in our own limbs we feel not the sap that every spring renews the green life of the trees.
>
> But Harry! you live over again, as I recall your image before me. I see you, plain and palpable as in life; and can make your existence obvious to others. Is he, then, dead, of whom this may be said?
>
> But Harry! you are mixed with a thousand strange forms, the centaurs of fancy; half real and human, half wild and grotesque. Divine imaginings, like gods, come down to the groves of our Thessalies, and there, in the embrace of wild, dryad reminiscences, beget the beings that astonish the world. (252)

Harry's silent voice, "buried secrets," and "ocean grave" stimulate the narrator to an act of redemptive imagination and articulation. Yet the end product of that act is to generate a series of "grotesque" metaphors—not just centaurs but a "zebra" in a "striped Guernsey frock" and a "silken quadruped-creole"—for a Harry already troped as "girlish" (253). Internalized, imaginative redemption of the past leads the narrator away from an understanding of Harry's "secret." It enacts an increasingly hyperbolic chain of tropes which moves toward repression of the sorrow at its origin.

Redburn's metaleptic and hyperbolic reverie recuperates the "Dreams" chapter of *Mardi*. Redburn at sea avows that he "felt as if in a dream all the time" and expects "to hear myself called to, out of the clear blue air, or from the depths of the deep blue sea" (64). The blueness of sea and sky recalls the experience of sailing for the Marquesas in *Typee*. *Redburn* recapitulates the threatening yet liberating power of the sea in Melville's first three novels. Only now the acknowledgment of death as a condition of meaning—the necessity of metaphor—provokes a swerve away from the solipsistic quest for vocal authority. Redburn experiences not a figure of his own centrality but a chain of metaphors which deny internalized resolution by refusing to reveal the secret self which Harry carries to his grave. His hyperbole returns him to his touching but superficial "reminiscence" of Harry's circumstances on ship. Gilman characterizes this "technique of symbolism" in *Redburn* as "proleptic" in that it "elaborates his higher meaning from the foundation of real things" (226). Gilman pinpoints Melville's reining in of his earlier figurative "extravagance" in returning his flights of fancy to facts rather than expanding or internalized "invention." Instead of being situated in the center of an "endless sea," an all-encompassing temporal moment, the figural imagination of *Redburn* is fixed between irredeemable and unknowable beginning and end points set by death.

Contemplating the failure of his guidebook, a metaphor for the unknowability of the past, Redburn says to himself, "Guide-books, Wellingborough, are the least reliable books in all literature; and nearly all literature, in one sense, is made up of guide-books" (157). "Every age," he proclaims, "makes its own guide-books, and the old ones are used for waste paper." Only "the one Holy Guide-book" "will never lead you astray, if you but follow it aright." Following the Bible "aright," however, necessitates a proper reading, and when called upon to translate a passage for the semiliterate cook, Redburn has to conclude that "it was a mystery that no one could explain; not even a parson" (82). Writing thwarts the single-minded recovery of truth by requiring metaphoric interpretation. A reader can never appropriate the viewpoint of the author of a book, and vice versa, because "authors, they say, never read their own books; writing them, being enough in all conscience" (87). The truth that lies in an authorial past, like the past of the Bible or the future revealed to Blunt in his *Bonaparte Dream Book,* remains "cast by means of figures, in some perplexed and difficult way" (90). One cannot trade the in-between world of metaphors for "that play of freedom & invention accorded only to the Romancer & poet."

Melville's engagement with a nexus of images tying sea, dreams, the past, imagination, and literary authority together in his early novels comes to a head, in *Redburn,* in an extraordinary statement on the nature of figurative language and death. Newly on board, Wellingborough is swamped by the proliferation of nautical terms which he is expected to respond to. He concludes that "sailors have a great fancy for naming things" (82), and that "I should not be surprised, if there were a great many more names, than things in the world" (66). He wonders,

> whether mankind could not get along without all these names, which keep increasing every day, and hour, and moment; till at last the very air will be full of them; and even in a great plain, men will be breathing each other's breath, owing to the vast multitude of words they use, that consume all the air, just as lamp-burners do gas. (66)

Redburn's recoil from nautical jargon repeats and inverts the experience of being filled up and taken over by one's own internalized voice in "The Calm." Both passages insist on hyperbole, the repressive plenitude of language. In *Typee,* hyperbole augments the persuasiveness of the narrative voice and thus aids in the novel's metaleptic resolution; in *Mardi,* hyperbole associates the repressive, inward voice with the becalmed, synecdochic expansiveness of its verbal freedom; in *Redburn,* hyperbole reinforces the mediate, limited, metaphoric nature of literary expression, its inability to capture, in any definitive way, the hidden truth. Things are ultimately a secret kept from words. The only future which language can establish is one choked by more words. The image of our "breathing each other's breath" tropes, metaphorically, the relationship of author and reader and raises the question of the audience in the impossible mode of "confession" which, from the title page on, fragments the dream of a redeemed past. To reveal one's secret is to exhale one's breath in words which unite only to kill.

Names—language, authorship, voice—in *Redburn* fill up the "in-between" space of human activity, "cast" the meaning of the self "by means of figures," occult (through a hyperbolic multiplication of words) the irreducible otherness and muteness which death introduces into meaning. Like Blunt, who can "with difficulty read at all" (90), the quester after expansive or redemptive truth awakes with a "wonderful dream" in head and falls to "ciphering." The effort corresponds metaphorically to the act of "making merry in the house of the dead." Blunt's humorous divination is interrupted as the crew of the *Highlander* is called to save her from impending collision. *Redburn* often shifts rapidly between serious and amusing anecdote. The degradation of Booble-Alley yields to a kaleidoscopic description of dockside life in which a horse backs into the water on order from a parrot; an ominous ramble through a landscape guarded by "man-traps and spring-guns" gives way to an enchanting meal with three "charmers." Melville punctuates his poignant novel with a wealth of lively, comic incident—Redburn's visit to the captain, the attack of the twins on Max, the crew's final salute to their officers—which create a tonal counterpart of its essential doubleness of standpoint. The book is sad and funny at the same time.

Melville's comedy leans as heavily on metaphoric relationships as do his serious themes. "What is a horse," he asks, "but a species of four-footed dumb man, in a leathern overall?" (197). In the presence of the three "charmers" eating buttered muffins, Redburn exclaims, "I wished I was a buttered muffin myself" (214). *Redburn's* passion for comparison engenders a steady stream of seriocomic doublings—Harry and Carlo, whaler and man-of-war's man, cook and steward, Liverpool and New York, Horatii and Curiatii, boy and man, reminiscence and confession. Not satisfied with one set of triplets, it offers a second with contrasting personalities. Rarely has a novel lived up so well to the flippant generalization that, although "the mere fact of their being twins always seemed curious," "I hardly know why this should be; for all of us in our own persons furnish numerous examples of the same phenomenon" (269).

In his humorous treatment of the dock "truck-horses," Melville asserts that "there are unknown worlds of knowledge" in the quadruped who "toils for his masters, half-requited or abused, like the biped hewers of wood" (197). In an October letter to Lemuel Shaw, he complains of being "forced" to write *Redburn* and *White-Jacket* "as other men are to sawing wood" (*Letters* 91).[8] He concludes:

> And while I have felt obliged to refrain from writing the kind of book I would wish to; yet, in writing these two books, I have not repressed myself much—so far as *they* are concerned; but have spoken pretty much as I feel.—Being books, then, written in this way, my only desire for their "success" (as it is called) springs from my pocket, & not from my heart. So far as I am individually concerned, & independent of my pocket, it is my earnest desire to write those sort of books which are said to "fail."—Pardon this egotism. (91–92)

As in the cases of both Redburn and Harry, the repressed "heart" promises only "failure." Yet the acknowledgment of a desire to fail is "egotism"—an evocation of a genteel superiority no longer necessary for self-expression. The "higher purpose" of *Mardi* has been "repressed" by the rhetoric of "more names than things"—of metaphors which bypass the secrets of the deep dive. Yet that rhetoric stands on its own—"I have not repressed myself much—so far as *they* are concerned; but have spoken pretty much as I feel." Authorial identity splits seriocomically into "heart" and "pocket" "individually concerned, & independent" of each other; however the split does not prevent Melville's ethos from presenting itself honestly. Like the truck horse, he may contain "unknown worlds of knowledge," but he is not uncomfortable with his "half-requited" toil.

The limited, unredeemed, seriocomic world of *Redburn* and its detached doubled and doubling narrative perspective give Melville a sense of authority originating neither in exotic experience nor in "freedom & imagination." He can speak "pretty much as I feel" out of the contingent concerns of the "pocket," which Ishmael will later invoke to climax his catalog of reasons for sailing before the mast. The sympathetic worldliness and realistic, metaphoric insights of the novel offer a comfortable alternative to the "higher aims" learned from Blair and enable a work of concerted humanity and democratic wisdom. For all its overt fragmentations, *Redburn* achieves a forceful rhetorical and ethical focus. The social insights and judgments which it conveys are among Melville's most persuasive. Its accomplishment carries over into the equally rapidly composed

White-Jacket and gives *Moby-Dick* its pre-Hawthorne continuo of local-color vividness and straightforward sympathy.

Melville's new, "honest" or realistic voice demonstrates its power and coherence throughout *Redburn*, and in so doing establishes the terms in which his next dialectical leap will occur. The clearest instance is the treatment of Jackson—after Wellingborough and Harry the most important character in the novel. Jackson is the one person in *Redburn* repeatedly described in metaleptic and synecdochic terms. Even though the sailors, by never speaking of him, attempt to "repress" the "recollection" in their "secret hearts," Melville asserts that "*his* death was *their* deliverance" (296–97). In death he plunges into the sea "like a diver" (295); Redburn exclaims, metaleptically, that "I can never think of him, even now," without being reminded of grand examples of past evil (276). Jackson calls to mind a whole host of the "illustrious damned" (276), and his entire "overawing" self is distilled synecdochically in the "deep, subtle, infernal looking eye" which Redburn says (metaleptically) "haunts me to this day" (57).

At the same time that Jackson continually suggests "deep" inwardness, expansive grandeur, and the interplay of past and future, he provides constant reminders of death in the lurid "piracies, plagues, and poisonings" of his tales and memories, in his reminders of departed shipmates and dangers to be faced, and his own imminent prospect of "dying like a dog" (58). Like death itself, Jackson functions as a principle of negation, the denial of hope, meaning, or resolution in the metaleptic and synecdochic powers which he evokes. Redburn comes to see him through the window of pity rather than hate, "woe" rather than "wickedness" (105); pity demands distance, a sense of metaphoric difference, and it tallies the doubleness which Redburn reads in Jackson's "evil eye"— hatred born of Jackson's envy of the "young and handsome" Redburn, who gives him a metaphoric point of contrast to his own quickening decay (58).

Jackson's special enmity for Wellingborough turns the crew against the youth and makes him an "Ishmael" who begins to hate his shipmates—a response which he must "pray against" in order to avoid becoming a "fiend" like Jackson himself (62). Later, Redburn's relationship to Harry echoes and inverts his responses to Jackson. Harry's peculiarities, like Jackson's, make Redburn identify with him and stand aloof from the crew. Both relationships end in a sense of unbridgeable difference and in pity; both introduce Redburn to the face of death and isolation. One cannot condemn him for abandoning his "brother" without taking into account the hard truths of death and distance learned from his encounters with Jackson.

In *Typee*, Tommo's nemesis is his own prior and threatened muteness, represented by sea and valley; Taji's is the disabling synecdochic structure of the narrative within which he must rove; lacking such figural "extravagance," Redburn finds his in the eye of a shipmate. Jackson's "evil eye" recalls the "big eyes" of the adventurer who had caught his childhood fancy—the supposed result of hunger, another trial which Redburn continually undergoes. Jackson's antipathy embroils Redburn in a subtle calculus of similarity and difference which grounds the complex network of metaphoric relationships that enmesh him throughout the novel. The lesson of distance from metaleptic and synecdochic "egotism" which Redburn learns from Jackson's negative example prepares him for the survival, the tales and voyages beyond his "first," which is the only positive hope in a story figurally conditioned by death. Metaphor—trope of the accommodation of unbridgeable differences—may not restore a lost past or secret inner self, but it inspires the naming of more names. If its processes lead ultimately to death, to the conflict of different identities frighteningly troped by the image of breathing of each other's breath, the honest facing of the fact carries considerable persuasiveness in its own right. *Redburn* offers a partial glimpse at a notion which Melville will confront later: the only thing which ultimately calls for metaleptic redemption or synecdochic appropriation is death; all else finds provisional meaning in systems of metaphoric relationships "cast by means of figures" in the in-between world conveyed by "the vast multitude of words."

The danger in the powerfully coherent metaphoric vision which emerges and begins to reveal its implications in *Redburn,* and correspondingly begins Melville's recoil toward a new rhetorical program, is that all metaphoric relationships ultimately reduce to the interplay between survival and death. Such a totalizing perspective threatens to collapse rhetorical figuration as a mode of enablement and dialectical growth. In order both to admit and to bypass the threat, Melville begins to explore a more radical and self-conscious way of engendering tropological change than that which generated his first two figurative departures—the shift from the irony and metalepsis of *Typee* to the synecdoche and hyperbole of *Mardi* and then to the metaphors of *Redburn.* Melville's new technique involves subjecting his master tropes to catachresis, to a reversal or misapplication which calls their logic into question; by actively derailing one rhetorical program, space for another is cleared.

Melville's metaphoric rhetoric in *Redburn,* by ringing incessant changes on the interplay between survival and death, opens the possibility of its own undoing; catachresis is courted, for example, in the way the metaphoric "brotherhood" between Harry and Wellingborough becomes so complex and emotionally conflicted, so subject to the burden of unredeemed pasts and unrevealed secrets, and so interwoven with Redburn's responses to Jackson that it loses both its clarity and it power to evoke genuine sympathy; Melville's authorial voice threatens to become too distanced, too wrapped up in exploring the terms of its own ethical authority, to sustain a compelling Wellingborough-Harry relationship.

Melville's rhetoric does not finally, in the Redburn-Bolton relationship, give in to catachresis because the rhetorical movement of *Redburn* from the synecdochic internalized world of *Mardi* toward a sympathetic, metaphoric realism is so rapid and dramatic; metaphor plays an aggressive role in his departure from the distressing disablement attending his earlier figures. The relationship between Wellingborough Redburn and Harry Bolton is moving in its exploration of the possibilities and difficulties of achieving a sympathetic voice in a harsh world rather than as a narrative fact. Melville's treatment of the emigrants, less central to the overall rhetorical program of the novel, pushes his metaphors even further toward catachresis.

In his final chapter on the emigrants, Melville comments feelingly on those who are reported dead at sea: "What a world of life and death, what a world of humanity and its woes, lies shrunk into a three-worded sentence!" (292). For them, there are fewer words than things; their difference is that of a tale not told, a figurative order foreclosed, a new secret instituted. Rather than strung out metaphorically, various lives are "shrunk" into a litotes (understatement) which signs their common fate. The death which disables synecdochic resolution throughout the novel now institutes its counterpart: the fate of Redburn himself, as well as of Harry, it suggests, can be troped by three words—dead (buried) at sea.

Melville exaggerates the synecdochic, and thus rhetorically backward-looking, nature of his treatment of the emigrants, by arguing, in support of their right to immigrate, that "the whole world is the patrimony of the whole world" (292). Synecdoche gives way to a tautology which combines the expansiveness of the former figure with the metaleptic temporality of "self-siring." Tautology produces a catachrestic collapse of the earlier figurative structures into each other. Furthermore, it haunts the larger rhetorical fabric of *Redburn*. Wellingborough imagines that his glass ship hides "gold guineas, of which I have always been in want, ever since I could remember" (8). The ship's secret recesses answer a subsequent need—the lack of money which gives true continuity to his identity and to his identity with Melville as author. A redeemed selfhood, in the metaphoric world of the novel, cannot be achieved through superficial financial satisfaction, yet the hope of such satisfaction originates the quest for redemption, for the means to get on one's feet again. The glass ship figures Redburn's self in terms projected back on it by his subsequent understanding of himself; rather than metaphoric, the ship is tautological, a locus of self-fulfilling prophecy.

Tautology, in the cases of the glass ship and the emigrants, suggests the possibility, inimical to the overall rhetoric of *Redburn*, that it may ultimately be the outward self, the self of the pocket rather than that of the heart, as White-Jacket will learn, which remains unaccountable, unrevealed, fateful—the locus of occulted synecdochic or metaleptic structures. Tautology permits Melville to overlap and slide between figurative strategies. It bespeaks an emerging self-consciousness which will come to fruit in the vertiginous rhetoricity of *Moby-Dick*. In *White-Jacket*, Melville continues to explore the implications of the realistic, metaphoric voice of *Redburn*, but he also begins the process of gathering up and integrating the figurative strategies central to his first four novels. *Moby-Dick* culminates this process of integration, and as a result masterfully climaxes the first phase of his rhetorical development, characterized by a brilliant exploration of tropes central to high Romantic literature. After *Moby-Dick*, Melville's rhetoric will become increasingly dominated by figures, such as tautology, which depart from the mainstream literary art of his day, and it will become increasingly involved in catachrestic gestures which give his ethos a post-Romantic cast.

7

"The strong shunning of death":
White-Jacket

I wondered whether I was yet dead, or still dying. But of a sudden some
fashionless form brushed my side—some inert, coiled fish of the sea; the
thrill of being alive again tingled in my nerves, and the strong shunning
of death shocked me through.
—Melville, *White-Jacket*

*W*hite-Jacket, written immediately after *Redburn* in the
summer of 1849, combines the rhetorical insight of Melville's two previous
novels with the vocal coherence of *Omoo*. It demonstrates how quickly he gains
control over and becomes comfortable with the results of his figurative experiments. Setting aside the subversive force of tautology which tints his treatment
of the emigrants, it integrates the synecdochic perspective of *Mardi* with the
metaphors (and engagement with death) of *Redburn* in a spectacularly unified
ethos. *White-Jacket* flies apocalyptic colors, in a way that none of his earlier
works has, as its deadly world expands rhetorically to appropriate the dialectic
of origins and outcomes which *Typee* had put into play in establishing Melville's
voice.[1] Apocalypse takes its place alongside death among his central literary
themes, making it possible to argue that delight in the intellectual insights and
persuasiveness of his fourth and fifth novels, as much as financial pressures,
explains their "maniacal" pace of composition.

In *White-Jacket*, death, doubleness, the disjunction between self and other,
and the secret inwardness of truth again condition meaning, only now the
provisional, in-between, shipboard world expands synecdochically to include
everything. The glass-ship metaphor for selfhood, with its hidden treasure,
becomes the world-ship in which "the vast mass of our fabric, with all its store-
rooms of secrets, forever slides along far under the surface" (399). Key tropes
from *Redburn* inflate in a manner which recalls the microcosmic island-hop-
ping of *Mardi*, although *White Jacket* avoids bagginess because of the metaphoric program and the focus given by the presence of death, inherited from its
immediate predecessor. By balancing figurative programs, the novel swerves
equally from the fragmented perspective of *Redburn*, the ironic Romance of
Typee valley, and the internalized "metaphysics" and "conic sections" of *Mardi*.

White-Jacket carefully elaborates the figures of secret selfhood and inner treasure which initiate the quest for selfhood in *Redburn*. The "remarkable" Nord keeps his past "barred and locked up like the specie vaults of the Bank of England" (52). White-Jacket at first delights in a garment "like an old castle" full of "mysterious closets, crypts, and cabinets" with "snug little out-of-the-way lairs and hiding-places, for the storage of valuables" (36). Such tropes of inward selfhood expand, at crucial points, like the Mardian sea; arraigned before the mast, the narrator feels "my man's manhood so bottomless within me" (280). Yet inner meaning again succumbs to muteness: White-Jacket reveals no name; the Commodore's power remains both "dumb" and possessed of "the strange power of making other people dumb" (21); pickpockets force the narrator to "mason up" his jacket and sail "pocketless" (37). Language displays even greater repressive powers than in *Redburn*: Jack Chase's hyperbole quiets the whaleman whose tales insult the maintop (16); Captain Claret offers no rebuke when Mad Jack rightfully countermands his orders (110–11); the Articles of War impose a deadly silence on their victims (294).

On the *Neversink*, the inner self is deeper but more thoroughly repressed than on the *Highlander*. There is no privacy; one's pockets are picked, and one's poetry "published." Life must be led in surface terms; one stands out in a crowd; in spite of its secret recesses, the ship offers no place to hide. Redburn's sense of alienation and doubleness now seems so absolute as to preclude not merely the accomplishment of temporal redemption but any thought of it; death expands into a condition of life so pervasive as to apocalyptically cancel the hope, the quest for an articulated identity, implied by the dialectic of "confession and reminiscence" which shapes *Redburn*. Thus, "the anticipated millennium must have begun upon the morning the first worlds were created" (186); "our final haven was predestinated ere we slipped from the stocks at Creation" (398); "the Past is dead, and has no resurrection" (150).

The utter, preemptive foreclosure of redemptive temporal figures in *White-Jacket* removes much of the tension associated with the split narrative perspective of *Redburn*. The narrator addresses the "subject full of interest" of where he will be next year by remembering "just where I was" on a particular day "of every year past since I was twelve years old" (173). He keeps the day, when he can, by eating a meal of lamb, peas, and sherry, a ritual which celebrates and tropes the repetitive rather than the redeemed nature of life. Nothing is to be expected from "shadowy reminiscences"; no keys to the secret self lurk in the past. In the man-of-war world of *White-Jacket* every detail adds to a totalized social order; the only alternative to repressive, repeated ritual is an uncanny experience of "bottomless" selfhood experienced under extreme duress—under threat of flogging or in falling from the topgallant yardarm. Escape is impossible; the most threatening phrase from the Articles of War—"shall suffer death"—"falls on your ear like the intermitting discharge of artillery" (293), and its apocalyptic message follows you "through all eternity, like an endless thread on the inevitable track of its own point, passing unnumbered needles through" (296). In contrast to the ending of *Mardi*, where Taji can propose "then let us fly," the idea of escape here evokes the response, "Nay, White-Jacket, the landless horizon hoops you in" (295).

The "three words" from the Articles of War "that hung those three sailors" in *White-Jacket* repeats the repressive litotes of the "three worded sentence" into which shrinks "what a world of life and death" in *Redburn's* discussion of the emigrants. Unrevealed truths, "cast by means of figures, in some perplexed and difficult way" in Melville's previous novel, here yield to rules which are "brief and to the point" (293). One is thrown back on the obvious, for "there are no mysteries out of ourselves" (398). There is no enabling, metaphoric doubleness, for "we are precisely what we worship" (321). The utter, repressive contingency of life under the Articles of War reduces the self to solipsism, to an apocalyptic synecdoche comparably paralyzing to the catachrestic tautology of the formula, "the whole world is the patrimony of the whole world," in *Redburn*.

Without the quest for temporal redemption, the ultimately futile hope, that shapes *Redburn*, the comparisons, sublimations, and logical relations responsible for a sense of progress and accumulating understanding in the earlier novel reduce to synecdochic repetition. Voice, in *White-Jacket*, may "shape eternity" (321) but not the conditions of a humane individuality. Nord, to survive, must "isolate and entomb himself" (52); the only expression of his "bottomless manhood" available to the narrator when "arraigned before the mast" is an act which would make him "a murderer and a suicide" (281). The "higher purpose" of synecdochic questing in *Mardi* gives way to a circular allegory of life as a voyage "homeward bound." We know where we are going because we have always already been there, yet articulation is forbidden; we sail under "sealed orders." Death offers our only contact with the inner self, and the synecdochic pressure of the man-of-war world returns all meaning and all hope to that self: "each man must be his own saviour" (400). Where Melville's previous works have enacted the quest for authority, temporal redemption, or self-understanding, *White-Jacket* enacts personal apocalypse, the suicidal gesture of Ishmael's repetitive return to the sea at the start of *Moby-Dick*.

White-Jacket demonstrates the startling power of Melville's rhetorical approach to literary creation. A seemingly subtle shift or new balance among his key tropes enables a dramatic change in tone and vision. Just as his new protagonist revels comfortably in the nautical jargon threatening to Wellingborough (and generates whole chapters out of salty arcana such as "dunderfunk"),

Melville both exaggerates and takes for granted his lessons of death, fragmentation, and secretness. The eye for pointed detail which ranged freely in *Redburn* becomes fixated on shipboard ritual; the internalized or hidden visions of selfhood at the center of his two previous novels prepare the ground for apocalypse. Realism blossoms into allegory, satire into Jeremiad. Even in performing a mere "job" like "sawing wood," Melville cannot resist the "certain something unmanageable" in himself which drives him to constant rhetorical experiment. *Redburn* elaborates a metaphoric world cradled in the disabled hope for metaleptic redemption drawn from *Typee*; *White-Jacket* marries that world to the pneumatic synecdoches of *Mardi*. Melville's new tropological environment goes hand in hand with the discovery of new themes—apocalypse (and millennialism)—and it also inspires a dramatic revisit to earlier ones—the sea, daimonization by voice, death. So his art progresses: "Tho' we put one leg forward ten miles—its no reason the other must lag behind—no, *that* must again distance the other—& so we go till we get the cramp & die" (*Letters* 83).

All of the rhetorical forces of Melville's first five novels gather and begin the accelerated interplay central to *Moby-Dick* in the passage which describes White-Jacket's fall from the yardarm. Against the background of Tommo's experience of sailing for the Marquesas, Taji's calm, and Redburn's glass ship, White-Jacket's fall gives an index of Melville's growing virtuosity. The passage is a rhetorical tour de force so haunted by backward- and forward-looking themes, figures, and insights that it demands careful scrutiny.

> Ten thousand pounds of shot seemed tied to my head, as the irresistible law of gravitation dragged me, head foremost and straight as a die, toward the infallible center of this terraqueous globe. All I had seen, and read, and heard, and all I had thought and felt in my life, seemed intensified in one fixed idea in my soul. But dense as this idea was, it was made up of atoms. Having fallen from the projecting yard-arm end, I was conscious of a collected satisfaction in feeling, that I should not be dashed on the deck, but would sink into the speechless profound of the sea.
>
> With the bloody, blind film before my eyes, there was a still stranger hum in my head, as if a hornet were there; and I thought to myself, Great God! this is Death! Yet these thoughts were unmixed with alarm. Like frost-work that flashes and shifts its scared hues in the sun, all my braided, blended emotions were in themselves icy cold and calm.
>
> So protracted did my fall seem, that I can even now recall the feeling of wondering how much longer it would be, ere all was over and I struck. Time seemed to stand still, and all the worlds seemed poised on their poles, as I fell, soul-becalmed, through the eddying whirl and swirl of the Maelstrom air. . . .
>
> As I gushed into the sea, a thunder-boom sounded in my ear; my soul seemed flying from my mouth. The feeling of death flooded over me with the billows. The blow from the sea must have turned me, so that I sank almost feet foremost

through a soft, seething, foamy lull. Some current seemed hurrying me away; in a trance I yielded, and sank deeper down with a glide. Purple and pathless was the deep calm now around me, flecked by summer lightnings in an azure afar. The horrible nausea was gone; the bloody, blind film turned a pale green; I wondered whether I was yet dead, or still dying. But of a sudden some fashionless form brushed my side—some inert, coiled fish of the sea; the thrill of being alive again tingled in my nerves, and the strong shunning of death shocked me through.

For one instant an agonizing revulsion came over me as I found myself utterly sinking. Next moment the force of my fall was expended; and there I hung, vibrating in the mid-deep. What wild sounds then rang in my ear! One was a soft moaning, as of low waves on the beach; the other wild and heartlessly jubilant, as of the sea in the height of a tempest. Oh soul! thou then heardest life and death: as he who stands upon the Corinthian shore hears both the Ionian and the Ægean waves. The life-and-death poise soon passed; and then I found myself slowly ascending, and caught a dim glimmering of light. (392–93)

As he falls, White-Jacket experiences the same repressive narrowing of focus endemic in the entire ship-world of the novel, the radical imaginative litotes of "all I had seen, and read, and heard, and all I had thought and felt in my life, seemed intensified in one fixed idea in my soul." His "fixed idea," however, fails once more to give a clear, unfragmented "peep" at inward identity, since "dense as this idea was, it was made up of atoms." In the apocalyptic world of *White-Jacket*, only death promises a unified view of the self, in this case the "collected satisfaction" that the end will come in "the speechless profound of the sea."

White-Jacket, in midair, expects the "speechless," voice-effacing emersion which threatened Tommo at the end of *Typee*. What actually comes to pass is dramatically different and tropes the changes which Melville's rhetoric has undergone since his first novel. As in "The Calm" in *Mardi*, while White-Jacket falls, "time seemed to stand still, and all the worlds seemed poised on their poles, as I fell, soul-becalmed, through the eddying whirl and swirl of the Maelstrom air." Daimonization accompanies temporal suspension: "There was a still stranger hum in my head, as if a hornet were there; and I thought to myself, Great God! this is Death!" The inner voice of death represses feeling: "All my braided, blended emotions were in themselves icy cold and calm."

As he falls, White-Jacket experiences what seems to be the reduction of all meaning to the repressive, all-encompassing, inner voice of death. Yet when he lands, his inward sense of himself is torn from him, and death enfolds him from without: "My soul seemed flying from my mouth. The feeling of death flooded over me with the billows." Inner "calm" gives way to "the deep calm now around me." The rhetoric and thematics of Melville's early works culminates in an experience of death as both inner and outer stasis—repressed, daimonic voice within and alienated, externalized soul. The "bottomless" self and the sea concatenate to repeat the fatal message of the deep dive in *Mardi.*

In the next instant, a "fashionless form" intrudes on White-Jacket's fatal, enveloping, inward-outward awareness, and "the strong shunning of death" shocks him "through." He is saved from the nihilistic rhetoric of his fall by "some inert, coiled fish of the sea." The incident dramatically modifies Melville's treatment of the sea, which now tropes salvation as well as the threat of muteness and the authoritative truth buried in an inarticulate past. Salvation by the sea, central theme of *Moby-Dick,* begins a corresponding alteration in and return to figures of metaleptic enablement and a swerve away from the synecdochic and metaphoric orders which have characterized the sea since *Typee.*

White-Jacket hangs "vibrating in mid-deep"; voice returns to him, shorn of the cloak of repressive calm: "What wild sounds then rang in my ear!" "Oh soul! thou then heardest life and death." Death, the unitary trope of all meaning, is replaced by two distinct voices, as feeling returns: "One was a soft moaning, as of low waves on the beach; the other wild and heartlessly jubilant, as of the sea in the height of a tempest." The apocalyptic unity of both self and world in *White-Jacket* bows to a new sense of doubleness associated with a repeated image of the beach—a return to the locus of the final drama of enablement in *Typee.* "Hearing" the sea becomes another figure for salvation, a key to inner-outer communication that replaces the abortive confessing, speaking, naming, and authoring associated with the deadly trope of "breathing each other's breath" which pervades Melville's two worldly works.

Redburn and *White-Jacket* explore the implications of a rhetoric of fragmentation, secret inwardness, alienation, and repression which finds voice in metaphors of loss, of the crippling wound—"such a scar that the air of Paradise might not erase it." Melville explores this side of his ethos with such unblinking courage that it leads him from disabling synecdoche through disabled metaphor to the frighteningly powerful repressiveness of hyperbole and litotes. His exploration of the set of figures is strong, energetic, and solipsistic in the most dangerous sense. From a rhetoric which doubts its own authority, he has turned to a rhetoric so willful that it begins to raise doubts about the world and the act of voicing which it embodies. White-Jacket's truthfulness is as controversial as Redburn's good faith.[2] Melville's own disclaimers provoke continued concern over the intentions and circumstances which his ethos projects.[3]

The problematic nature of Melville's narrators, narrative perspectives, and authorial identity reflects an art which conceives and responds to itself in rhetorical rather than philosophical or representational terms. In his first five years as a practicing writer, Melville invests himself unreservedly in his exploration of the possibilities of literary voice in general and his own voice in particular. He tests the accessibility and the limits of a number of the major figurative techniques sanctioned by both the prescriptions of Blair and the literary Romanticism of his day. He reaches an understanding of how these figures can be made to cross over from the voice to the structure to the thematic content of a novel. He learns how to embody his impatient, dialectical self-consciousness in an art of bold revision and departure. He comes to identify his own authority with processes of change and growth rather than stable goals or accomplished refinements. He becomes comfortable with his habit of reacting to his previous work, experimenting, and working out the implications of his experiments all within the course of a single novel—a habit which suits his breakneck composing process and distaste, shared with Tommo, of "right-about retrograde movement."

Melville's first five novels, however one evaluates their individual artistic accomplishments (and I evaluate them very highly), together detail the maturation of a literary genius marked by first-rank rhetorical courage, insight, and persuasiveness. The novels give him a panoply of achieved techniques rare in scope and penetration, in its varieties of spellbinding vocal power. They also make him itch for a sense of purpose commensurate with his talents, the mere exercise of which no longer convinces him of his authority; and they leave him with understated but gathering doubts about the rhetorical underpinnings of the Romanticism of his day.

Moby-Dick reflects its circumstances in the most fortunate way. It calls on and integrates the rhetorical strategies developed by Melville to this point, yet it does so with a new self-consciousness in regard to the dangers of art in which truth is inevitably "cast by means of figures." It finds a perfect theater for the "resurrection" which Melville imagines at the end of *White-Jacket*. It makes good on the inherent scope of Melville's signature theme, the sea. It derives a new sense of purpose from the example and encouraging fellowship of Hawthorne and from the metaphysical discussions with George Adler which take such a prominent place in Melville's journal account of his 1849 trip to Europe. It sows the seeds of a further dialectical departure, which will answer its grand, synthetic voice with a radical and equally productive leap into the post-Romantic rhetorical and ethical environment which will occupy Melville's genius for the rest of his career. "All this, and more than this" is the novel which follows *White-Jacket*.

"So as to kill time": *Moby-Dick*

> My mother dragged me by the legs out of the chimney and packed me off
> to bed, though it was only two o'clock in the afternoon of the 21st June,
> the longest day in the year in our hemisphere. I felt dreadfully. But there
> was no help for it, so up stairs I went to my little room in the third floor,
> undressed myself as slowly as possible so as to kill time, and with a bitter
> sigh got between the sheets.
> —Melville, *Moby-Dick*

*M*oby-Dick has often been cited for inconsistencies born
of Melville's composing process,[1] yet its ethos, its rhetoric, achieves a concerted
mastery unmatched in American literature. If Melville is referring to his own
work in asserting that "there are some enterprises in which a careful disorderliness is the true method" (361), the "disorderliness" of *Moby-Dick* shows his
"care" in the organized way it embraces the dialectical "method" central to his
prior literary growth. In *Mardi, Redburn,* and *White-Jacket* tropological departures intrude and predict later ethical change; in *Moby-Dick,* they are reinte-
grated into the structure of the novel, and their logic is exhausted internally.
What Hayford and others see as compositional stages can be read as rhetorical
layers or programs—perhaps in the guise of the "particular subordinate allegories" mentioned in Melville's 1852 letter to Sophia Hawthorne (*Letters* 146). The
voice of the novel defines, interrelates, and finally encompasses these layers in a
way which transcends their contradictions.

Moby-Dick displays three distinct figurative layers. Although they relate
partly to the three stages proposed by Hayford, they look forward and backward to each other in ways which a sequential composing process cannot
explain. Even the first and ostensibly "earliest" of them, before either Queequeg
or Ahab take center stage, evidences the high rhetorical ambitions which Bezanson attributes to the project from the start (176–77): Having announced the
work in June of 1850 as "a romance of adventure, founded upon certain wild
legends" (*Letters* 109), Melville seems ready to return to the "freedom and
invention" of *Mardi* a full year before his famous avowal to Hawthorne that he
can write only "banned" books (*Letters* 128).

Right at its start, *Moby-Dick* announces its dialectical "method" by both
reviewing Melville's achieved figural system and posing a tropological question

central to both its subsequent rhetorical environments and his ongoing development. In "Loomings," Melville adopts the retrospective posture of Redburn's "confession and reminiscence," yet he takes steps to repress the deadly metaphoric logic which makes Wellingborough's narrative perspective comparable in its duplicity to that of Tommo. Ishmael reiterates the question of origins, into which he thinks he can "see a little" (7), but he splits the question in two. He first addresses the suicidal drive which sends him before the mast and which provokes his meditation on the sea as synecdochic "key to it all." The sea reveals the "ungraspable phantom of life"—reflected image of a selfhood out of reach of narcissistic desires.

> And still deeper the meaning of that story of Narcissus, who because he could not grasp the tormenting, mild image he saw in the fountain, plunged into it and was drowned. But that same image, we ourselves see in all rivers and oceans. It is the image of the ungraspable phantom of life; and this is the key to it all. (5)

The mirroring surface of the water predicts the intervention of death—in a manner inherited from the metaphoric order of *Redburn*—between ego and double, internal and external grounds of identity. *Moby-Dick* begins very much in the rhetorical mode of Wellingborough's reflections on his glass ship, yet in spite of Ishmael's fascination with the "springs and motives" that "induced" his voyage, he refuses to measure himself against a lost childhood self. His retrospection swerves from that of Melville's earlier novels and finds, in the second aspect of his framing of the question of origins, a dramatic new focus.

The second part of Ishmael's question addresses the particular whaling voyage at hand; it calls forth a rhetorically unprecedented answer. In exploring the inner world of his compulsions, Ishmael concludes:

> By reason of these things, then, the whaling voyage was welcome; the great floodgates of the wonder-world swung open, and in the wild conceits that swayed me to my purpose, two and two there floated into my inmost soul, endless processions of the whale, and midmost of them all, one grand hooded phantom, like a snow hill in the air. (7)

The end of "Loomings" explains the origin of Ishmael's quest—why "the whaling voyage was welcome"—metaleptically in terms of its goal, the white whale. His viewpoint predicts Ahab's obsession with Moby-Dick. Yet Moby-Dick at this point in the tale is unknown to Ishmael; the whale cannot, except "preposterously," function as an inducement. As a logical explanation of his quest, the white whale is impossible, catachrestic. Furthermore, it too is a "phantom," a duplicate of the ungraspable synecdochic selfhood which, lying on the other side of death, is "the key to it all" in the earlier Narcissus passage. It both combines and calls into question Melville's key figurative strategies.

Moby-Dick accrues additional figurative presence in "Loomings" by mediating both the doubleness of the "two and two" procession of imaginary whales and, in the manner of White-Jacket's fall, the outer world of "wild and distant seas" and Ishmael's "inmost soul." Moreover, its confusion of goals and origins mediates the necessary temporal doubleness of first-person narrative by permitting Ishmael to speak as if from a moment which concatenates the onset and the aftermath of his adventure. The hegemony of the white whale in the springs and motives outlined in "Loomings" introduces into Melville's rhetoric a type of figure closer to Emersonian symbolism than any Melville has previously employed. The whale raises the question of a trope so forceful as to displace the endless dialectics of self-representation central to Melville's narratives. It takes on the daimonizing power of the hyperbolic sea/language nexus that hitherto locates the interplay between mute experience and the potentially deadly freedom of "more names than things"; only now it wears the garb of an overarching temporal, causal, and psychological unity.

The white whale in "Loomings" challenges the figural underpinnings of Melville's previous work. He has structured his first five novels around the search for enabling relationships between a present vocal authority and an unredeemed past or alienated otherness couched in images that evoke his preliterary life. His rhetoric seeks to ground identity on persuasiveness. It defines an ethos committed to testing the limits of its own freedom and engagement and to exploring the figurative substructure of literary art. It responds to his quest for authority by reaching for means that permit it to "re-collect the broken past, to remember the dismembered"—an enterprise which Bainard Cowan calls "the defining concern of allegory" (10). In de Man's terms, it reveals its "allegorical" nature in its unflinching acknowledgment of the doubleness, the fragmented temporal perspective, at the heart of any authentic representation of the human condition. In contrast, the white whale in "Loomings" raises the possibility of a symbol which transcends dialectic, which absorbs the terms of meaning into itself and forecloses contradictory perspectives, which is more persuasive for its momentary awesomeness than for its historical or narrative itinerary, which relates the literary word directly to what Eco calls a "theology,"[2] and which undermines "the part and parcel allegoricalness of the whole" (*Letters* 146).

The posing, in "Loomings," of the question of the symbolic to Melville's earlier "allegorical" rhetoric by no means signals his capitulation to transcendentalist poetics. In an 1851 comment to Hawthorne, he asserts:

> What nonsense! Here is a fellow with a raging toothache. "My dear boy," Goethe says to him, "you are sorely afflicted with that tooth; but you must *live in the all*, and then you will be happy!" . . . N.B. This "all" feeling, though, there is some

truth in. You must often have felt it, lying on the grass on a warm summer's day. Your legs seem to send out shoots into the earth. Your hair feels like leaves upon your head. This is the *all* feeling. But what plays the mischief with the truth is that men will insist upon the universal application of a temporary feeling or opinion. (*Letters* 131)

Ishmael, in his fascination with the whale, clearly risks falling, like Ahab, into the trap of insisting on "the universal application of a temporary feeling." The idea of a symbolic rhetoric, however, of an authorial selfhood freed from the project of troping and redeeming its origins, promises a persuasiveness of its own, associated with Goethe and the other Romantics which Melville had been reading and discussing with friends since he first heard Emerson lecture early in 1849. With typical gusto, Melville sets out to explore the implications of the dilemma. It is not the specific symbolic nature of the whale—its particular "theology"—which engages him but rather its power both to unify and to force into catachresis the terms on which the articulation of an authentic and persuasive literary ethos has seemed up to this point to depend.

In confronting his established rhetoric with the symbol of the whale, Melville inspires a global reconsideration of his key themes: the muteness of the sea, the deadly repressive power of language, the secret interiority of identity, the problematics of self-siring, the nature of greatness, and the "expanding soul" of art. Along the way he broaches provocative new issues: the nature of memory and a corresponding rhetoric of repetition, the temporal implications of salvation, the circular structure of fictional selfhood. The growth of these issues, and the new tropological environments which they necessitate, out of the face-off between "allegory" (Melville's achieved rhetoric) and "symbolism" (the figurative power of the whale) determines the masterful ethical coherence of *Moby-Dick*.

The early chapters of *Moby-Dick* follow up on "Loomings" by multiplying figures which suggest a fate, a book already finished, a set of synecdochic circumstances like those of *Mardi* which, because they preempt the articulatory power of death in the Narcissus image, set the stage for the unifying rhetoric of the whale as "key to it all." Melville replays the vibrant sense of inner-outer articulations attending White-Jacket's fall into the sea, but he returns to the seriocomic realism of *Redburn* in order to defer the theme of resurrection associated with "the strong shunning of death" in the earlier moment. He revisits his previous rhetorical breakthrough in a context burdened but also sharpened by the intrusion of the whale.

As Ishmael searches for lodgings in the cold New Bedford December, he avers that an "old writer—of whose works I possess the only copy extant" says of the winter wind that "it maketh a marvellous difference, whether thou lookest out at it from a glass window where the frost is all on the outside, or whether thou observest it from that sashless window, where the frost is on both sides, and of which the wight Death is the only glazier" (10). Immediately thereafter he rhapsodizes on the case of a freezing derelict, whom he calls "Lazarus." Only death, in a parallel image to the surface of Narcissus's fountain, names the articulation between inner self and external world.[3] One can do nothing about it, since "it's too late to make any improvements now." "Lazarus" awaits a resurrection which cannot be troped, since "the universe is finished; the cope-stone is on, and the chips were carted off a million years ago" (10). Melville's imagery denies the personal, apocalyptic time of *White-Jacket:* it places origins and ends at an unreachable remove and thereby denies his tropes their earlier purchase.

Ishmael responds to his entrapment in a deadly "in-between" world in a dramatically different manner than any of Melville's earlier heroes: he engages in a spectacular act of self-naming. In announcing, "Call me Ishmael," he predicts his own end and unifies his own perspective, in a manner which echoes the figure of the whale. One symbolic construction, one experience of "the all" ("the key to it all"), confronts another. Entering the Spouter-Inn, he faces the "portentous, black mass" in the painting by the entryway (12). His attempt to read into the image a meaning "cast by means of figures" gives way to a simple, literal-symbolic answer—a whale—which unifies "aggregated opinions" and forecloses allegorical interpretation. Throughout the early chapters of the novel, Ishmael unerringly confronts, recognizes, privileges, and follows a series of signs leading to the whale, to his single, overwhelming future.

At the Spouter-Inn, Ishmael displays a defensive isolation in tune with his autotelic pseudonym: "No man prefers to sleep two in a bed. In fact, you would a good deal rather not sleep with your own brother. I don't know how it is, but people like to be private when they are sleeping" (16). He poses himself as lonely, fated quester after the symbolic whale. His self-naming concatenates the origins and goals, causes and effects, of his adventure and denies allegorical redemption. He proposes no alternative or end to his suicidal voyages. "Ishmael" combines a "preposterous" metaleptic temporality, synecdochic generality of feeling ("No man prefers"), the repressiveness of a litotes—"Call me Ishmael"—which hides any prior identity, and a taste for incessant metaphoric comparisons which validate the "damp, drizzly November" in his soul. All figurative possibility returns to his name.

The rhetorical environment which dominates the early chapters of *Moby-Dick* recapitulates Melville's previous techniques, now preempted by the over-arching figures of the whale and Ishmael's assumed identity. Ishmael shows every inclination to define his personality in terms of his role, to reduce, as symbolism does, ethos to fate. The teleology of the two figures offers no cure for a sense of selfhood oscillating between solipsism and narcissism, since "the copestone is on, and the chips were carted off a million years ago." Yet the exaggerated humor of the novel's beginning suggests that its portentous loomings represent "the universal application of a temporary feeling." Symbolism returns Melville's voice to irony, to the enabling doubleness of *Typee*. This irony prevents the novel from promising the totalized perspectives dominant in Melville's fiction since *Mardi* and prepares the way for Queequeg and for the second, more significant, rhetorical environment of *Moby-Dick*. On this second level, rhetoric begins to reveal previously unavailable powers which answer, allegorically, the symbolic forces that confuse and challenge it at the start.

The rapidity with which Queequeg redeems Ishmael's "splintered heart" signals Melville's discomfort with a rhetoric dominated by symbolism, by the grand confrontation between his autotelic protagonist and Moby-Dick as locus of "the key to it all." Queequeg's significance is first signaled by his tattoos, of which Ishmael decides, "It's only his outside; a man can be honest in any sort of skin" (21). Ishmael reads Queequeg, in contrast to both Melville's prior use of tattooing and the permeable skin of "Lazarus," as a case of strict inner-outer distinction, the inviolability of the inner self. Yet his initial reading, suggestive of the tragic secrecy central to *Redburn* and *White-Jacket* in its evocations of the fear of death—Queequeg's shrunken heads, tomahawk, and dangerous smoking in bed—quickly falls away as Ishmael comes to experience a more happily integrated selfhood than any of Melville's narrators has yet evidenced: "No more my splintered heart and maddened hand were turned against the wolfish world. This soothing savage had redeemed it" (51).

Queequeg's early centrality and later disappearance from Ishmael's tale composes one of the novel's most obvious points of "disorder." It signals the conflicting rhetorical levels with which Melville is working. It re-poses the twin questions of the interplay between inner and outer self—repeated in Father Mapple's "far, far upward and inward delight" (48)—and of the possibility of a metaleptic—"redemptive"—relationship with the past. It reintroduces a synecdochic model of sociability—a joint-stock company world—previously preempted by the universal but deadly sea of "Loomings." Queequeg's rhetorical level of *Moby-Dick*, which extends much further into the experience of the tale than does Queequeg's physical presence, forces a major reevaluation of the notion of symbolism with which the novel begins.

The rhetorical departure which characterizes Queequeg's layer of *Moby-Dick* emerges in the title experience of "The Counterpane." At the beginning of his report of the experience, Ishmael avows, "My sensations were strange. Let me try to explain them" (25). Like Redburn musing on his glass ship, he returns to an originary childhood spring and motive in order to "explain" himself. His explanation is both oblique and rhetorically telling. He concludes, "Now, take away the awful fear, and my sensations at feeling the supernatural hand in mine were very similar, in their strangeness, to those which I experienced on waking up" (26). The repetition of his "sensation" serves to "explain" himself, even though he cannot "settle" if the original experience was "reality or a dream" (25). Memory, the repetition of a strange but inexplicable sensation, explains Ishmael's feeling by giving him a heightened and ongoing, if problematic, sense of identity: "But waking in the morning, I shudderingly remembered it all, and for days and weeks and months afterward I lost myself in confounding attempts to explain the mystery. Nay, to this very hour, I often puzzle myself with it" (26).

In "The Counterpane" Melville invokes a counterpart of the "preposterous," metaleptic time of *Typee* in order to wed memory and repetition together as keys to the self as seeker after meaning—"I often puzzle myself with it." Remembered experience plays the role of repeated telling in *Omoo* to authorize an ethos able to report and "explain" its confrontation with the meaning of experience. Melville indicates a new appreciation of repetition as a trope, a figure of thought and expression, distinct from those at the center of his earlier work. Repetition denies the stasis of metonymic or synecdochic time without imposing the closed, circular, antecedent-consequent overlap characteristic of *Typee*'s metaleptic ending. It resolves ironic difference without insisting on the logical similitudes and comparisons of *Redburn*'s metaphors. It protects against the linguistic repressiveness of hyperbole and litotes. It puts in play an experience and corresponding figure of time which inserts itself between the "temporary feeling" and "universal application" of transcendental symbolism and thus undercuts the totalizing power of the whale. It resurrects an event which remains undecidable in its own terms—"reality or a dream"—yet which affirms an identity, repeated later in "A Squeeze of the Hand," attuned to a mix of precise yet figuratively "expanding" incidents. It is the central trope of the central, second, rhetorical level of *Moby-Dick*.

What Ishmael remembers above all in "The Counterpane" is the horrible weight of time, the dismal calculation that "sixteen entire hours must elapse before I could hope for a resurrection" (26). Facing a sentence as inexorable as the Articles of War in *White-Jacket*, he undresses slowly "so as to kill time" and, after a failed plea for clemency, goes to bed "feeling a great deal worse than I have ever done since" (26). When he awakens, the supernatural hand rests in his "for what seemed ages piled on ages." His remembered experience of time predicts key passages later in the book: in "The Symphony" Ahab feels the weight of "piled centuries since Paradise" (544); on the third day of the chase, time "held long breaths with keen suspense" as if "gold-beaten out to ages" (565). As in Tommo's experience of sailing for the Marquesas and "A Calm" in *Mardi*, a heightened sense of self emerges out of a fearful suspension of time.

"The Counterpane" departs from Melville's earlier metonymic, synecdochic, and hyperbolic temporal suspensions on the basis of the repetitive operation of memory. First, looking back on the earlier experience from the point of view of its repetition promises to "explain" its meaning to the self; second, Ishmael asserts, "Take away the awful fear, and my sensations at feeling the supernatural hand in mine were very similar, in their strangeness, to those which I experienced on waking up and seeing Queequeg's pagan arm thrown round me" (26). Ishmael's "redeemed" heart achieves his earlier, hoped-for, temporal "resurrection" by repeating the incident with its "awful fear" removed. Memory, in reproducing a "strange" event in dramatically altered circumstances, permits the speaking (explaining) self to recapture an important sense of self-awareness shorn of its original paralyzing fright. Ishmael awakens not to his earlier isolation and entrapment in time but to Queequeg's redeeming "bridegroom clasp."

The "Counterpane" experience heals Ishmael of his sense of fragmentation—his "splintered heart"—yet doubles his speaking voice into one which is satisfied by the incident as self-explanation and one which is still "lost" in "confounding attempts to explain the mystery." His earlier and later experiences of selfhood coexist in memory; neither absorbs the other synecdochically or metaleptically; neither is repressed by a surplus of words over things or "explained" metaphorically. Neither takes precedence as a "key to it all." Rather than "killing" time, "The Counterpane" ushers in a model by which past and present can interact without absorbing or misreading each other. Memory presents a past which one can "see" without needing to "see into" in an endless search for springs and motives. It presents a past whose muteness and otherness no longer evokes a feeling of "awful fear."

Melville's emphasis on memory and repetition in the second rhetorical layer of *Moby-Dick* derives from his response to the extraordinary influence of Hawthorne on his art and authorial identity. In *The School of Hawthorne*, Brodhead discusses at length Hawthorne's gift to Melville of a "prophetic" mode of literature characterized by a definition of literary writing as an internal search for knowledge, a reliance on allegory, and an interest in daimonization—human character shaped by fetishistic fixation. Hawthorne's numerous tales of obsession clearly prefigure Ahab's fascination with the white whale; more significantly, they exemplify and elaborate the context within which repetition reveals to Melville its ethical implications.

In describing the fetishism in *Moby-Dick*—Ahab's obsession—David Simpson stresses the circular function of the whale as "both the object on whom revenge must be taken and at the same time the image of the lost [phallic] member which must be conquered and regained" (80); Ahab's quest to avenge his lost manhood, like all fetishistic "phallicism," "is a metonymic activity that seeks to persuade its user and his audience that it is in fact synecdochic" (73). In my terms, the catachrestic concatenation of metonymy and synecdoche gives a false appearance of metaleptic resolution, of a circularity which enables rather than paralyzes. Such fetishistic rhetorical confusion characterizes both Dimmesdale's and Ahab's beliefs. Hawthorne's "prophetic" fiction works not by instituting symbols but by mapping their social and psychological implications in allegorical (tropological) terms. Hawthorne's art is ethical in the fullest sense of the word. Its rhetorical sophistication (possibly born of his contact with Samuel Newman at Bowdoin)—its unwillingness to accept conventional figurative strategies at face value—gives its voice, Hawthorne's own ethos, exemplary complexity and power.

Melville takes more from Hawthorne than Ahab's blindly fetishistic rhetorical identity. He sees in his compatriot a telling instance of the new sense of time which his use of the figure of repetition in "The Counterpane" (and throughout *Moby-Dick*) opens to view. In a characteristically dialectical manner, Melville's reading of Hawthorne's achievements and significance as an American author undergirds his particular revision of Hawthorne's "prophetic" rhetorical program. It may be that the cooling off in their relationship after the dramatic intimacies of 1851 and 1852 owes as much as anything to the realization among two master rhetoricians that their ethical uses of current literary techniques diverge and conflict radically. Melville's response to Hawthorne as harbinger of a new view of time begins with his famous essay "Hawthorne and His Mosses," written in early August 1850 at just the point when, several months into the writing of *Moby-Dick,* he makes the acquaintance of his fellow author.

Melville's revision of Hawthorne's rhetoric involves the relationship between repetition and the "great Art of Telling the Truth" (*PT* 244) lauded in "Hawthorne and His Mosses." The relationship is worked out in terms of the essay's comparison between Hawthorne and Shakespeare, a comparison which parallels the impact of Queequeg on Ishmael in *Moby-Dick* by establishing a context which enables the redemptive repetition of earlier insight. "Hawthorne and His Mosses" harks back to Melville's comments on Shakespeare and Emerson in his 1849 letter to Duyckinck. At that time, he expressed the wish that Shakespeare could speak without "the muzzle which all men wore on their souls in the Elizabethan day" (*Letters* 80). In his essay on Hawthorne, Melville avers that "great geniuses are part of the times"; Shakespeare is "sure to be surpassed" because "it is not so much paucity, as superabundance of material that seems to incapacitate modern authors" (*PT* 246). Hawthorne, not Emerson, is the modern author whose genius, while not overshadowing that of Shakespeare, repeats it in a way which keeps us from having to oscillate in Shakespeare's rainbow.

Hawthorne repeats Shakespeare's telling of the truth "covertly, and by snatches" (244). Yet Hawthorne's modernity permits him to speak more freely, with a soul at least partly unmuzzled. His example gives American literature a future destined to redeem its secondariness vis-à-vis its exemplary British antecedents. Just as Ishmael, in response to his "Counterpane" experience, transcends the moment to "puzzle" about it "to this very hour," Melville declares in "Hawthorne and His Mosses," "As I now write, I am Posterity speaking by proxy" (253). His enthusiasm results from a vision of literary progress which escapes both self-siring and the piled weight of ages. Progress, a new version of the "expanding soul" of art, results from the repetition of "the great Art of Telling the Truth" in a changing and enlarging context.

The temporality which the trope of repetition permits Melville to carry over from his view of Hawthorne to Ishmael's second-level explanation of himself in *Moby-Dick* is progressive and open-ended. For all their nineteenth-century milieu, Melville's earlier novels have contained no vision of progress. They have focused on an irredeemable past, retrograde cultural movement (the corruption of the islanders), and personal apocalypse. Now Melville builds from repetition to "resurrection" to "redemption" in progressive terms. Repetitive, progressive time denies the "all" of symbolism and sets the Shakespeare-Hawthorne axis against the transcendentalism of Emerson and Goethe, yet it ultimately undercuts Hawthorne's particular, "prophetic" form of allegory as well, an effect which becomes increasingly obvious as both the second level of *Moby-Dick* and Melville's continuing interchanges with Hawthorne work out the implications of his rhetorical program.

On receiving Hawthorne's favorable response to *Moby-Dick,* Melville effusively describes his sense of redemptive fellow-feeling:

> Whence come you, Hawthorne? By what right do you drink from my flagon of life? And when I put it to my lips -lo, they are yours and not mine. I feel that the Godhead is broken up like the bread at the Supper, and that we are the pieces. Hence this infinite fraternity of feeling. . . . Once you hugged the ugly Socrates because you saw the flame in the mouth, and heard the rushing of the demon,— the familiar,—and recognized the sound; for you have heard it in your own solitudes. (*Letters* 142)

Melville's hyperbolic "demon"—always associated in his work with his voice—is quite different from Hawthorne's, which separates and isolates his characters and forecloses their futures rather than promoting what Melville calls a "pantheistic" sense of communion. What the letter glosses over is the power of repetition to deny causality in an aggressive manner, to turn Hawthorne and himself into instances of each other and confuse questions of influence. In *Moby-Dick*, Melville deals with this power by making the redeeming openness to the other which Ishmael gains from Queequeg the grounds for his participation in Ahab's fetishistic quest. The implications of a repetitive rhetoric thicken in a way which prepares for the novel's third level, or figurative program, and ultimately for the spectacularly radical rhetoric of *Pierre*.

At the close of his November 1851 letter to Hawthorne, Melville invokes his new sense of time.

> Lord, when shall we be done changing? Ah! it's a long stage, and no inn in sight, and night coming, and the body cold. But with you for a passenger, I am content and can be happy. I shall leave the world, I feel, with more satisfaction for having come to know you. Knowing you persuades me more than the Bible of our immortality. (*Letters* 143)

Hawthorne's repetitive participation in a process of "changing" promotes a "persuasive" redemption of the Bible which opens, for Melville, belief in an accessible, indefinite future. At the end of "Cetology," he explicitly relates this new sense of time to authorship.

> But I now leave my cetological System standing thus unfinished, even as the great Cathedral of Cologne was left, with the crane still standing upon the top of the uncompleted tower. For small erections may be finished by their first architects; grand ones, true ones, ever leave the copestone to posterity. God keep me from ever completing anything. This whole book is but a draught—nay, but the draught of a draught. Oh, Time, Strength, Cash, and Patience! (145)

The open future of "posterity" implies a state of endless "draughting" and "changing." One is redeemed by a sense of the past as a step in a repetitive yet authorizing and "persuading" process that radically alters Melville's previous rhetoric, devoted to a closed "universe" in which "the copestone is on, and the chips were carted off a million years ago."

As Ishmael sits in his room with Queequeg in "A Bosom Friend," he describes the "evening shades and phantoms gathering round the casements, and peering in upon us silent, solitary twain" (51). His "redeemed" state externalizes and holds at bay the "phantom" of life which, in "Loomings," occupies the "midmost" position in his "inmost soul" in the guise of the "grand hooded phantom" of Moby-Dick. Along with a progressive sense of time, repetition ushers in a selfhood satisfied by its own provisional location in the "grand programme of Providence" and by the persuasiveness of its necessarily limited explanations. It is this insight which distinguishes Ishmael's perspective from Ahab's. In terms of the second-order rhetoric which dominates most of *Moby-Dick*, Ahab's quest for revenge is an exact mirror image of the redemption experienced by

Ishmael, and his reading of the whale as "the gliding great demon of the seas of life" (187) repeats the daimonic selfhood characteristic of Melville's earlier tropology. Brodtkorb suggests that Ahab denies the present in his concentration on the future (80); more tellingly, Ahab can be said to fetishize and be daimonized by an irredeemable past. Revenge necessitates a memory with all its "awful fear" intact, a need to "kill time" by both fixing and canceling a single originary experience.

Ahab circles, without progress, in the world given by his compulsions, as Tommo does in the metonymic vale of the Typees, yet he fetishizes his quest by viewing it in the synecdochic terms of Taji. Blind to the catachrestic structure of his enterprise, he accepts the whale as a totalizing symbol and attempts to appropriate its power; as a result, he meets all the bad ends which Melville's works to this point have enumerated—immersion, entrapment, muteness (living out another's prophecies), suicide, isolation, fragmentation. His outer person so perfectly represents the fixated origin of his soul that he becomes a living mnemonic, a "visible reminder" of the wound which dominates his inmost self. He admits none of the "changing" which signals Melville's new rhetoric; he sees no escape from the burden of time except through fulfillment of its predetermined, symbolic portent.

In Ahab, Melville pushes his earlier rhetoric to its logical conclusion, signaled by the figure of tautology. Haunted by the question, "Is Ahab, Ahab?"[4] Ahab ultimately asserts, "Ahab is for ever Ahab, man. This whole act's immutably decreed" (561). The attempt to define one's present meaning in terms of the quest for redeemed or revenged origins, when combined with synecdochic temporal paralysis, ultimately implies an illogical—tautological—self-siring. To explain one's authority on the basis of the genealogy of that authority, to dovetail experiential and speaking selves, amounts to rhetorical tail-chasing. The past is irrecoverable to the ethical present not because it is ineluctably other but because it has no irreducable otherness, no difference, nothing of its own to hold on to: it is completely, tautologically determined by the act of speaking which brings it to life.

Ahab is a magnificently poignant figure because the deadly absurdity of his quest tolls the knell of Melville's entire, preceding ethical enterprise. With him, the figurative substructure of Romantic fiction collapses into tautology. We are not sure what of value survives his "fiery hunt." Ishmael's task becomes to explain his survival, not his origins, and to find a source of authority or persuasiveness in his unforeseen and undeserved good fortune. Whatever originary meaning or Shakespearean lesson Ahab's tragedy reveals is reabsorbed into its own tautologically circular perspective; it gives Ishmael nothing to go on; he is conscious of making up whatever causality lies in the past of his experiences; their value depends on his voice.

In turning Ishmael's story to good account against the comprehensive negative example of Ahab's absurd tragedy, Melville gives his voice and his tale over to the repetitive, progressive, open-ended sense of time at the center of his interactions with Hawthorne. The lion's share of *Moby-Dick* measures its plot in terms of a repetitive series of lowerings and a comparable series of gams which only haphazardly move it forward but which exemplify the endless variety of contexts within which a whaleman may choose to "explain" himself. Ishmael refuses to fix the origin of his redeemed but inexplicable identity; his name, like "Typee" in *Omoo*, stands for a past undergone, but he has no surviving shipmates to authenticate him; he must name and authorize himself. The only way that he can escape from the catachrestic effect of an act which is necessarily tautological is to deny determinate origins and ends and seek persuasiveness in repetitive, temporally open-ended description, in a recuperation of the seemingly endless details of the voyage, without "settling" their essential tropological order. Looking back, he can trace his redeemed identity to his initial depression, fascination with the sea, desire to sail from Nantucket, selection of the *Pequod*, submission to Ahab, experience of the final tragedy of the hunt, finding of Queequeg's coffin, or rescue by the *Rachel*. Each of these incidents makes figurative sense; each offers to "kill time" by organizing past, present, and future in respect to an event which bridges the gap between "springs and motives" and outcomes. Ishmael refuses to choose among them.

Ishmael's use of multiple origins and repetitive structures as a key to escape from figures of meaningfulness set by Ahab's tragedy climaxes in the novel's exploration of a trope of selfhood as a circle with the seemingly redemptive quality of mildness at its center, a trope which, in its association with Ahab, signals both the accomplishment and the end of the powerfully authoritative identity sought by Melville's earlier rhetoric.[5] Mildness bridges all rhetorical levels of *Moby-Dick*. The dusting of the Late Consumptive Usher in "Etymology" "somehow mildly reminded him of his mortality" (xv); Narcissus reaches for his own "tormenting mild image"; through the redeeming offices of the "soothing savage," Ishmael finds an inner calm which is repeated, later on, in the calm center of the rushing circle of whales in "The Grand Armada." In "The Symphony" Ahab almost succumbs to the influence of the "mild, mild wind, and a mild looking sky" (545), and when Moby-Dick is first spotted, his "mighty mildness of repose" (548) repeats and appropriates the redeeming quality. Finally, when Ishmael reaches Queequeg's coffin at the "vital centre" of the "closing vortex," he is "buoyed up" "on a soft and dirge-like main" which preserves him unharmed by sharks and sea-hawks (573).

Mildness cannot work its magic unless, in contrast to Ahab's response in "The Symphony," it is internalized, taken to heart; it remains subject to inner-outer articulation. In "The Castaway," Pip becomes an idiot when his "ringed horizon began to expand around him miserably" (414). His experience inverts that of "The Grand Armada" in which the boat is threatened by the "outer circles" of whales "all violently making for one centre" (390). The survival of the self lies in the relation between center and circumference articulated by Ahab when he says to Pip, "True art thou, lad, as the circumference to its centre" (535). Ahab's mistake is in imagining that the horizonless idiot can serve as circumference to his center. Later on, his own head becomes the "centre" of the white whale's "ever-contracting" and "planitarily swift" circles (551). When Ahab collapses after the first day's chase, Melville comments that "in their pointless centres, those noble natures contain the entire circumferences of inferior souls" (552). For a center to contain circumferences may appear noble, but it figures the inward collapse of Ahab's identity and authority—his fatal third-day feeling of his bones "damp within me, and from the inside wet my flesh" (564).

Circumference and center, in the extraordinary, incessantly repeated circular figure which climaxes *Moby-Dick,* fix the new terms of inner-outer articulation. Ahab's example teaches the instability of the model. At times his "far inland, nameless wails" overwhelm and deny outer experience, reducing his defiance to solipsism; at other times his outer engagements collapse in on and swamp the inner self. When the two balance, and one senses an inner "mildness" protected from the ravages of experience, it is crucial to remember that one's sense of "universal" redemption is only a "temporary feeling" subject to incessant "changing." Melville's key figure of selfhood reveals its full field of meaning only through repetition. Repetition and its corresponding sense of unstable balance then carry over from Ishmael's selfhood to his voice in the novel's "Epilogue," which begins with the quote from the Book of Job, "I only am escaped alone to tell thee" (573).

The "Epilogue" to *Moby-Dick,* in its quote from Job, raises the question of the relationship between Ishmael's survival and his act of telling. Rather than assert a metaleptic or causal contact between the authority of experience and the persuasiveness of voice, Ishmael repeats the essential point of the Job quote in order to explain the presence of his voice: "Why then here does any one step forth?—Because one did survive the wreck" (573). As in "The Carpet-Bag," he finds himself in possession of "the only copy extant" of his tale. Both his own story, at the end of which the sea rolls on "as it rolled five thousand years ago" (572), and the "old black-letter," cited earlier, which inspires Ishmael to muse on the completion of the universe "a million years ago" (10), express a rich but subtle experience of "afterness" which alters the sense of time felt by Melville's earlier narrators.

Tommo finds the Typees hovering on the verge of inevitable corruption, their fate deferred but sealed; Redburn fails to save Harry; White-Jacket envisions no escape from the Articles of War; Ishmael's survival, on the other hand, his absolute outliving of the past, originates the speaking act. The "copestone" is on the "universe" of his adventure, but his writing answers Father Mapple's question, "What is man that he should live out the lifetime of his God?" (48). In an 1851 letter to Hawthorne, Melville writes, "As soon as you say *Me*, a *God*, a *Nature*, so soon you jump off from your stool and hang from the beam. Yes, that word is the hangman. Take God out of the dictionary, and you would have Him in the street" (*Letters* 125). By "aftering" an idea, words "hang" it. To write the story of a godhead is to live out its lifetime and define "what is man." The afterness of words explains Melville's sense that he has "written a wicket book"; words cancel godliness and supplant the conditions of fate rather than "remembering" a dismembered past.

Afterness turns survival into an expressive ethos which projects a future that may repeat the past but which is not doomed to circle back in attempting to redeem it. The future is opened to the endless "changing" associated with Melville's claim to be "Posterity speaking by proxy." *Moby-Dick* draws a sharp distinction between the order of nature, which is the order of fixed origins in a completed past, and that of art, which projects itself forward in unceasing revision and recontextualization. The sea, for the first time in Melville's career, is "aftered" and abandoned as the inevitable locus of vocal authorization. A "draft of a draft" implies infinite regress, not tautology, and it promises the progressive future denied by Ahab. It counters both the static finality of symbolism and the tropological dialectics of allegory as construed by Melville to this point. Its radical posture points to the third level, or rhetorical environment, of the novel.

Throughout *Moby-Dick* Melville reiterates Ishmael's experience of a liminal afterness by musing on and questioning the implications for futurity of predetermined phenomena: is the whale getting bigger or smaller; can one ever hope to read his hieroglyphic brow? "The Doubloon" suggests that the process of interpreting symbols will continue "in the resurrection" (435) without yielding a unitary answer. A book is an open-ended sequence of "Extracts" that rewards its author with escape from "splintered hearts" only in the afterlife (xviii). The figurative program of *Moby-Dick*'s third level permits Melville to reinterpret his authorial self-discovery not as a birth but as a resurrection into a new and latter-day (i.e. after-day) context, a regermination followed by incessant change.

I am like one of those seeds taken out of the Egyptian Pyramids, which, after being three thousand years a seed and nothing but a seed, being planted in English soil, it developed itself, grew to greenness, and then fell to mould. So I.

Until I was twenty-five, I had no development at all. From my twenty-fifth year I date my life. Three weeks have scarcely passed, at any time between then and now, that I have not unfolded within myself. (*Letters* 130)

In *Moby-Dick* the "aftering" of vocal power frees Melville from his own previous rhetoric—a defetishizing which distinguishes his ethos from Hawthorne's. In exclaiming, "Oh, Time, Strength, Cash, and Patience!" he speaks the concerns of authorship in terms of a worldly present rather than a narrated past: the writer must canvass his current resources in order to speak to posterity rather than chase the ghosts of a lost childhood in hopes of combining persuasiveness with an authenticity that recalls Blair's privileging of "knowledge of the subject" over invention. Authority—authorial identity—demands a dialectical leap beyond the antithesis of symbolism and allegory, a leap which gathers momentum throughout the novel and emerges into full consciousness in the dizzying problematics of "The Whiteness of the Whale."

"The Whiteness of the Whale" afters itself in relation to the rest of the narrative: "But how can I hope to explain myself here; and yet, in some dim, random way, explain myself I must, else all these chapters might be naught" (188). Ishmael's apologetic explanation purports to revise and redress a lack in his narrative: "What the white whale was to Ahab, has been hinted; what, at times, he was to me, as yet remains unsaid" (188). Yet in reaching to "explain," Ishmael strikes not to the "innermost idea" of either the whale or himself but instead "of this hue" (189).

In ending "The Whiteness of the Whale" with the rhetorical question "Wonder ye then at the fiery hunt?" (195), Ishmael suggests a satisfying explanation similar to that which launched the second level of *Moby-Dick* in "The Counterpane"; indeed, every term of the earlier chapter, and the tropological program which it embodies, returns in heightened but skewed form. Whiteness presents "an abhorrent mildness, even more loathsome than terrific" (189), and it repeatedly conjures up "phantoms" (192, 193 twice). The act of remembering gives rise to a riot of associations, an endless accumulation of parallel figures, as if the repetitive rhetoric of the novel's second level were uncontrollably speeded up. Nowhere else does *Moby-Dick* give itself over to such vertiginous troping, and nowhere else does it so clearly prefigure the rhetorical excesses of *Pierre*. In being grounded on a general quality—whiteness—rather than a distinct prior experience, Melville's allegorical logic loses its moorings and recalls the deadly hyperbole of "more names than things" which threatens to use up all available air in *Redburn*.

The danger which "The Whiteness of the Whale" courts is nothing less than the fetishization of language itself, an endlessly repetitive yet fixated circulation of tropes that reduces explanation—the ethical articulation of selfhood—to a "dumb blankness, full of meaning" expressive only of death, of the "charnel-house within" (195). Under the sign of tautology, the "white-lead chapter about whiteness" threatens to bring its explanation under the "white flag" of Ishmael's "hypo" (194). Death, clothed in whiteness, seems likely to reinhabit and take over the signifying structure of all tropological assertions. Furthermore, whiteness, "by its indefiniteness" "shadows forth the heartless voids" (195); it destroys both center and circumference of selfhood and replaces it with an abstract "intensifying agent." By "shadowing forth" all things, whiteness makes local explanations inconceivable. It moves us further away from an allegorical explanation of what the whale meant to Ishmael.

The figurative chaos of "The Whiteness of the Whale" gets much of its subversive power from nominalization, a process which will dominate the first half of *Pierre*. In giving center stage to created nouns like "whiteness" and "indefiniteness," Melville exemplifies the ability of language to deny and at the time emphasize absence, to voice that which has no tangible substance. The chapter gives instance after instance of the missing center which it circles. Derived verbs accompany nominalizations: whiteness "shadows forth" the heartless voids. "Shadows forth" confuses subject and object by locating itself in relation to the nonexistent entity or background from which it projects. Whiteness incessantly calls to account that which is "nameless" or "colorless," which escapes yet is invoked by the process of figurative representation.

In "The Whiteness of the Whale," Melville's tropological rhetoric reaches into the grammatical level of language to challenge the logic of subject and predicate. At first blush, the boldness of this departure seems catachrestic in the exteme—even deconstructive—yet explanation, not absurdity, is its goal. The program behind Melville's experiment, and its relationship to the second-order rhetoric central to *Moby-Dick*, lies in his reconsideration of the redeeming memory which grounds Ishmael's new experience of time in "The Counterpane." Melville shifts from an understanding of memory drawn from Blair to a new model, close to that of Hegel, a philosopher discussed in his long, peripatetic conversations of 1849 with George Adler (Leyda, *Log* I, 322). A double sense of memory—Hegel's distinction between *Erinnerung* and *Gedächtnis*—underlies the figurative thrust of Melville's new voice in "The Whiteness of the Whale."[6]

Hegel's *Erinnerung*—"interiorization"—offers a counterpart to the internalization which paralyzes *Mardi;* what one interiorizes becomes part of oneself, like one's first language, and is called up without thought. *Gedächtnis*—"thinking memory"—relies on a secondary order of mnemonic signs and categories which are used, like the grammatical rules of an unfamiliar language, to call up memories which are not immediately and intuitively accessible. Ahab's desire to strike through the pasteboard mask of reality exemplifies his desire to confront Moby-Dick as an interiorized presence whose power has become part of his own identity, rather than as a constructed symbol; Ahab rejects *Gedächtnis* for *Erinnerung*. "The Whiteness of the Whale" broaches a contrary sense of memory by addressing a state of mind whose reality must be inferred from signs of the absence which it would redress—a "dumb blankness full of meaning." By breaking down the grammatical logic of language, Melville seeks not to destroy its representational function but instead to enable it to construct a memorable model, figure, or mnemonic for the conventionally inexpressible. Fiction depends not on what has been interiorized but on what can be given to memory by thought.

In the second rhetorical level of *Moby-Dick,* memory generates a redemptive sense of time; in "The Whiteness of the Whale," the process of constructive or thinking memory both kills and reconstitutes time in a way which brings the representational systematics of language in line with an ethics of repetition. Ishmael explains what the white whale was to him through a long digression on whiteness; the whale remains an "unsaid" locus for the operation of voice as "intensifying agent," a figure which returns to the theme of tattooing as represented by Lem Hardy rather than Queequeg—"so beautifying an operation" which authorizes an unthinkable selfhood through the conscious imposition of superficial markings.

The rhetoric of "The Whiteness of the Whale" repeats instances of the "dumb blankness full of meaning" of allegorical figures until their "dumb blankness" generates a sense of meaning, an "explanation" of a selfhood rendered inexplicable by the necessary afterness of voicing. How can Ishmael hope to explain what the whale was to him, when his innermost understanding of "all" is overwhelmed by his experience of survival? Yet explain he must, "else all these chapters might be naught." His digression frames the essential rhetoricity of his situation, the need to project his interiorized world outward, reconstruct its springs and motives in terms accessible to an audience, a posterity, and to figure the pasteboard mask rather than seek to strike through it.

In "The Whiteness of the Whale," language is saved from a fetishized, catachrestic "dumb blankness" by reconstituting in externalized rhetorical and ethical terms, by thinking the memory of, the shadow or phantom of the whale which lies inexpressible in Ishmael's "innermost soul." The whiteness of the whale figures the space, the tangible absence, of the whale, which becomes "key to it all" by being survived, aftered, written. The repetitive time of the second layer of *Moby-Dick* counters the totalizing power of Ishmael's adventure construed in Ahab's terms as a symbol-allegory antithesis; the nominalizing voice of its third layer matches that sense of time with a rhetoric which linguistically evokes the catachrestic structure of the outlived past. It evolves a tropology of incompleteness, a grammatical decentering of traditional figures which opens them to an ethic of "changing"—of instability, relativity, dependence on context—which projects the process of explanation into the future. What the white whale means to Ishmael, without which the book "might be naught," is given to the reader, to posterity, to further "draughts" to resolve.

"The Whiteness of the Whale" concludes that "the invisible spheres were formed in fright" (195): the originary is not that which is lost but loss itself, the cruel invisibility which characterizes the internal sense of "heartless voids" shadowed forth by any figurative representation of the past. For the first time, Melville considers that the center of his authorial selfhood is occupied not by some spring and motive hidden in the muteness of his seagoing adventures but rather by the constructed memory of muteness as the condition of his voice. The totalizing power of whiteness reaches back to the beautiful, disarticulating blue of sea and sky which thwart and entrance Tommo early in *Typee*. In one breath, Melville speaks the collapse of Romantic allegory—the impossibility of a satisfying, defensive redemption of the past—and the necessity of rhetoric, of the tormenting, indeterminate "changing" put in play by the quest for mildness, for a sense of identity or authority which, he now realizes, can become "the key to it all" only if it leaves "the copestone to posterity."

"The Whiteness of the Whale" ushers in the post-Romantic (or what can be called "Victorian") phase of Melville's career, characterized by iconoclasm in regard to representational rhetoric and a growing fascination with the nuanced surface of human life. Rather than making him fearful of language, *Moby-Dick* heightens his sensitivity to the constructed, stylized nature of experience and the silences, phantoms, and undecidable absences which haunt such characters as Isabel, Hunilla, Don Benito, Israel Potter, and, most dramatically, the Confidence-Man. To be resurrected or redeemed into voice, Melville now realizes, "afters" one from determinate origins and brings a new responsibility for one's rhetorical circumstances—one's authority in regard to one's audience and one's stance vis-à-vis the paralyzing "superabundance of materials" available to modern literature.

After *Moby-Dick*, Melville will never again take for granted the imperative to self-representation as essential to fiction, and he will never again assume the stable authority of either common rhetorical figures or the temporality which they imply. Above all, he will never repeat the grand allegory of emergence which his first six novels trace. *Moby-Dick* writes the final chapter of a story exemplary in pre-twentieth-century literature—the story of an author uncovering, exploring, and judging, with unsurpassed boldness and insight, a dizzying

range of rhetorical structures—figures of speech and thought—central to persuasive *ethopoeia* in his day. Melville's courage and intellectual impatience leave
him, like Ishmael, an "orphan" of his own success. His deep dive into the
"inmost leaf" of Romantic literary figuration gives him a heightened sense of
the rhetoricity of his enterprise. With *Pierre* he sets forth on the endless sea of
a quest for alternative techniques and ethical modes. Some that he discovers
will seem prescient—postmodern—and some perversely idiosyncratic. In either
case, the tale of Melville's next stage of development, although not so grand in
convential terms as that capped by *Moby-Dick,* is equally compelling. It describes a voice seeking not to ground an authoritative identity but rather to
analyze its own assumptions and methods and plant the seed of a persuasiveness no longer doomed to oscillate in the rainbow of a complex and problematic past.

9

"Nimble center, circumference elastic": *Pierre*

This history goes forward and goes backward, as occasion calls. Nimble center, circumference elastic you must have.
—Melville, *Pierre*

*P*ierre is *often seen as a book "invalidated by the sickness of despair" (*Pierre* [Murray] xciii)—the product of Melville's "exhaustion and burning out on the themes of authority and genealogy" (Sundquist, *Home* 145) or of his "taking refuge in silence" (Feidelson 201). These views give a negative biographical slant to Melville's abandonment of the search to ground a persuasive identity which culminates in *Moby-Dick*. Yet *Pierre* also displays the "ebullient and assimilative inventive faculty" (Braswell 211) of a voice struggling to outgrow Romantic conventions, and its analytic zeal and penetration make it arguably "the best psychological novel that had yet been written in English" (Higgins and Parker, *Critical Essays* 265). Rhetorically, it gives birth to Melville's entire later career.

What Higgins and Parker, Brodhead (*Hawthorne, Melville, and the Novel* 181), and others see as Melville's mastery and midstream abandonment of psychological portraiture in *Pierre* has clear rhetorical roots. Unlike *Moby-Dick*, *Pierre* reaches the limits of a tropological program and then changes perspective without providing the interaction among layers responsible for its predecessor's large-scale coherence. Melville's seventh novel does not circle back on itself in an encompassing manner. Its rhetorical departure is too radical: *Pierre's* critique of the figurative means of self-presentation fundamentally alters Melville's approach to fiction.

Early in his relationship with Isabel, Pierre casts his decision to leave home in terms carried over from *Moby-Dick*.

> Listen. But without gratuitous dishonor to a memory which—for right cause or wrong—is ever sacred and inviolate to me, I can not be an open brother to thee, Isabel. But thou wantest not the openness; for thou dost not pine for empty nominalness, but for vital realness; what thou wantest, is not the occasional openness of my brotherly love; but its continual domestic confidence. Do I not speak thine own hidden heart to thee? (192)

0 9

Pierre sees himself as having a stable identity, linked to his "sacred" memory of his father. This identity enables him to speak for the "hidden heart" in order to escape from the "empty nominalness" which threatens to subvert relationships between language and reality in a manner carried over from both the "more names than things" of *Redburn* and the "dumb blankness full of meaning" of "The Whiteness of the Whale." Pierre reiterates the question of how language and memory interact to ground a "redemptive" vision of selfhood, and he looks forward to a process of "changing" which will keep his authority as the last Glendinning intact.

Pierre's quest for meaning functions on the level of authorial ethos in a new way because the novel's third-person point of view detaches its events from the vocal act, in effect foreclosing the circularity at the center of Melville's earlier fiction. This denial of the temporal figures linking actor and speaker subverts the authority of the past—of "sacred" or redeeming memory—on both levels of the narrative: Pierre confronts the unreliability of memory as a key to meaningful action; Melville integrates such a wealth of autobiographical detail into the novel that its tragic outcome appears to be an act of "self-annihilation" (*Pierre* [Murray] xvii). In both cases, the critical energy of *Pierre* leads away from the "prophetic" vision of *Moby-Dick*. The future is not freed but problematized by the undecidability of the past.

The first half of *Pierre* works out the implications of the rhetoric of "The Whiteness of the Whale" in terms of its protagonist's insights and choices. Midway through the novel, however, the narrator, as if exasperated, stands apart from and begins to analyze his hero in a way which recuperates, in exaggerated form, the ironic ethos of *Typee*. Although Melville reasserts his earlier rhetorical belief that "the visible world of experience" is "that procreative thing which impregnates the muses," he qualifies the pronouncement by suggesting that success which depends on the memory of "some rich and peculiar experience in life" will "almost invariably" dissemble the quality and originality of the writer's thought (259). Remembering, the narrator implies as he observes Pierre's literary struggles, must give way to the possibility of forgetting. As a result, even the redemptive repetition, "afterness," open-ended future, and "thinking" memory (*Gedächtnis*) which enable "Ishmael" to address posterity by proxy are called into question. The novel spirals to a close in a spectacularly heightened rhetorical self-consciousness that refigures relationships among self, world, and voice.

In the beginning of *Pierre*, the protagonist confidently assumes his ability to access a process of redemptive repetition based on the adequacy of memory. Pierre has taken his father's place and expects to repeat, and thus further memorialize, his father's greatness. His identity brooks no challenge, since he is

"companioned by no surnamed male Glendinning, but the duplicate one reflected to him in the mirror" (8). He is ignorant of Narcissus's deadly lesson of
speculation because his reflected self-image is reinforced by his name, by a
process of "nominalization" which is not viewed as "empty" but filled by the
authoritative image of his father's official portrait. The past, thus anchored and
institutionalized, promises a bright future.

What Pierre's early confidence dissembles is that his reflected or nominalized
identity is not self-adequating but instead grounded on his mother's vision in
him of "her own graces strangely translated into the opposite sex" (5). His
synecdochic "companionlessness" depends on an unwittingly incestuous relationship with her. When Pierre begins to suspect that his mother loves not him
but "her mirrored image" (90), the grounds of his identity crumble; he comes
to doubt the validity of his father's portrait and to see its truth as a constructed
memory (*Gedächtnis*) reflecting his mother's selfishness. Rather than face his
own incestuous complicity in the fetishizing of his identity, he turns to Isabel—
who reaffirms that his face resembles his father's (158)—for legitimation.

Pierre's family pride chains him to "the empty air of a name," the authority
of which is "more endurable than a man" (10) because there is no fixed ground
against which it can be measured. His identity hangs on a process of "endless
descendedness" (9) which mirrors the indeterminate temporality asserted by
Ishmael. As long as he accepts his mother's constructions, he inhabits the center
of a seamless, fetishized world, metonymically timeless like Typee valley, yet
claiming the synecdochic significance of his lineage. When his faith collapses,
he has no experience of "afterness," like that of Ishmael, out of which he can
"draught" an ongoing selfhood.

The dissembled instability of Pierre's identity characterizes his experience of
love, which the narrator wryly describes as having "more to do with his own
possible and probable posterities, than with the once living" (32). Ignoring the
tautological self-siring on which his love is based, Pierre asserts its synecdochic
force in a manner which repeats both the becalming hyperbole of *Mardi* and
the dire circumferences of *Moby-Dick*. To Pierre, "Time and space can not
contain Love's story" (34); love "sees ten million fathoms down," and in its eyes
"the mysteries of life are lodged" (33). "By ten thousand concentric spells and
circling incantations," love "glides round and round him" (34). Love fixes Pierre
in a static, synecdochically expansive world whose authority is shored up by
phantom memories of a "sacred" past.

Into the immobile circle of Pierre's youth enters Isabel's face, a duplicate of
his father's. The face, in replacing one image of beauty—his mother's—with
another, appropriates the synecdochic power of love and takes over the center
of his world. It constitutes an alternative past which rearticulates time in a

manner just as fetishistic as that which it replaces: "vaguely historic and prophetic; backward, hinting of some irrevocable sin; forward, pointing to some
inevitable ill" (43). It calls up "phantoms" (42, 49, 53) of a lost memory, "an
empty echo . . . of a sad sound, long past" (38). Pierre has "the vague impression, that somewhere he had seen traits of the likeness of that face before" (49).
Isabel's similarity to an unofficial "chair-portrait" of his father, given to him by
his aunt and kept to himself, offers a duplicate identity, derived from a different
memory, which contradicts his mother's version.

Neither Pierre nor his mother attempts to reconcile the two paternal images
or sees them as instances of the contextualized truth, the "changing" central to
Ishmael's ethos. Pierre's obsession with Isabel's face as the "inscrutable thing"
which opens before him "the infernal catacombs of thought" (51) duplicates
Ahab's fetishistic obsession with the whale (and prefigures Claggart's fascination with the "handsome sailor" in *Billy Budd*). The narrator, lacking Ishmael's
contradictory experience and sense of memory, finds himself caught up in a
play of possibilities which disarticulates the circular figure on which selfhood
depends in *Moby-Dick:* "This history goes forward and goes backward, as
occasion calls. Nimble center, circumference elastic you must have" (54). Isabel's face calls up "one infinite, dumb, beseeching countenance of mystery,
underlying all the surfaces of visible time and space" (52).

Pierre's first response to Isabel is to "banish the least trace of his altered
father" (87) from his thoughts, a reaction which he realizes promises none of
the redemption which he seeks. His next is to "make a sacrifice of all objects
dear to him"—to hold Lucy "ransom for Isabel's salvation" (105). The impulse
to sacrifice either memory or world, self or other, corresponds figurally to
Ahab's reliance on revenge to "kill" time. Melville tags Pierre's thought with the
tautological formula "eye for eye, and tooth for tooth" (105) in recognition of
its self-destructiveness. None of the alternatives which he ponders offers escape
from a Romantic rhetoric which hangs identity on the absolute, conflicting
possibilities of redemption and annihilation.

Pierre's dilemma is raised from the level of fulsome pathos to that of psychological and rhetorical insight by its institution not just of alternative fetishizings
of self and world but of the catachrestic Romantic conflation of beauty and
death. The "mournfulness" of Isabel's face makes it beautiful "in a transcendent
degree" and invites him to "champion the right" (107). "He now gazed upon the
death-like beauty of the face, and caught immortal sadness from it. She seemed
as dead; as suffocated,—the death that leaves most unimpaired the latent tran-
quillities and sweetnesses of the human countenance" (112). Mistaking death
for transcendence, trope for symbol, Pierre commits himself to its power. Isabel
speaks to him with the combined force of "Memory and Prophecy," against

which he has no "reserve" (112). He exclaims, "From my heart's depths, I love and reverence thee; and feel for thee, backward and forward, through all eternity" (113).

Pierre's abandonment of his mother and Lucy for Isabel superimposes a synecdochic image of death on his established, incestuous, pattern of self-definition. This shift has the dramatic rhetorical impact of replacing figures of reflection and circularity, the Romantic fetishism carried over from *Moby-Dick* and from Hawthorne's fiction, with a more radically negative vision. The "dumb blankness full of meaning" embodied in the repetitive, constructed memories of absence central to "The Whiteness of the Whale" ushers in a rhetoric of death whose subtlety and power the rest of the novel elaborates. Isabel's face "kills" not just Pierre's metaleptic dream of eternal, backward and forward love but the processes by which memory can be figured either redemptively or proleptically, as *Erinnerung* or *Gedächtnis*.

The concern for memorial and epitaphic remembrance—memory which preserves and which kills—introduced into *Pierre* by Isabel's deathly beauty receives elaboration and analysis both in the second half of the novel and throughout Melville's later career.[1] It inspires a series of rhetorical experiments and perspectives which give his work its elusive "postmodern" cast. The first half of the novel sets the stage for the second half's departure by elaborating with increasing boldness its parodic critique of the rhetoric of selfhood. Thus, from their first meeting on, the interaction between Pierre and Isabel replays and subverts the key formulas central to the vocal authority of *Moby-Dick*.

Isabel's initial story repeats and exaggerates Ishmael's "Counterpane" experience. It tells a similar story of loneliness, temporal entrapment, and "awful fear." Ishmael cannot "settle" if his remembrance is "reality or a dream"; for Isabel "the solidest things melt into dreams, and dreams into solidities" (117). Although Pierre "often, in after-times" credits "this first magnetic night" with the origination of the "Pantheistic master-spell" which holds him (151), Isabel disperses origins in an infinitely regressing past: "My brother . . . a second face, and a third face, and a fourth face peep at me from within thy own. Now dim, and more dim, grows in me all the memory of how thou and I did come to meet" (117–18). In a parody of the Narcissus image in *Moby-Dick*, she gazes in the "smooth water behind the house" and sees "the likeness—something strangely like, and yet unlike, the likeness of his face" (124). Even to herself she signifies the father which is the ungraspable phantom of life—the key to it all—for both her and Pierre. Yet it is not the authority of the father but of her "likeness" to "the likeness of his face" which she puts in play. Like "The Whiteness of the Whale," the "likeness of his face" grounds meaningfulness on the power of a problematic nominalization.

In a move calculated to alert the reader to his parodic recapitulation of "The Whiteness of the Whale," Melville graces the meeting between Pierre and Isabel with a spectacular and absurd proliferation of nominalizations. Isabel cannot recall "the blankness, and the dimness, and the vacant whirlingness of the bewilderingness" (122), although she remembers her first "sweet idea" of "the infinite mercifulness, and tenderness, and beautifulness of humanness" (122). In her guitar music, Pierre hears "sounds of melodiousness, and mournfulness, and wonderfulness" (126). In *Moby-Dick*, the meaningfulness of nominalization is linked to the first-person attempt to say what the white whale means to Ishmael; it makes sense as a rhetorical gesture only in the context of "afterness." In *Pierre*, the protagonist gives it originary significance, a move which mixes Romantic and anti-Romantic formulas.

Pierre takes Isabel's nominalized and nominalizing "mysteriousness" not as a decentering force which will free him from the past but instead as "unchangeable" (141): she "soared out of the realms of mortalness" to become for him "transfigured in the highest heaven of uncorrupted Love" (142). Rather than generating a "posterity" as Hawthorne does in relation to Shakespeare in "Hawthorne and His Mosses," the "resurrection" of the "likeness" of Pierre's father is taken as a time-killing synecdoche which, as we have seen, only thinly veils the presence of death. Rather than submitting himself to a process of "draughting," Pierre, like Ahab, declares his topmost greatness: "Henceforth, cast-out Pierre hath no paternity, and no past; and since the Future is one blank to all; therefore, twice-disinherited Pierre stands untrammeledly his ever-present self" (199).

Pierre's self-fetishizing declaration culminates the psychological portraiture of the novel's first half. In declaring himself free, he merely displaces his incestuous relationship with his mother onto an incestuous relationship with his sister. His sense of himself is governed by classical repetition-compulsion, and the nominalizing rhetoric of the novel circles not the dumb blankness full of meaning at the center of language but rather the unconscious space of repressed incest. Without Ishmael's experience—however "ungraspable" or "unsettled" it may be—the circular pattern of enablement espoused by Melville's earlier, first-person, narrators can promise neither redemption nor freedom. The fictional act reduces to a trope of fatality: Pierre is portrayed "learning how to live, by rehearsing the part of death" (305).

The impingement of death on meaning, which comes to the fore in the middle of *Pierre*, rather than leading Melville down the road to despair, promotes a leap out of the psychological and once again into the rhetorical. The rhetorical equivalent of death is silence, a silence which denies even *Gedächtnis*—the constructed presence of memory. Halfway through *Pierre,* Melville begins an exploration of the rhetoric of silence which institutes the most breathtaking— and theoretically complex—rhetorical departure of his entire career. To see the second half of the novel in terms of its rhetorical exploration of silence enables one to see how the energy and analytic zeal of Melville's voice survives the collapse of the conventions of fictional self-representation which the novel's blithely horrifying ending climaxes.

The silence which broods over the face of book 14 of *Pierre* frames the central question of Melville's post-Romantic art: "How can a man get a Voice out of Silence?" (208). This question takes the place of Father Mapple's "What is man that he should live out the lifetime of his God?" in determining the itinerary which verbal self-representation must take in the novel. A third-person, unlike a first-person, narrator speaks "out of Silence": there is no previously inscribed tale to repeat. For Dryden, among others, the effect of such questions is dire; it produces a work in which "words and things are equally fictitious" (*Melville's Thematics* 120). Yet Melville elaborates the question in surprising ways in applying it to Pierre's situation.

Silence is an inevitable concomitant to meaning, since "all profound things, and emotions of things are preceded and attended by Silence"; it is "the general consecration of the universe" and "the only Voice of our God" (204). Moving from his grand pronouncement to an analysis of Pierre's dilemma, Melville comments that "certainly, all must admit, that if for any one this problem of the possible reconcilement of this world with our own souls possessed a peculiar and potential interest, that one was Pierre Glendinning at the period we now write of" (208–9). Silence, in *Pierre,* is external. The "world" may speak a message of silence, but "our souls" do not. The problem of fictional rhetoric is not to avoid lapsing into silence but to reconcile the "empty nominalness" of inner plenitude—the "more words than things" which memory constructs—with the objective silence, the death, on which meaning depends in "the universe."[2]

Melville's departure from first-person narrative in *Pierre* goes hand in hand with his concern for speaking out of a context dominated by death and silence. His earlier perspective always implies an afterness which makes death inconceivable, a survival whose meaningfulness is at stake but whose existence cannot be gainsaid. The authorial identity which first-person fiction attempts to ground always already exists; self precedes self-representation; one cannot say what one has no memory of. As a result, the "everything profound" which silence "precedes and attends" remains outside consideration. Third-person narrative, by rendering "nimble" the center and "elastic" the circumference of fictional selfhood, permits the voice of the narrator to emerge out of a previously inarticulate verbal space. By constituting itself as a voice out of silence, narrative can confront the meaning of death without falling into the endless figural displacements of "The Whiteness of the Whale."

The rhetorical departure which Melville announces in the middle of *Pierre* has a variety of practical and theoretical implications which cannot be couched in terms drawn from his earlier works. It represents a post-Romantic or post-modern, but not deconstructive, turn. By problematizing the representational logic of his voice, he seeks to discover its presentational authority: the search for silence is a search for the voice of both "death" and "our God"—for the persua-sive presence of an utterance whose potential is not predetermined by its narra-tive (figural and temporal) context. It is the search for a voice which does not imply the entire history, the portfolio of memories, of a fictional speaker. *Pierre* by no means ends this search, which will lead Melville, after 1857, to the putative objectivity of both history and the "measured forms" of verse; but the novel sets the terms that the search will take well into his poetic career.

The terms in which Melville frames the dilemma of his third-person narra-tive correspond to a startling degree to the highly rhetorical psychoanalytic theory of Nicolas Abraham. I will call on Abraham, whose work provides an important transition between classical Freudianism and the early work of his friend Jacques Derrida, in order to clarify the systematic and prescient nature of Melville's rhetorical departure in *Pierre*. Melville inserts the idea of silence into his psychological portraiture in exactly the way Abraham seeks to revise psy-choanalytic discourse on the basis of what he calls its "anasemia."

"Anasemia" for Abraham names the "scandalous anti-semantics" of psycho-analytic discourse—the fact that its terms signify in relation to each other, within their own closed economy, but refuse determination by ordinary lan-guage. Thus, "the language of psychoanalysis no longer follows the twists and turns (topoi) of customary speech and writing. Pleasure, Id, Ego, Economic, Dynamic, are not metaphors, metonymies, synecdoches, catachreses; they are, through the action of discourse, products of de-signification and constitute new figures, absent from rhetorical treatises" ("The Shell and the Kernel" 20). Psychoanalysis traces the itinerary of "psychic representatives" which mediate between such anasemically defined realms as the Somatic and the Psychic. These "psychic representatives," "like the symbols of poetry, are mysterious messages from one knows not what to one knows not whom" (21). For Abra-ham, a poetic symbol "makes allusion to the unknowable by means of an un-known, while only the relation of the terms is given." He concludes, "All au-thentic psychoanalytic concepts may be reduced to these two structures (which happen to be complementary): symbol and anasemia" (21). These structures provide the only meaningfulness available in the context of "the non-presence of the self to itself" (19).

Silence, death, and the "only Voice of our God" impose a condition of anasemia on the representation of selfhood in *Pierre* by projecting the figures—memories—on which an experientially based authority depends onto the screen of a silent universe. In *Moby-Dick* the "invisible spheres" are "formed in fright"; in *Pierre,* that which lies outside the spoken history of the self is neither invisible nor frightening, but mute. Fiction depends not on rhetorical representations of established meaning but on transactions between unfigured realms—in Pierre's case, the silence of the external world and the incest at the center of the internal. Shorn of even constructed experience—*Gedächtnis*—the key elements of fiction become purely relational. Characters, for example, give up all pretense of realism; they function like Fedallah, the one genuinely anasemic personage in Melville's earlier fiction. *Pierre* reads like an allegory for which the keys to figurative meaning have been lost.

Likewise, Melville's earlier rhetorical (tropological) strategies lose their power to evoke stable temporal and phenomenological modes of experience—redemption, internalization, comparison, alienation, and so forth. The idea of a privileged set of figures of speech that reflect key figures of thought gives way to a nimbleness and elasticity untrammeled by the structures of memory, by the patterns of redemption and prophecy. The overarching power of death and its rhetorical counterpart, silence, forces Melville to reconstitute his rhetoric in new terms. His search for alternative tropes—for the principles of an authoritative voice freed from a phenomenology built from represented memories—yields a number of structures central not just to the outcome of *Pierre* but to his subsequent fiction as well.

Pierre's transcendentally centered vision of love is one of the first and most obvious aspects of the novel to fall victim to anasemic revision. Since transcendence is associated in Isabel with death, love comes to reveal different bases than those imagined by Pierre. Melville comments, as his protagonists travel to New York, "The love of the most single-eyed lover, almost invariably, is nothing more than the ultimate settling of innumerable wandering glances upon some one specific object" (217). This reinterpretation of love is one of a number of instances in the novel which institute a dramatically new relationship between inner and outer aspects of subjectivity. Rather than dive deep into the self, reach the center of the circle, or interiorize the world, *Pierre* calls for an outward projection of identity. One comes to know oneself by reading external reflections—embodiments—of the incorporeal voice of the soul: "All the great books in the world are but the mutilated shadowings-forth of invisible and eternally unembodied images in the soul; so that they are but the mirrors, distortedly reflecting to us our own things" (284). Love, if not permitted its worldly measure, will remain self-love.

In *Moby-Dick*, Narcissus attempts to penetrate the surface of life in order to grasp the deep, unitary image of himself, which is "the key to it all." In *Pierre*, that surface, in all its multiplicity and distortion, offers a more concrete image of the "shadowed-forth" self than deep-diving can hope to reveal. The only clear, unitary meaning is death (silence), the condition of anasemia imposed on our desire for redemptive, proleptic, or memorable self-presence. Compared with egocentric Romantic ideals, the utilitarian views of "the every-day world's people" are far more likely to reveal the complex nature of truth. Melville's emerging view of the self corresponds to Abraham's definition of consciousness as an "organ" capable of "objectifying the various modes of nucleo-peripheral relationship in relations of the Ego to external Objects" (25). To Abraham, we constitute ourselves through consciousness as "Objects of the Object" (25); in *Pierre*, identity must find its outward place and learn how to read its embodied, worldly reflection if it hopes to escape narcissistic self-mystification.

Melville's new view of the self tallies the "superabundance of materials" which he describes as daunting modern writers in "Hawthorne and His Mosses." His throwing of Romantic self-presence into anasemia determines an objectivity which places Pierre's illusions in relief. Pierre turns to writing in the hope of disclosing a deep identity; instead he knits himself into a fabric of elaborating relationships which plays out the deadly force of his repeated, incestuous gestures. What he must come to face are the self reflected in his worldly actions and the silence which the universe gives back to his Romantic dreams. The difference between Pierre's task and the Narcissus image of *Moby-Dick*, as Isabel's specular experience demonstrates, is that self and reflected self are separated by the gap between spoken and silent meaning, living subject and portrait. The "Object" which consciousness must constitute itself as "Object of" is an otherness which refuses to conform to the terms of meaningfulness set by a rhetoric of self-presence. The speaking subject must learn to align its voice with images reflected from an objective external world if its truth—the "Godly" (i.e. persuasive or creative) force of its articulations—is to emerge. The "universe" of *Pierre* resists the personification (prosopopoeia) inherent in Melville's earlier formulations, including his figure of the sea as a reality to be explored through an act of "diving" parallel to the inward-turning quest for the essential soul. Death has no phenomenological voice.

When Pierre begins to understand the implications of objectivity, of the active engagement with the world necessary to identity, he misjudges the subject-object, speaking-silent, inner-outer dichotomy in which he is caught. Instead of searching for new relational formulas, he reads the silence of the world into his own identity and once more dissembles the incest which his life acts out. He proposes the ethical silence of the world as a condition of his own identity: "Look: a nothing is the substance, it casts one shadow one way, and another the other way; and these two shadows cast from one nothing; these, seems to me, are Virtue and Vice"; he goes on to assert that it is the law "that a nothing should torment a nothing; for I am a nothing" (274). Pierre's inward projection of ethical meaninglessness contradicts its own passive, nihilistic posture by leading directly to his outward expression of sexual desire for Isabel: "Swiftly he caught her in his arms: 'From nothing proceeds nothing, Isabel! How can one sin in a dream?' " (274). He remains unable to see the reflected duplicity of his incest-centered selfhood.

Incest, in *Pierre,* becomes a master figure for the tautological self-siring or self-fetishizing critiqued in Melville's earlier work. It signals the desire to construe oneself in the model of "self-reciprocally efficient hermaphrodites" (259) capable of denying both the essential silence of the world and the constructed and objective nature of ethos. Incest does more than equate the self with itself in a way which denies metaleptic or proleptic time, it destroys the inner-outer, self-world, speaking-silence balance without which human meaning, in *Pierre,* is inconceivable. It not only paralyzes but short-circuits narrative time by trapping Pierre in the fatal secondariness dictated by his mother. It keeps him "learning how to live, by rehearsing the part of death" (305).

Incest as trope, figure, or rhetorical structure underlies both Pierre's failure as a writer and Melville's abandonment of his earlier search for the grounds of an authoritative authorial identity. In both cases, the attempt to mine one's own past, memories, or inner self generates a blindly fetishistic subjectivity capable only of continuing the repetitive, inward-turning dance of death against which its rhetoric struggles. Pierre's manuscript serves only to defend against another book—that of his incestuous life—"whose unfathomable cravings drink his blood" (304). For Melville, autobiographical first-person narrative can complete its circle only in suicide; otherwise it is doomed to repetition; the persona narrators of his earlier work start each novel with the same desire to escape the meaninglessness which the world imposes on self-authoring; their successes, momentary at best, depend on ever-heightening rhetoric rather than discovery of the metaphysical grounds of an authoritative identity; like Pierre, they are "fools of Truth."

Pierre circles back not to redeem but to chastise itself. Melville embodies its critical logic in a repetitiveness from which death is the only escape. Shortly after Pierre's Enceladus vision reveals its "doubly incestuous" nature to him (347), the three protagonists encounter, in a museum, a third iteration of the father's painted likeness. Pierre, seeing the "resurrection" of his earlier portrait, realizes that "the original of this second portrait was as much the father of Isabel as the original of the chair-portrait. But perhaps there was no original at all" (353). His feelings become "untranslatable into any words that can be used." Silence and repetition are his only choices, and both signify and lead to death. The difference between Pierre's original and final states comes with the realization that he is caught in the middle, not at the end, of the "endless descendedness" which was his former glory. Repetition traps him within his own "empty" or "nominalized" memories. Yet as the novel drives toward its triple *Liebestod*, its relentlessly repetitive structure frees Melville, as narrator speaking "out of silence," to revise earlier figures in a way which protects his ethos from the plight of his protagonist. In so doing, it returns to the radical irony which started Melville's search for authority in *Typee*.

The figurative economy which enables Melville's voice to rise above his tale emerges in a cluster of images deriving from the authorial ethos of *Moby-Dick*. In the summer of 1851, Melville had described himself to Hawthorne as "one of those seeds taken out of the Egyptian Pyramids" and in the same breath as having "unfolded within myself" to reach "the inmost leaf of the bulb" (*Letters* 130). In *Pierre* he again figures the search for the truth of the self: "The old mummy lies buried in cloth on cloth; it takes time to unwrap this Egyptian king. . . . By vast pains we mine into the pyramid; by horrible gropings we come to the central room; with joy we espy the sarcophagus; but we lift the lid—and no body is there!—appallingly vacant as vast is the soul of a man!" (285) A few pages later, he writes, "Deep, deep, and still deep and deeper must we go, if we would find out the heart of a man; descending into which is as descending a spiral stair in a shaft, without any end, and where that endlessness is only concealed by the spiralness of the stair, and the blackness of the shaft" (288–89); and still later, "There now, do you see the soul. In its germ on all sides it is closely folded by the world, as the husk folds the tenderest fruit; then it is born from the world-husk, but still now outwardly clings to it" (296).

Rather than being a locus of self-presence or resurrection, the inner self, as figured by tomb, shaft, and seed, now betokens vacancy, blindness, and the clinging husk of the outer world.[3] Yet more important for Melville's voice than his revision, in line with the general thematics of *Pierre*, of inner-outer dialectics, is the manner in which his images relate to each other rhetorically. The ending of *Moby-Dick* gives multiple instances of a single, key trope (center and circumference), but the effect of this technique in *Pierre* is significantly different. In *Moby-Dick* each iteration adds to and amplifies the accumulated meaning of the figure; the instances recall and relate to each other to build toward a coherent vision. In *Pierre*, the images occur in seeming rhetorical isolation, as if the narrative voice did not remember its previous formulas. Melville's descriptions of the vacant vastness, clinging worldliness, or endlessness of the soul do not dovetail logically with each other. Each is a self-contained, oracular pronouncement. We are back in a rhetorical world of momentary, dramatic, exaggerated, and disconnected ironic effects much like that of "Fragments from a Writing Desk."

The strangely ironic and unfocused interplay of Melville's images, of which the example cited above is only one among the many which clot the second half of the novel, brings to a halt its progress toward ethical resolution; it bogs down in fascinating but desultory narrative speculation, or else moves forward by fits and starts in unpredictable directions. Both narrative time and the memory processes on which it depends are destabilized; things remembered—explicit or evoked—resist integration into a coherent, expanding ethos; one rhetorical flourish encounters the next, without any teleology holding them together; the "continuous imaginative presence" of the narrative voice seems to be playing games, multiplying whimsical possibilities, or else trying to make up its mind. None of its formulations slows the inexorable march of Pierre's tale toward its tragic fate.

A key to the rhapsodic rhetoric of the second half of *Pierre* comes at the end of the chapter in which Pierre encounters Plotinus Plinlimmon: "And here it may be randomly suggested, by way of bagatelle, whether some things that men think they do not know, are not for all that thoroughly comprehended by them; and yet, so to speak, though contained in themselves, are kept a secret from themselves? The idea of Death seems such a thing" (294). In the terms generated by the novel, the process described in the passage is one of "silent memory," a precursor to Freud's notion of the unconscious. Figures are seen as enactments of a level of memory unavailable to voice. Death may not be spoken or integrated into articulate selfhood, but its hegemony is clear. From the perspective of the inward "dive," death is an impossible concept; it is a condition of existence which is not present to consciousness. From a worldly point of view, the notion of death is adequate to its manifestations: it and silence trope, on different levels, the essential circumstance—unavailability of both a prior self awaiting resurrection and a speakable future—for which voice must account. Inner and outer, nominalized and embodied meanings relate to each other anasemically through the operation of literary figuration—Abraham's "poetic symbols."

The presence of the unconscious or of "silent memory" in *Pierre* disarticulates the temporality associated with Melville's previous rhetoric of self-establishment. As Pierre contemplates his mother's death and the presentments which it arouses in regard to himself, Melville announces "presentment" to be a "judgment in disguise," for "while still dreading your doom, you foreknow it." Melville asks, "How foreknow and dread in one breath, unless with this divine seeming power of prescience, you blend the actual slimy powerlessness of defense?" (287) Later on, when Pierre attempts to justify Lucy's impending arrival, he credits her with the power of "presentment"; Isabel cannot understand; she translates: "Hath she that which they call the memory, Pierre; the memory?" Pierre responds that "we all have the memory," but Isabel, in spite of her clairvoyance, demurs, claiming "but very little" (314). Isabel recognizes that all understanding, all foresight, relies on memory, and that memory carries the unspoken weight of judgment. All three protagonists are being backed by the silent memory of Pierre's unacknowledged incest into increasingly "slimy" defensive postures.

Silent memory, in *Pierre*, underlies presentment—the foreknowledge which depends on judgment, on the past. Unless that which is silent—death, or in Pierre's case, incest—is understood in terms which permit its worldly reflection to be read, it will remain unconscious and continue to force life into patterns determined by repetition-compulsion. It will kill time, just as Freud's unconscious can kill psychological time by fixating the personality and Abraham's "crypts" can force the self to act as if out of feigned, and thus unanswerable, unconscious syndromes. Pierre is daimonized by unspoken judgments; Plinlimmon's face haunts him with the seeming knowledge that he and Isabel are not married (293); Delly echoes Plinlimmon's insight (329); the portrait opposite No. 99 presents a message of "incest and parricide" to him (351). In his desire to create a "love deep as death" (307), he is pushed forward by silent memories out of the unresolved past, the equivalent in Melville's rhetorical terms of Freud's return of the repressed. He can expect neither redemption nor change; an unspoken judgment remains final.

The narrative voice, Melville's ethos, in *Pierre* is left in a posture of combined presentment and "slimy" defensiveness vis-à-vis the iron-railed plot of the novel. Rather than attempting an incestuous involvement with it, it elaborates, with extraordinary energy, figures calculated to mediate between its own "empty nominalness" as a "voice out of silence" and the unacknowledged content of its past in Melville's earlier work. Wanting instinctively to make phenomenological—that is, redemptive or prophetic—sense out of its voice, it finds itself a "fool of Truth" caught in the endless repetitions necessitated by the avoidance of synecdochic self-fetishizing. As an art devoted to stripping to the inmost leaf or excavating the mummy of an authoritative identity, it finds itself ironized by the emptiness of the sarcophagus, the clinging tenacity of the husk.

The solution which *Pierre* offers to the impasse of Melville's rhetorical program, and by analogy to its protagonist as well, depends on the outwardness of silence (death). Silent memory is objective memory; it signifies genuine as opposed to nominalized experience. In order to ground a self which is not incestuous, self-fetishizing, and empty, memory must acknowledge its external history in the way that the unconscious, in psychoanalytic discourse, must reveal its patterns of cathexis. Rhetoric, ethos, in *Pierre* must give up its re-demptive or prophetic agendas and become a talking cure. In terms of Melville's art, this means that the voice instituted by the quest to establish an authoritative identity must be disorganized and retroped in terms which reflect the outward, repetitive patterns of its incestuousness. The fictional rhetoric leading up to *Pierre* flirts in key places with Melville's recognition of the need to find a way of figuring death, yet each time this happens it produces momentary catachreses which only temporarily call into question the self-defined invincibility of voice. In *Pierre,* the implications of this impasse are followed up. If Melville's art were to resolve it on the level of plot and theme, then Pierre would have to find a way to unlive his incestuousness. But that would leave Melville's voice unchanged. Instead, Pierre is sacrificed in order to break the mold of an art which circles back on itself in perpetual auto-valorization. In the process, the ever-heightening rhetoric of Melville's developing career is stripped to the bone.

Pierre's suicidal end tolls the knell not only of the thematics of Romantic fiction (along with the values of the Duyckinck circle with which Melville broke early in 1852) but also of its tropological structure. Synecdoche dominates Pierre's vision of himself and his love at the center of an expansive world; metonymy organizes his regressive fantasies and the static temporality within which his incest locates him; hyperbole emerges in the exaggerated nominalizations which characterize his relationship with Isabel; metaphor structures the fatal parallel between his life and his own attempt at writing, as well as correspondences between Isabel and Lucy, and among the apostles; metalepsis determines the backward and forward movement of time promised by Isabel's story. What survives Pierre's downfall, out of Melville's earlier rhetoric, are radical irony—an irreducable incongruence between voice and voiced—against which his entire process of development, starting with the "Fragments from a Writing Desk" and *Typee,* can be measured; a deep respect for the irreducible objectivity of death, related rhetorically to the presence of silent memory; and the ana-semic figuration which permits Melville's post-Romantic hard-mindedness to take fictional wing.

In killing off Melville's earlier rhetorical program, *Pierre* reveals itself to be a desperate but not a despairing book. Melville is willing to give up the grand, prophetic authorial image of *Moby-Dick* in return for freedom from the repetition of worn-out figural patterns and for a new means of engaging the "super-abundance of materials" lying without. Although his move from New York to

Pittsfield necessitated withdrawal from urban literary engagements and contro-versies, his fiction in the years following *Pierre* combines a muted, flexible authorial presence with a broad range of "the gritty real-life stuff he increas-ingly seized on, after exhausting his Pacific experiences, to make into fiction" (*CM*, "Historical Note" 273)—places inhabited and visited, occupations and working environments, historical documents, political issues, buildings, furni-ture and works of art, newsworthy characters and events. His art takes on a more specific and contemporary flavor, and it uses its combined rhetorical freedom, underlying irony, and honesty in the face of death in an impressive variety of ways. What it loses is the large-scale architecture enabled by the rhetoric of self-actualization at the center of his first-person novels, and *Clarel* proves even this loss temporary.

10

"A dream of the eye": Magazine Fiction

And there, the invisible painter painted to her view the wave-tossed and disjointed raft, its once level logs slantingly upheaved, as raking masts, and the four struggling arms undistinguishable among them; and then all subsided into smooth-flowing creamy waters, slowly drifting the splintered wreck; while first and last, no sound of any sort was heard. Death in a silent picture; a dream of the eye; such vanishing shapes as the mirage shows.
—Melville, "The Encantadas"

*T*he *rhetoric* of Melville's magazine fiction builds on that of *Pierre* as *Omoo* builds on *Typee*. Rather than sustain the shrill pitch of the novel, however, the works published from 1853 to 1856 return to the modulated prose and focused concerns which characterize his earlier sequels.[1] Where they experiment, as Bickley, Dillingham (*Melville's Short Fiction*), Rowe, Seelye, and Sundquist ("Suspense and Tautology") show them to, their experiments involve application of the *Pierre* rhetoric rather than bold departure. Having razed his Romantic ethos, Melville mortars in the carefully selected bricks of a new one. He writes as fast and obsessively as ever, but with stunning rhetorical precision.

The immediate and enduring success of Melville's magazine fiction proves that there is nothing willfully inaccessible about the voice which emerges in *Pierre*.[2] The short stories were well published, well recompensed, and generally well reviewed.[3] In spite of the 1851 statement to Hawthorne that "what I feel most moved to write, that is banned,—it will not pay. Yet, altogether, write the *other* way I cannot" (*Letters* 128), Sealts concludes that "by contributing to such publications Melville did not have to prostitute himself by writing 'the *other* way'" (*PT* 513). Reviewers repeatedly praised the tales for "vividness" and "brilliancy" of imagination: rather than ask once again for a return to nautical realism, they accepted considerable "freedom & invention," now shorn of the excesses of *Mardi*. For all his family's concern over his career and state of mind, Melville was better in tune with his public than he had been since *Typee*.[4]

Melville's magazine fiction hones to impressive sharpness five distinct aspects of his *Pierre* rhetoric. The first and most important is the radical irony, discussed at length by Seelye and Sundquist, which separates narrator from character in the second half of the novel and establishes the "troubling distance" between "experience or preception and its representations" throughout the tales (Dryden, "From the Piazza" 65). Melville not only masters the ambiguity-producing machinery of third-person narrative, his first-person narrators, like that of "Bartleby, the Scrivener," can no longer be trusted even to the extent that we trust the morally confused Redburn, self-mystifying Ishmael, and rhapsodic Taji.

Melville's second borrowing from *Pierre* is a fascination with silent memory, with evocations of a phantasmic past that bear on life in unspeakable ways and function as "presentments"—defensive foreclosings of the future. Silent memory is the condition for narrative to constitute itself as a "voice out of silence," an ethos whose authority is not given, in the manner of Hugh Blair, by antecedent experience or status. Silent memory underlies the pathos of Bartleby's dead-letter office past, Hunilla's untellable experiences in "The Encantadas," and Benito Cereno's deadly memory of "the negro." Unable or unwilling to articulate, much less redeem, a lost past, all three are given over to "an inability to use language that leads inexorably to silence—often the silence of death" (Barnett 60).

The third aspect of the *Pierre* rhetoric espoused by Melville's magazine fiction is renewed interest in the "world-husk" of human identity, the outward circumference of selfhood essential to any peep at inner motives. The worldliness of Melville's post-Romantic rhetoric leads from a realization that "linguistic masquerades consolidate political hierarchies" (Hauss 20), to the increased engagement with contemporary social issues detailed by Dimock, Fisher, Karcher, and Rogin. It underlies his interest in how people relate to each other on bases other than shared quests or trials. Finally, it explains the easy rapacity with which he appropriates the documentary sources of "Benito Cereno" and *Israel Potter.*

The fourth rhetorical quality carried over from *Pierre* is "anasemia"—the organization of key terms so that they are meaningful only in relation to each other. Rhetorical anasemia underlies the bemusing, counterpoised pairs which populate Melville's tales—from Turkey and Nippers in "Bartleby the Scrivener" to black and white in the "gray" (*PT* 46) world of "Benito Cereno." Anasemia draws attention to the figural relationships linking terms together rather than to their absolute meanings. In his magazine fiction, Melville detaches it from the apocalyptic psychodrama of *Pierre* and plies it as a transportable rhetorical technique. It joins with silent memory to give his descriptions the air of "dreams of the eye"—a commanding but muffled ethical resonance.

The final point of rhetorical contact between *Pierre* and Melville's magazine fiction is the inescapability of death as a condition of meaning. Death is the outward counterpart of inner silence (silent memory), and it is equally present, although literally unspeakable, as an aspect of voice. Authorial ethos in Melville's post-Romantic rhetoric occupies the space between silence, out of which it comes, and death, toward which it points.[5] Like Ishmael before him, the narrator of "Bartleby, the Scrivener" steps forward as sole voicer of an otherwise lost but deadly tale that, unaccountably, gives his own life its focus. More comfortable with the rhetorical implications of death than ever before, Melville continually probes the figurative structures which link it to the authority of literature.

The power of Melville's *Pierre* rhetoric shines brightest in his three most famous magazine stories: "Bartleby, the Scrivener," "The Encantadas," and "Benito Cereno." Published in 1853, 1854, and 1855 respectively, the three tales reveal not just Melville's vocal mastery but a pattern of development culminating in the elaborate self-consciousness of *The Confidence-Man.* As he gets used to his post-Romantic voice, his rhetoric becomes at once more intrusive and more controlled. He also recognizes that short fiction gives him the freedom to employ unusual narrative perspectives, and as a result the narrators of his tales lie at the center of their exploratory energy. By 1855 he is consciously working close to the bone of the verbal structures implicit in *Pierre.* He is also preparing the ground for a notion of literary authority measured in terms derived from the central social and political issues of his day—a stance which will surface fully in the splendid historicity of *Battle-Pieces.*

"Bartleby, the Scrivener" displays a rhetorical playfulness which counters its claustrophobic content. Like the first few chapters of *Moby-Dick,* it summarizes, in abbreviated form, a number of the key tropological patterns of Melville's earlier fiction and then subjects them to catachresis; like *Pierre,* its vocal authority outweighs its nihilism. Nowhere is Melville's sheer rhetoricity—the charisma of his ethos—more obvious than in his "Bartleby" narrator, whose provoking slipperiness tallies that of the great narrators created by Browning and other contemporary British poets.[6] In choosing an unreliable narrator, Melville moves from the synecdochic, redemptive, and prophetic viewpoint of his Romantic fiction to a sardonic but engaging perspectivism, a "poetry of experience" in Robert Langbaum's terms, characteristic of Victorian literature.

The narrator of "Bartleby, the Scrivener" at first puts in play both the metaphoric comparisons and contrasts that link and distance Redburn and Harry in Melville's fourth novel and the radical irony that raises *Pierre*'s narrator above his hero. Yet his voice is so hyperbolic and self-reflective, as he sets out to "penetrate to the predestinated purpose" of his life (*PT* 37) and at the same time "cheaply purchase a delicious self-approval" (*PT* 23) by befriending Bartleby, and so thoroughly infected by the epidemic litotes which Bartleby's "I would prefer not to" unleashes, that his account returns to the antic vocal comedy of Melville's early "Fragments from a Writing Desk." We are left wondering whether to read the final synecdoche—"Ah, Bartleby! Ah, humanity!"—as a cry of pain and revelation or as a melodramatic gesture typical of the "slimy" defensiveness which the narrator of *Pierre* criticizes in his hero's judgments (*P* 287). Is the tale—to echo *Redburn's* subtitle—a contrite "confession" or a solipsistic "reminiscence"? Neither we nor the narrator himself are given the means to decide. The opposing interpretations which Rowe lists (119–20) remain unresolved not because Bartleby functions as Derridian *différance* (Rowe 137) but because none of their terms is grounded or valorized: they remain anasemic. Melville's rhetoric of self-conscious overstatement and understatement refuses to provide decisive information, even on an allegorical level.

"Bartleby, the Scrivener" gets away with its narrator's anasemic duplicity because almost everything else in the story participates in comparable patterns. Turkey and Nippers complement, mirror, and relieve each other in a gratuitous yet portentous way; so do the narrator and Bartleby, and all the tale's counterpoised ethical viewpoints. Yet as Sundquist shows to be the case in "Benito Cereno," ironic opposition tends to dissolve into tautology: that which appears different functions similarly. The narrator's "recondite documents" have no more authority than Bartleby's "dead letters." Redeemed narrator and unredeemed character are "predestinated" fools of the same truth. Language—communication, expression, understanding—comes too late to fend off death. Without a past on which its authority can stand, voice tells only its own story. The narrator lacks both the prior experience and the track record of repeated yarn-spinning on which Melville's Romantic nautical fiction bases its "interest." The tale instances what Louise Barnett calls "the withdrawal of the Melvillian protagonist from speech" (59).

What "Bartleby, the Scrivener" is left with in its denial of metaleptic quest, synecdochic drama of ethical emergence, and imperious irony is a silence of past and future which reduces hope to "presentiments of strange discoveries" (*PT* 28). The narrator compensates for this silence with assumptions: "Yes, as before I had prospectively assumed that Bartleby would depart, so now I might retrospectively assume that departed he was" (*PT* 35). Throughout the tale, assumption and preference circle in an exquisite but entropic minuet of balanced ethical possibilities.[7] The drama of the story lies in its spectacular casuistry, its playing of one supposition against another until the entire substructure of the Christian moral order troops by in carnival dress. "Bartleby, the Scrivener" reminds us that we live in an anasemic world linked to each other by an elaborate monkey-rope of tropes on the basis of which our pretenses claim the authority to speak.

The ostensible struggle of wills at the center of "Bartleby the Scrivener" is really a struggle of rhetoric. The narrator inhabits a world, much like our own, where any rhetorical stance must give way in the face of material exigencies. The truths of the "pocket"—selfhood's circumference—outweigh those of the "heart"; the latter are always figured, unstable, and dependent on external manifestations for authority. Into this world steps Bartleby, who will die for his rhetoric. As the tale progresses, it becomes clearer that what he "prefers" is not what is at stake—he prefers to oppose whatever the narrator suggests. At stake is maintaining, at all costs, a verbal formula. Human life, his rhetoric suggests, demands choice. In the face of inevitable death, only litotes—the understatement of "I prefer not to"—demonstrates the freedom of the will; not given to make sense of fate, Bartleby rhetorically reduces it. He perishes out of preference. The narrator, trapped by his own Romantic ethos, can summon up neither the verbal nor the material power to refute Bartleby's formula. It puts into catachresis the figurative structure of his own authority. The redemption which Bartleby offers him by way of fellow feelings "hardly to be resisted" remains ambiguous, since it is couched in the very terms that his unshaking preference subverts. In Gregory Jay's words, the lawyer "represents a center that both claims to ground a structure as its origin and yet appears only as an effect of that discursive system" (22). His responses to Bartleby remain anasemic.

Bartleby's unresolved relationship with the narrator of "Bartleby, the Scrivener" combines verbal with visual figures in a manner both similar to the picturesque interplay between Tommo and the inhabitants of Typee valley and characteristic of Melville's magazine fiction, praised by reviewers for its descriptiveness. In a replay of the metaleptic "I can never forget" of *Typee,* the narrator comments on his first view of Bartleby: "I can see that figure now— pallidly neat, pitiably respectable, incurably forlorn!" (*PT* 19); when the narrator attempts to dismiss him, Bartleby stands "like the last column of some ruined temple . . . mute and solitary in the middle of the otherwise deserted room" (*PT* 33); and when he visits Bartleby in the Tombs, the narrator describes, without interpretation, the suggestive setting: "The surrounding walls, of amazing thickness, kept off all sounds behind them. The Egyptian character of the masonry weighed upon me with its gloom. But a soft imprisoned turf grew under foot. The heart of the eternal pyramids, it seemed, wherein, by some strange magic, through the clefts, grass-seed, dropped by birds, had sprung" (*PT* 44). Lacking a speakable past and thus an authoritative meaning and at the same time replete with the visual trappings of synecdochic authority, Bartleby's life becomes a "dream of the eye," a series of tableaux whose picturesqueness forecloses whatever "meagre" resolution the narrator's "imagination" can supply (*PT* 99). In the end, language and physical world bypass each other: words, ever "on errands of life" can only "speed to death" (*PT* 99).

"Bartleby, the Scrivener" demonstrates the limits as well as the attractions of Melville's *Pierre* rhetoric. Having subverted the intentional structure of his Romantic tropes—irony, metaphor, synecdoche, metalepsis, hyperbole/litotes—by denying memory, the voice of the past, Melville is left with a set of powerful new figures—tautology, repetition, nominalization, anasemia, presentment (silent memory), and death—which are brilliantly effective in creating a rich visual and verbal ambiguity but unsuited to the task of giving large-scale movement or teleology to narrative. For the moment, Melville accepts the challenge of short fiction and sets out to craft resonant and economical dreams of the eye. In "The Encantadas," his patience with his *Pierre* rhetoric at flood tide, he produces a genuine masterpiece of the picturesque.

"The Encantadas" paints a world not merely bypassed by language but in which human language has no bearing: "The chief sound of life here is a hiss" (*PT* 127). Memory, confused in the narrator's mind with "the magic of my fancy" (*PT* 129), is represented mutely and visually by "the ghost of a gigantic tortoise, with 'Memento ****' burning in live letters upon his back" (*PT* 129). As the foreshortened motto (*memento mori*) suggests, the only human thing to be remembered is death, and the only appropriate response silence. Where "Bartleby, the Scrivener" rests on a rhetoric out of tune with the large-scale movements of narrative, "The Encantadas" cancels all motion: "To them change never comes" (*PT* 126). None of Melville's other works is as consciously conceived in descriptive terms, as an ethically provocative but anasemic sketch, a "dream of the eye."

As with White-Jacket's fall in Melville's fifth novel, the relatively monochromatic prose of "The Encantadas" frames a stunning rhetorical flight—"Sketch Eighth: Norfolk Isle and the Chola Widow." Here Melville evolves the subtly intrusive narrative viewpoint essential to "Benito Cereno." The narrator does not stand critically apart from his tale as does that of *Pierre;* he presents himself as a first-person witness to the rescue of Hunilla. In this role, however, he displays none of the self-conscious tendentiousness that makes the narrator of "Bartleby, the Scrivener" at once fascinating and frustrating. When Hunilla begins to recite her tale, the tale's perspective moves closer to third-person narrative. Hunilla's pathos lies not in her responses, for "she but showed us her soul's lid, and the strange ciphers thereon engraved; all within, with pride's timidity, was withheld" (*PT* 155).[8] Instead it derives from responses that the narrator makes available in imagining her experiences. He does not play the ventriloquist and put words in her mouth, but in speaking for himself, he brings to life the range and depth of human meanings inherent in her ordeal.

> So instant was the scene, so trance-like its mild pictorial effect, so distant from her blasted bower and her common sense of things, that Hunilla gazed and gazed, nor raised a finger or a wail. But as good to sit thus dumb, in stupor staring

on that dumb show, for all that otherwise might be done. With half a mile of sea between, how could her two enchanted arms aid those four fated ones? The distance long, the time one sand. After the lightning is beheld, what fool shall stay the thunderbolt? (*PT* 154)

By guarding both Hunilla's and his own discretion—protecting in turn what she hides and what he imagines her to hide—the narrator asserts an identity, a narrative complicity, with her which takes a giant step toward the dissolution of irony which Sundquist notes in "Benito Cereno." Hunilla's memories remain silent, permitting the narrator to supplement them out of his own store of memorable or fanciful images, like that of the "thunderbolt" quoted above. Melville's authorial ethos permits Hunilla to gain rhetorical force not through a synecdochic inflation of local into universal circumstances à la Goethe in Melville's 1851 letter to Hawthorne (*Letters* 130–31) but instead by the operation of an ongoing process of sympathetic identification.

In "Benito Cereno," Melville's "Norfolk Isle" narrator will gain in intrusiveness until he appears to be determining rather than interpreting his character's experiences. Amasa Delano walks the deck of the *San Dominick* like a puppet in a dumb show, subject to a parade of "assumptions" more exaggerated even than those of the "Bartleby" narrator. His judgments are permitted to stand, and the reader to accept them, even when the narrator knows better. Melville comes to recognize that the structure of sympathy and the structure of duplicity in fiction coincide. Sorting out the implications of this dilemma becomes a key goal of *The Confidence Man*. In "Norfolk Isle and the Chola Widow," however, the closeness which Melville establishes between narrator and character results in a pathos unseen since the Launcelott's-Hey chapter of *Redburn*.

Tropologically, "Norfolk Isle and the Chola Widow" lies halfway between the irony of *Pierre* and its tautological reduction in "Benito Cereno." The sketch works by simile. The "fellow-feeling" which Melville handles with kid gloves in "Bartleby, the Scrivener" here draws people together—narrator, captain, sailors, and widow. Neither ironically counterpoised nor tautologically identified, they show themselves to be distinct but ethically aligned. Simile works differently from the metaphors of *Redburn*, in which death inhabits the bridging of differences and words exhaust the breathable air. The effect here is closer to the sacramental "small voice of silence" which Stan Goldman finds in *Clarel*—the sharing of an embracing reverence for "a spot made sacred by the strongest trials of humanity" (*PT* 151).

For a brief moment, in "Norfolk Isle and the Chola Widow," Melville combines silent memories and vivid pictures—the truths of heart and pocket, center and circumference—into a dream of the eye whose rhetoric opens unexpected, almost sentimental, emotional registers. What the tale lacks—why Melville reacts against rather than builds on it—is time. Unlike Tommo, Hunilla attempts to count the days of her ordeal, but cannot; there are too many. Time eludes the rhetorical capacities of the picturesque. When Melville writes that "time was her labyrinth, in which Hunilla was entirely lost" (*PT* 156), he writes of his own voice.[9] Without a tropological environment that permits the exfoliation of temporal relationships, no narrative progress is possible: "The distance long, the time one sand" (*PT* 154). Hunilla is rescued from isolation by a "mysterious presentiment" (*PT* 175) that returns her tale to the complex temporal tropes of *Pierre* and "Bartleby, the Scrivener." She rides out of the story at the point in time when, "last seen," her future and the narrator's past—anasemically related—mark each other's diverging trajectories.

In "Benito Cereno," Melville's magazine rhetoric, the rhetoric of picturesque but static dreams of the eye, clashes consciously with his itch for large-scale narrative and temporal movements. This tension emerges most clearly in the strained and complex relationship between the narrator and his protagonist, Captain Delano. Rather than the sympathy and closeness of "Norfolk Isle and the Chola Widow," or the first-person comedy of "Bartleby, the Scrivener," the narrator returns to the irritated condescension of *Pierre,* further aggrandized by an unbridled manipulativeness unseen in Melville's earlier works. If Sundquist is right in asserting that the two finally blend together tautologically, that blend results from ethical authority rather than limitation. They merge on the narrator's terms.

Melville's ethos in "Benito Cereno," although lacking the pathos of "Norfolk Isle and the Chola Widow," displays renewed confidence and drive. He attempts to solve the problem of temporal progress by having his narrator push the story forward in an unrelenting game of clues, assumptions, and gathering suspense. For the first time in a major work, Melville's narrator not only teases the reader but forces his characters to become accessories to the game, as when Delano comments on the key worn by Cereno, "So, Don Benito—padlock and key—significant symbols truly" (*PT* 63), one of many examples. That Melville gets away with it—that the tale, for all its perspectivist cynicism, is so moving—bespeaks the depth of his rhetorical mastery. As in *Omoo,* he revels in the sheer exercise of newly acknowledged vocal powers, and the reader is swept along willy-nilly.

In "Benito Cereno," Melville dissembles his outrageous ethical willfulness through a combination of new and old techniques. Sundquist notes his regular use of "double negatives"—a form of litotes, practiced by the narrator of "Bartleby, the Scrivener," and even more central to *The Confidence-Man.*[10] Litotes gives the narrator a cagey deference, as when he asides, in regard to Delano's good nature, "Whether, in view of what humanity is capable, such a trait implies, along with a benevolent heart, more than ordinary quickness and accuracy of intellectual perception, may be left to the wise to determine" (*PT* 47). The passage warns us against Delano's stupidity and at the same time excuses it. As a result of the suspension of possibilities, the reader is caught up in a process of trying to weigh rationalizations even more tendentious than those of the "Bartleby" narrator.

Along with litotes, Melville employs a class of more intrusive tropes, called "conjectural expressions" by Seelye, who counts 115 instances in the tale (105). The narrator of "Benito Cereno" incessantly qualifies his perceptions and judgments with phrases like "presuming that," "it might have been that," "possibly," and "perhaps," along with a host of more complex formulas. Seelye's "conjectural expressions" correspond to the classical figure of aporia, in which genuine or pretended doubt is expressed. Combined with litotes, the effect of aporia on "Benito Cereno" is not so much to suggest, as Seelye asserts, "the deceptiveness of events" as to make it obvious that the narrator is withholding the truth. The suspense in the story results from our understanding that the narrator knows more than we do and can be expected to inform us later.

Melville's shift from the unreliable first-person narrator of "Bartleby, the Scrivener" to the sympathetic third-person one of "Norfolk Isle and the Chola Widow" to the manipulative one of "Benito Cereno" reflects a self-consciousness which will flower in *The Confidence-Man.* For a voice to have no past is for it to have extraordinary freedom. From a post-Romantic rhetorical perspective, to exercise that freedom in an act of sympathy is no more ethically authoritative than to use it in a tour de force of persuasive duplicity. The relationship between the ethos of a work of literature and its content—between voice and voiced—is arbitrary, subject at any point to the incursion of radical irony. Fiction does not work by facts; everything meaningful can be faked or questioned.

Melville uses his newly understood narrative freedom to refine the picturesque rhetoric of his magazine fiction. No passage from the mid-1850s better reveals the accomplishment of his "dreams of the eye" than the description at the beginning of "Benito Cereno."

> The morning was one peculiar to that coast. Everything was mute and calm; everything gray. The sea, though undulated into long roods of swells, seemed fixed, and was sleeked at the surface like waved lead that has cooled and set in the smelter's mould. The sky seemed a gray surtout. Flights of troubled gray fowl, kith and kin with flights of troubled gray vapors among which they were mixed, skimmed low and fitfully over the waters, as swallows over meadows before storms. Shadows present, foreshadowing deeper shadows to come. (*PT* 46)

The passage owes its effect to figures typical of Melville's post-Romantic art: repetition ("everything," "gray," "shadows"); a general atmosphere of understatement; simile ("like waved lead," "kith and kin"); the delicate aporia of the repeated "seemed"; and presentment ("foreshadowing deeper shadows to come"). It also uses a Romantic figure, prosopopoeia (personification), in a post-Romantic, anasemic, manner. The sense of inner, human qualities projected outward ("troubled," "fitfully," "foreshadowing") and of external qualities portending human response ("mute," "gray") disperses without a clear referent. The passage denies memory, a context which would focus its psychological resonance. Visually suggesting much, phenomenologically it leads nowhere. The complex and careful interplay of inner and outer which is a major theme from *Mardi* to *Pierre* never materializes. It has the same quality of static restlessness as "the distance long, the time one sand" in "The Encantadas."

"Benito Cereno" reflects the dilemma at the center of Melville's career. His development shows a dialectical oscillation between moments of seeking a rhetoric strong enough to answer his purposes and moments of seeking a purpose worthy of his rhetorical strength. The drama of emergence which culminates in *Moby-Dick* embodies the first, and the exploration of post-Romantic techniques which culminates in *The Confidence-Man* the second. His poetry will again repeat the pattern: *Battle-Pieces* and *Clarel* address the meaning of history and of the historical bases of religion, and the two late volumes return to the self-conscious search of the artist for appropriate objects. As Melville approaches the end of his first cycle, not yet aware of how much further *The Confidence-Man* will take him, he adds to the ending of "Benito Cereno" an extraordinary summary gesture which reveals the extent and direction of his development.

The problem "Benito Cereno" poses for Melville is how to shuck off Captain Delano once his preconceptions no longer generate suspense. Melville solves it by interposing Don Benito's deposition. If Delano is hampered by ignorance and stupidity, Cereno bears the burden of forbidden wisdom. He has undergone Romantic adventures in a post-Romantic world; the truth of his terrible ordeal will brook no hearing. Like Hunilla, he must swallow a past which can neither be redeemed nor articulated. Torn between the "dumb blankness" of Delano and the silent memory of Cereno, Melville interposes documents, suspends the dilemma, and retreats into a worldly, ostensibly nonfictional prose. The strategy appears to answer the strange question which interrupts Hunilla's account in "The Encantadas": "If some books are deemed most baneful and their sale forbid, how then with deadlier facts, not dreams of doting men? Those whom books will hurt will not be proof against events. Events, not books should be forbid" (*PT* 156). Documents, in "Benito Cereno," bridge the gap between deadly events and the silence they evoke.

Melville's genius lies in bringing Delano and Don Benito together in a final conversation, even though there is little for them to share. Neither ironically

distanced nor related through tautology or similitude, they predictably fail to
touch.

> "You generalize, Don Benito; and mournfully enough. But the past is passed; why
> moralize upon it? Forget it. See, yon bright sun has forgotten it all, and the blue
> sea, and the blue sky; these have turned over new leaves."
>   "Because they have no memory," he dejectedly replied; "because they are not
> human."
>   "But these mild trades that now fan your cheek, do they not come with a
> human-like healing to you? Warm friends, steadfast friends are the trades."
>   "With their steadfastness they but waft me to my tomb, señor," was the fore-
> boding response.
>   "You are saved," cried Captain Delano, more and more astonished and pained;
> "you are saved; what has cast such a shadow upon you?"
>   "The negro."
> There was silence, while the moody man sat, slowly and unconsciously gather-
> ing his mantle about him, as if it were a pall.
>   There was no more conversation that day. (*PT* 116)

As Melville's magazine career begins to draw to a close (only "I and My
Chimney" and "The Apple-Tree Table" follow "Benito Cereno"), he brings
versions of Bartleby and his employer back together. Unlike Bartleby, however,
Benito Cereno gives an answer to his rhetorically unsophisticated interlocutor's
request for an explanation. His answer, "the negro," is misunderstood because
it is literal. Don Benito is irredeemable because he cannot forget the actual
experiences he has gone through—because he has a memory, is human, ultimately finds his meaning outside the world of fiction. Delano, like the narrator of "Bartleby, the Scrivener," cannot understand because the truths of silence
and death bear on his world only as tropes; they are "cast by means of figures."
Fiction is the fool of truth, but truth is the silence of fiction. Melville has found
a way to give drive to his narrative, but without its earlier pattern of circling
back, ethos and experience, voice and voiced, freedom and authority, fail to
meet. Of all his characters, Delano most directly prefigures both the confidence-man and the strangely iron-railed inhabitants of *Billy Budd*. Lacking
memory, he lacks history, the ground on which, in *Battle-Pieces,* verbal authority will rest. He leaves Melville at the threshold of profound insights and profound questions regarding the rhetorical methods by which literature asserts
itself.

In 1855 Melville gathers the strands of his recent career together to begin his
most rhetorically self-conscious work. *The Confidence-Man,* published in 1857,
remains, in John Bryant's words, his "least accessible" novel, so complex "that it
is even difficult to render a reasonable plot summary without in some sense
betraying one's interpretive biases" (316). Yet its rhetoric, and thus its underly-

ing approach to literary art, grows firmly out of *Pierre* and the magazine fiction. It summarizes the rhetorical conclusions which Melville has reached at the end of a decade of preternaturally intense and productive experimentation with the structures of fiction. It offers a manifesto for post-Romantic literature. It reveals Melville at the height of his ethical development, still appropriating, exploring, challenging, and disabusing old forms and generating new ones of startling power. Like all of his major work, it mixes the highest of seriousness, stunning rhetorical risk-taking, and antic play. Its difficulty is matched only by its enduring freshness. *The Confidence-Man*, more than any of Melville's other works, gets us more elaborately and unsettlingly involved in the question of what happens when human beings address each other and their forms of address are given fictional representation.

11

"Mysterious touches":
The Confidence-Man

> Needless to say what distress was the unfortunate man's, when, engaged
> in conversation with company, he would suddenly perceive his Goneril
> bestowing her mysterious touches, especially in such cases where the
> strangeness of the thing seemed to strike upon the touched person.
> —Melville, The Confidence-Man

*T*he Confidence-Man summarizes and organizes the achieve-
ments of Melville's fictional rhetoric between Moby-Dick and 1857, just as his
whaling novel did for the first part of his career. It places on center stage the
incongruity between voice and voiced, and the resulting radical irony, proposed
by Pierre and explored in various ways by the magazine fiction, as an essential
condition of narrative.[1] The gap between voice and voiced, figure and figured,
disabuses The Confidence-Man of phenomenological representationality—of
the assumption that the ethos of a literary work puts in play a "continuous
imaginative presence" which has its own history or genealogy, sense of time,
and redemptive or prophetic ambitions. The ethical presence of fiction, Melville suggests, is as likely to dissemble as to authorize whatever past or system of
memories it claims, in the manner of Hugh Blair, as its basis.[2]

As is his wont, Melville shapes the thematics of his novel to reflect his
rhetorical agenda. The Confidence-Man enacts, on the level of event, the implications of its irony. Without memory, *ethopoeia* rests on either the coercive-
ness of language or unrationalized faith—in a word, on "confidence." The utter
clarity of Melville's rhetorical thinking gives rise to the novel's obscurity when
viewed through the lens of Romantic fictional conventions: in a manner which
exaggerates Captain Delano's role in "Benito Cereno," The Confidence-Man
moves and is motivated by verbal technique and figure rather than plot, character, and theme; the latter remain anasemic in the sense developed in Pierre and
the magazine fiction, a condition which underlies the novel's "entropic" economy, to use Lawrence Buell's astute term (20).

The aptest and most productive way to name Melville's rhetorical agenda in
The Confidence-Man is to call it "poetic." Poetry distinguishes itself from prose
on the basis of its concern for the organizational properties of its signifiers—

rhyme, rhythm, meter, line and stanza shape, patterns of figurative usage, repetition of rhetorical modes of address, and lyric sense of time. A poem, in the modern tradition, shapes and presents its own ethos through formal manipulation; the voice of a sonnet, for example, is always first and foremost that of *the* sonnet as a known convention. *The Confidence-Man* holds itself together by means of "poetic" rhetoric; the textual web spun by its key techniques dictates the style and content of its arguments (*logoi*). It organizes its figurative environment in tune with Melville's gathered insight into the nonrepresentational strategies which underlie the movement of narrative.

Viewing *The Confidence-Man* as "poetic" situates it in relation to the "lifelong interest" (Vincent vii) in verse demonstrated by the volume of poems Melville left with brother Allan (but never published) before sailing with his youngest sibling, Captain Thomas Melville, for San Francisco in 1860 (Leyda *Log* II, 615–16). Edwin Fussell (378) and Laurence Barrett (622), among others, have cited Melville's interest in the power of "forms, measured forms" as a key to his turn from fiction to poetry. What needs to be added is that the power of poetic forms for Melville lies in their de-Romanticizing of ethos, a process that comes to the fore in *The Confidence-Man*. The famous final line of the novel, "Something further may follow of this Masquerade" (251), predicts, more than anything, the verse which occupies the rest of Melville's creative life. The turn to "poetic" rhetoric is successful enough in Melville's eyes to inspire the engagement with history, in *Battle-Pieces* (1866), which in turn permits his return in *Clarel* (1876), to "old and crushing obsessions in the medium of eighteen thousand tetrameter lines" (Short, "Form as Vision" 554); Melville's final published novel heralds an ongoing aesthetic venture.

Like the world-ship of *White-Jacket*, the *Fidèle* has both open deck spaces and "quarters unseen," "confidential passages," and "out-of-the-way retreats like secret drawers in an escritoire" (15). Yet its "facilities for publicity or privacy" stage no interplay between inner and outer selves. Instead, *The Confidence-Man* offers an endless catalog of superficial behavior: fanaticism, belief, parsimony, weakness, ruin, charity, predation, and casual social interaction. The fear of being singled out as a "tool of Truth" is meaningless—anasemic—amid a "flock of fools, under this captain of fools, in this ship of fools" (15). Folly faces no possibility of redemption or "changing," no alternative, against which to measure itself. No one has anything of significance to hide; there is no secret "key to it all" lurking in the inmost soul.

The characters in Melville's earlier novels seek the "ungraspable phantom of life" in the reflected image of an inner selfhood. In *The Confidence-Man*, that phantom—the novel's only key to it all—walks among them as its eponymous hero. Rather than function as a "language machine" (Sussman 37), the confidence-man institutes and circulates the ironic structures which dominate the novel. He is inconceivable apart from his disguises—indeed, it is not even clear if he is one or several characters—yet his specific masks are incidental. It makes no difference whether or not anyone sees through him, because his victories have no impact on the world in which he operates, and his supply of victims is endlessly renewed. It is not even clear, especially in the second half of the book, who is tricking whom, if anybody: everyone in the work, narrator included, is a potential dupe, deceiver, and self-deceiver; no one wins or loses anything of serious value, is hurt, changes, or learns. The world of the *Fidèle* articulates itself as a self-referential (anasemic) April Fools' trick with no past or future and no causality except repetition.

A crucial aspect of Melville's rhetorical thinking is the realization that any figurative device or ethical structure implies a temporality, a set of relationships between past, present, and future. Rhetoric is inseparable from a theory of memory. *The Confidence-Man* is organized in terms of three distinct time-schemes which sort out in terms of divergent tropological programs. I will call these "authorial," or "prior," time; "genealogical," or "representational," time; and "textual," or "poetic," time. The differences among them and their peculiarities emerge in relation to the mythopoeia which is a central concern of *The Confidence-Man* and which Melville associates with the Romanticism he has been trying to escape since *Pierre.*

The Confidence-Man begins as a tale without a past in a mythical time and place: "sunrise on a first of April" (3) on the "cosmopolitan and confident tide" of the Mississippi River (9). Its first character appears "suddenly as Manco Capac at the lake Titicaca" (3). A key function of mythopoeia, as both Melville and modern commentators like Frank Kermode (39), Ernst Cassirer (II, 105), and Hans Blumenberg (149) realize, is to pin human experience to a larger or more meaningful time-scheme.[3] In this way, myth (fictional or otherwise) presents culturally and psychologically viable genealogies of human instrumentality, a function corresponding to Melville's attempt, in his earlier fiction, to associate the power of voice with a representable selfhood. *The Confidence-Man* incessantly projects its exploration of possibilities for human choice and action onto the screen of Christianity, Hinduism (in Franklin's argument), contemporary social or political exempla (Helen P. Trimpi), and other external frameworks. Yet, although Melville sets the stage for traditional mythopoeia in *The Confidence-Man,* he denies the synecdochic and metaleptic temporality needed to carry it out; the novel's apocalypses, as Warwick Wadlington points out, are apocryphal (138), and "a more unteleological fiction could not be imagined" (164). The various guises of the hero appear in an order which suggests no clear progress, no terminus, no developing focus. Each "avatar" seems original—

having no foreseeable relationship to those which precede—and yet repetitive, characterized by replicated methods, capabilities, arguments, and outcomes. The tale's mythopoeia better fits Claude Lévi-Strauss's description in *The Raw and the Cooked:* "Since it has no interest in definite beginnings or endings, mythological thought never develops any theme to completion: there is always something left unfinished. Myths, like rites, are 'in-terminable'" (6).

Lévi-Strauss's definition of mythic time differs from the traditional one in being structural and functional rather than representational; it describes myth as a pattern ("mythological thought") participated in ("like rites") rather than heard or understood. In *The Confidence-Man,* Melville introduces themes and elements having a traditional mythic resonance and then forces them into a rhetorical environment in which, lacking any sense of origins or goals, their function and structure rather than their meaning is highlighted. Mythic stories, in Melville's hands, degenerate into parables. They lose their power to tie human action to a representable world outside their own anasemic rhetorical environment. The authorial voice of *The Confidence-Man* explains itself through a tissue of parabolic interpolations (rationalizations, exempla, precepts) whose lessons reflect in microcosm the novel's larger structures and thereby add to its irreducible irony. Its parables are told, feigned, retold, reported, embedded within other tales, and circulated in a way which robs them of their ethical and temporal location, their access to a believable past. They function in the game of confidence, but they cannot be positioned within the causal logic of a larger ("genealogical") temporalty. An example will be analyzed in detail later.

The notion of fictional mythopoeia in *The Confidence-Man* defines the three time-senses that situate the novel in relation to Melville's earlier fiction. "Authorial," or "prior," time signifies the prearticulate past of silent memory, a temporal "otherness" out of which fictional consciousness, voice, and action are thought to emerge. "Genealogical," or "representational," time includes all the processes of memory which bridge the gap between an inarticulate past and a present ethos, which figure the emergence of voice out of what is "prior." "Textual," or "poetic," time denotes the temporal movements established by the surface or technical level of the novel's rhetorical environment. In the fictional mythopoeia of Melville's earlier novels, genealogical movements and processes, and their corresponding figures, perform the crucial function of connecting an authoritative but inexpressible priority—sea, childhood, innocent adventure, noble ancestry, and so forth—to a ritual participation in the immediate, "poetic" experience of discourse—its compelling formulaic movements.

In *The Confidence-Man* Melville's rhetoric cancels genealogical time, the central of the three temporal modes common to his earlier fiction. Cut loose from phenomenological conventions, from representing the emergence of ethical authority, the tale's key tropes generate their own temporal and relational movements, their own "textual" or "poetic" temporality; concurrently, "prior" time, now dis-figured and rendered inaccessible, haunts the narrative in the form of phantasmic echoes—silent memories of an inarticulate past. The resulting rhetoric is carnivalesque and polyvocal, but not chaotic. Melville focuses his attention on a limited set of temporal and poetic possibilities, which remain important to the poetry which he writes in the following decade.

Melville's bracketing of genealogical rhetoric in *The Confidence-Man* gives the novel a new perspective on death. In his bleakest previous work—*Redburn, Pierre,* "Bartleby, the Scrivener," and "The Encantadas"—the figurative operation of death determines the genealogical temporality of the desultory itineraries which his characters follow. Growth, survival, voice, and identity establish themselves by instituting death within a figurative program—in a word, by permitting art to register its human implications, even if these are inconceivable from a first-person narrative perspective. In contrast, death has no fictive force in *The Confidence-Man.* As in the story of Colonel Moredock, it is a matter of "metaphysics" which can only be reported parabolically in a world without genealogical time. In Melville's aesthetic manifesto, death, metaphysics, traditional mythopoeia, genealogical or representational time, and Romantic self-representation coincide, and he puts them out of play as a group. What remains—temporal priority and poetic textuality—is given almost surgically precise definition. Manuscript evidence of extensive revision (*CM* 401–99) reveals the care exercised by Melville in shaping his prose.

Melville's bracketing of genealogical time—the substructure of Romantic ethical self-representation from which he has been trying to free his literary practice—dramatically revises his treatment not just of the theme of death but of fictional character in general, another conscious enterprise of *The Confidence-Man.* He announces the lamblike mute, whose appearance at sunrise on April Fools' Day begins the novel, to be "in the extremest sense of the word, a stranger" (3). The "extremest sense" of the word in Melville's literary environment includes that of the "stranger" in Coleridge's "Frost at Midnight"—a ghostly portent of some unexpected arrival. The lamblike man, in both his "strangeness" and the texts which he holds up, forecasts the subsequent appearance of the confidence-man. His startling "white placidity" like an unexpected "sugar-snow in March" (6) recalls the "snow hill in the air" which initiates the complex troping of *Moby-Dick.* In a manner similar to the whale, the lamblike man functions proleptically to disrupt the normal order of causes and effects. His "placidity" recalls the "mildness" associated with inner selfhood in the earlier novel, and his silence mirrors the figurative world of *Pierre.* In the context of Melville's fiction, the lamblike man functions as a figure of priority, a locus of portentous but slippery echoes from the earlier novels. He seems "to have come from a very long distance" (6), but he has no discernible story or goal, no genealogy.[4]

The lamblike man's muteness prevents him from explaining or giving a persuasive rationale for the texts which he writes on his slate. They operate out of no ethical context except strangeness. *The Confidence-Man* begins with public rejection of the mute's writings; proceeds through denial or subversion of the various books, pamphlets, prospectuses, and contracts which appear throughout; and returns in the end to the barber's ineffective "No Trust" sign and the Apocrypha puzzled over by the old man in the cabin. To have a text is to have a past which has no bearing. A recorded identity, like the business card of Mr. Roberts, can only make one vulnerable. All characters in the book are strangers, if not "strangers still more strange" (8); they have no authorizing memories; they are disconnected and unrationalized. Character, in *The Confidence-Man*, comprises "mere phantoms which flit along a page, like shadows along a wall" (69).

Poetic time shorn of genealogical time produces characters whose textuality or inscribed identity has a future but no past. They are insubstantial yet portentous. The appearance of a character immediately opens a set of expectations and possibilities and announces further arrivals. Character in *The Confidence-Man* is all future, "originality" in the creative sense of the word; yet without stable memories—genealogies—to distinguish them, the characters in the novel appear all the same, part of a wave of dispersed transactions having a repetitive, poetic rhythm but no teleology. Originality as origination precludes originality as novelty in a world where all representable difference, all personal history, like that of the lamblike man, is phantasmic.

The lamblike man announces selfhood in fiction to be a stranger or phantom, holdover from some pretextual state as mute as the childhood of Casper Hauser, with whom he is compared (7). His appearance, "like some enchanted man in his grave," provokes the "epitaphic" comments of the onlookers (7–8). The past which he evokes is not his own but that of Melville's earlier fiction, the silent and empty "tomb" of *Pierre*. He suggests a priority which is authorial, located in a fictional pre-text, and without causal force in the poetic environment of *The Confidence-Man*. Like the white whale, the lamblike man announces a comprehensive tropological impingement; the novel is taken over by its trickster hero, original character, precursor of the radiant "cynosure" who gives his name to *Billy Budd*.

It makes no difference, in a world without genealogical representation, whether the confidence-man is one character or many. Although he is "the key to it all" in the novel, there is nothing for him to be the key to except his own poetic functions. Identity dissolves into textuality, into an ordered sequence of phantoms which flit along the page. The novel threatens to degenerate into the linguistic self-fetishizing implied by Henry Sussman's deconstructive argument. What saves it is Melville's understanding that freeing the poetic or textual level of art from genealogical rhetoric institutes not indeterminacy but new, and equally constraining, tropological patterns. As sweeping as the power of the confidence-man is, it puts in play a series of formal choices which once again defend Melville's aesthetic from the charge of nihilism.

When pushed from behind, the lamblike man indicates his deafness through "a pathetic telegraphing of his fingers" (6). His gesture picks up a motif introduced by Melville in describing "certain chevaliers," of which he says, "But as for their fingers, they were enveloped in some myth" (4). He populates the novel with "upstretched" hands (17), hands reaching into pockets (17, 21, 52), a character named Ringman (19), a company taking shares into its "own hands" (22), books in hands (25), "touchy disgust" (28), streaks left by fingers (32), people "not untouched" (33), gloved hands that avoid "touching anything" (36), a "master chord" and a "dangerous string" "touched" (42, 186), a "touching case" of "mysterious touches" (62, 61), hopes that "explode in your hand" (67), a "finger-post to virtuous action" (72), "fortune's finger" (206), hands laid on (132, 138) and off (132), snakes that "kill at a touch" (190), and numerous other pointings, handlings, and objects in or at hand. In addition, the imagery of hands and fingers in *The Confidence-Man* overlaps numerous instances of "extremities" either missing or endured. The "pathetic telegraphing" of the lamblike mute's fingers clarifies his strangeness. He gestures but does not touch in a world where touch tropes all transactions. To remain untouched or untouching in his evocation of an authorial past separates him from the other characters, whose lack of a past reduces them to a plight which is touching in both senses of the word.[5]

The beginning of *The Confidence-Man* establishes two realms—the world of touching fingers "enveloped in some myth" and the phantasmic but silent presence of the "lamb-like figure." The first defines the dramatic possibilities available within the poetically structured world of the novel and the latter the lingering specter of extratextual or intertextual authorial meaning. The two cannot "touch," in spite of the participation of the confidence-man in both. The latter incessantly intrudes on the former, yet its lack of access to representable temporal structures strips it of motive force. Rather than interact, the two generate disparate and equally unsettling tropologies: an epidemic of puns ravages the "touching" drama of the work, while its authorial voice spins off wildly in disabled, parabolic attempts at ethical rationalization. Melville remains hard-minded to the end, refusing either to qualify the catachrestic functioning of his figures or to moderate the irony which keeps them apart. If his first six years of authorship trace the search for a representable ethos, his second phase completes, in *The Confidence-Man*, a rhetorical experiment whose intent is to sweat demystified narrative principles drop by drop out of the flesh of a traditional (representational) fictional mythopoeia. His last published novel is his most composed; its poetry is precise and resolute.

The second chapter of the novel ensures the phantasmic nature of the lamb-like man by effacing his "last transient memory" (8). On his level, that of prior, or authorial, time, memory remains silent, and on the poetic level it lacks substantial force. The confidence-man's ability to manipulate or escape memory enables him to replace experience with fantasy, and thus to destabilize identity. When Ringman offers to "supply the void" in the memory of Roberts (20), he calls on the same punning locution used in the image of the empty sarcophagus in *Pierre:* the confidence-man both furnishes and redresses Roberts's mental emptiness. Roberts complains, "I hope I know myself" (19), but his hope is vain without a usable past.

When Black Guinea is asked, "Is there not some one who can speak a good word for you?" he answers "as if his memory . . . suddenly thawed back into fluidity" (13). But what his memory supplies is a proleptic list of the confidence-man's avatars and possible avatars to come. Guinea's memory forecloses the future as Charlemont does later in being "beforehand with the world" (185–86). Proleptic memory enables originality, but it turns the past into a phantom, "one I now dream of" (186). Charlemont shares the proleptic logic of the gimlet-eyed man, who responds to the charge that "the suspicious man kicks himself with his own foot" by asserting that "whoever can do that, ten to one he saves other folks' sole-leather" (30). In predicting a future whose only outcome is "touching" (kicking), proleptic memory evidences the "slimy" defensiveness raised in Pierre's discussion of "prescience" with Isabel. The future takes on the status of a judgment emerging out of an unavailable past, a projection of the negative content of silent memory. In the second half of *The Confidence-Man*, even the act of touching disappears among the phantoms and parables of the hall-of-mirrors conversation between Frank and Charlie, and Guinea's punning prediction that his references will prove him "wordy" of confidence comes to fruit (13). In the terms given by poetic time, the past puns a future determined by unstoppable, repetitive textual movements.

Guinea and Ringman begin the incessant punning which dominates the novel. A pun is one version of the rhetorical trope of syllepsis; the structure of the figure—unrelated signifieds inhabiting a single signifier—embraces echo and allusion as well as homophonic or homographic word-play.[6] In *The Confidence-Man*, virtually every important aspect of the work's "touching" transactions carries double meanings, often which contradict each other. Confidence—faith—is subverted by confiding; touching stories are only ironically touching; origination disables originality. Syllepsis is a global quality of life on the *Fidèle;* characters echo each other's appearance, language, and attitudes; incongruous allusions expand the sylleptic carnival of the novel to include numerous characters from contemporary America. Other writers like Emerson, Thoreau, and Poe stalk the tale in more or less obvious guises. The gimlet-eyed man who confronts Guinea memorializes the "discharged custom-house officer" (12) used by Hawthorne as narrative persona in the introduction to *The Scarlet Letter.* His oracular aphorisms, jaded view of human morality, and ability to see below the surface fit Melville's view of his old friend, and his self-characterization as a "seedy" thistle reflects Hawthorne's inseminatory role in Melville's career. Guinea offers a similar parodic image of Melville himself—"wordy" mummer forced to "swallow" his own "secret emotions" (11) for a few coins.

In choosing between Guinea and the gimlet-eyed man, the gathered passengers must choose between proleptic self-representation and "lame" naysaying. Both positions are caricatured "in extremity." Both sylleptically predict other characters—the grimy boy and the soldier of fortune. Their functional characteristics and the questions they raise, like those of many others on the *Fidèle,* reverberate throughout the novel to produce a zombie-jamboree of disabled aesthetic, philosophical, political, and moral postures. As Trimpi shows, the sylleptic rhetoric of *The Confidence-Man* makes it impossible to decide where to stop tracing allusions, echoes, and double meanings; rather than having clear limits, they fade off indefinitely into more and more oblique possibilities. The cacophony of ghostly voices and presences in the novel moves it from polyvocality, as defined by M. M. Bakhtin and noted by Wadlington, to a glossolalia in which all languages merge and blend. None of Melville's earlier works has as encompassing a voice; little separates the narrator from anyone else. Along with the syllepsis which dominates the dramatic action of the novel and the parabolic rhetoric which characterizes its self-conscious ethos, Melville draws on a third trope, litotes, which helps give the narrative style of the novel its extraordinary consistency.

Litotes characterizes the prose of the novel from the beginning. The first chapter employs such phrases as "not without epithets," "not unlike," "not without causing," "not wholly unaffected," and "not entirely ignorant." Litotes creates the throttled and somnambulistic effects which dog Melville's style throughout: "the merchant, though not used to be very indiscreet, yet, being not entirely inhumane, remained not entirely unmoved" (21). It is a different litotes than the laconic understatement of the Articles of War in *White-Jacket;* it has nothing to repress. As a "poetic" device, it creates a more radical form of the phlegmatic caginess or ironic detachment central to "Bartleby, the Scrivener" and "Benito Cereno." It suggests caution rather than preemptive defensiveness. Rather than denying the presence of other voices in the novel, it admits them—and then smothers them in qualification.

When the gimlet-eyed man asserts that money is not "the sole motive to pains and hazard, deception and deviltry, in this world" (32), he points not to a repressed but a phantasmic past. The devil's gulling of Adam and Eve can be rationalized (attributed to revenge) only on the basis of a view which ignores the proleptic authority of God essential to Christian myth. Similarly, Melville's confidence-man cannot be explained by reference to a single mythologized point of origin or causal-temporal pattern. The litotes of *The Confidence-Man* works, through qualification, irony, and negative understatement, to protect poetic language from genealogical determination while opening it to incessant phantasmic echoes; it signals Melville's unwillingness to engage, as he did in *Pierre,* a psychological vision of selfhood which preserves the notion of a center, even if that center is empty. The circular logic of parable in the work defines no "ringed horizon" or "inmost soul"; it spirals freely across the surface of the novel in a way which subverts accumulating meanings.

The "touching" story of the "unfortunate man" exemplifies the spiral movement of parable in *The Confidence-Man.* Initially, it promises meanings foreclosed by the understated, sylleptic world of the novel's action. On closer look, it demonstrates the careful manner in which Melville disarticulates the genealogical time on which authorial ethos depends. It teaches the reader how to take the other narrative parables in the novel, such as the story of China Aster, as well as Melville's digressions on the art of fiction. The tale is told by the merchant to the third avatar of the confidence-man, the Black Rapids Coal Company man, from whom he has bought bogus stock. He tells the story in order to counter the confidence-man's optimism. Ironically, the story has been told to him by Ringman, the trickster in an earlier guise, as the basis of a successful appeal for charity. The confidence-man has a chance to deny his own earlier argument, and he takes it with gusto; he offers a theory of confidence which refutes the grounds for earlier confiding; the merchant, previously both charitable and anxious to invest, is reduced to the cynical observation that hopes for human good "explode in your hand, leaving naught but the scorching behind" (67).

Melville introduces the parable of the unfortunate man with the qualification, "as the good merchant could, perhaps, do better justice to the man than the story, we shall venture to tell it in other words than his, though not to any other effect" (59). Given its rhetorical context, the story exemplifies the "ven-

triloquism," to use A. Robert Lee's term, which characterizes the telling of
Melville's parables and makes it impossible to position them as speech acts in a
determinate causal or temporal chain. Immediately following the tale, he interpolates another brief parable, about an American observing Sir Humphrey
Davy at a party in London, as an "anticipative reminder" (64) to the reader. The
second episode warns against a "hasty estimate" of the seemingly "jaunty"
confidence-man and suggests, against appearances, that the latter is capable of
sustaining "humanitarian discourse." Yet the confidence-man's argument to the
merchant relies on the proposition that the unfortunate man brought his sorrow on himself when he "tried to use reason" with his wife, Goneril, "instead of
something far more persuasive" (65). His oblique but unmistakable advocacy of
physical force then leads into a long rhapsody on behalf of sticking "behind the
secure Malakoff of confidence" rather than being "tempted forth to hazardous
skirmishes on the open ground of reason" (66). The "humanitarian discourse"
promised the reader proves to be a defense of battery.

During most of the discussion between the merchant and the confidence-
man, both voices are translated into the narrator's words. Melville draws us
away from and flattens the dramatic situation of the dialogue. He undercuts any
predictable sense of distinct identity in the two interlocutors and leads the
reader to expect narrative commentary in place of dramatic resolution. When
the conversation breaks up, Melville interpolates the first of his later-added
digressions on authorship, a discussion of consistency in character which apol-
ogizes for the inconclusive nature of the previous parable. The device of apostrophe which, in traditional fiction, adds a sense of accumulating ethical insight,
concern, or manipulativeness here prolongs a dizzying exercise in ventrilo-
quism, hedging, and qualification. The authorial voice spins off provocatively
from the fictional world of the novel, in a way which parallels a "comedy of
thought to that of action" (71), without permitting the two to interrelate in
terms other than those of the novel's global irony.

Melville's soliloquy on the art of fiction leads from parable to parabasis, a
modern version of the choral address to the audience in Greek old comedy. The
key to the figure's parabolic structure is its swerve away from a supposed
representational or logical center and into new discursive quadrants. When
Melville starts discussing the qualities of fiction, he does so to apologize for his
practice, yet it is not clear whether or not the apology is ironic, and just who is
being addressed. The theater of poetic indeterminacy—the novel's lack of tele-
ological logic—expands to include the reading audience. We become involved
in an "in-terminable" rite which refuses to fix our own "genealogical" position.
Do we, like traditional readers, stand back and take wisdom from the experience, or are we too passengers on the *Fidèle?* Melville's frequent "anticipative

reminders" both preempt and judge our possible responses; as in "Bartleby, the Scrivener," we lack the ethical distance which readers of Melville's earlier novels are granted. Our imaginative voice is intruded on and colonized by Melville's parabolic digressions.

The beginning of Melville's first digressive parable/parabasis repeats a key temporal figure from *Pierre:* "As the last chapter was begun with a reminder looking forwards, so the present must consist of one glancing backwards" (69). The notion of a "reminder looking forwards" repeats the proleptic memory which informs the confidence-man's itinerary, thus doubling on the level of ethos the tale's organizational logic. Melville almost immediately argues that consistency in character is unnatural and reductive: "Shall those who are not sages expect to run and read character in those mere phantoms which flit along a page, like shadows along a wall?" (69). If character is rendered unpredictable by its phantasmic nature, what sort of future is implied by a "reminder looking forwards"? Melville's time-sense courts catachresis, yet he elaborates:

> It might rather be thought, that he, who, in view of its inconsistencies, says of human nature the same that, in view of its contrasts, is said of the divine nature, that it is past finding out, thereby evinces a better appreciation of it than he who, by always representing it in a clear light, leaves it to be inferred that he clearly knows all about it. (70)

Later he contradicts himself once more by asserting that "the grand points of human nature are the same to-day they were a thousand years ago. The only variability in them is in expression, not in feature" (71). This last image, in contrast to his earlier defense of "inconsistency," returns to the enduring, speculative sea of *Moby-Dick*. The reader is left with an unresolved dilemma.

Melville's digression, for all its circumlocution, makes two assertions. First, to present something clearly is not to see it clearly; "clear light" in fiction washes out the "phantoms which flit along a page, like shadows along a wall" which are, ironically, the key to it all in *The Confidence-Man*. Truth in literature is phantasmic rather than representational. This is the case because human nature, although unchanging, is "past understanding." That is, it is beyond understanding in the past, lost in a past left unspoken by the proleptic memory, by the process of "reminders looking forward" which determines the poetic movements of verbal art. Literature is a "Voice out of Silence" doomed to "variability" in "expression"; its rhetorical inconsistency is its truth. It is a play of overlapping comedies, incessantly nostalgic for a foreclosed unity, incessantly multiplying voices out of a priority and elaborating an ethos whose ground can be figured only by an in-terminable carnival of syllepses.

Melville's first large-scale parable/parabasis in *The Confidence-Man* marks his achievement of a post-Romantic, postneoclassic rhetoric. His art no longer admits the necessity of tragedy, genealogy, or a redemptive or prophetic voice. His digression signals his own confidence in the ability of poetry to find powerful (pathetic) figurative patterns and shape arguments (*logoi*) around them. In *Battle-Pieces*, Melville will focus the demythologized rhetoric of *The Confidence-Man* on the task of figuring the available truth of the Civil War to those who survive it. In *Clarel* he will explore the interplay of historical, religious, and aesthetic grounds of confidence. Freed from the imperative to self-establishment, to explaining how the authorial voice got where it is, he takes on the worldly "materials" which he announced as essential to modern literature in "Hawthorne and His Mosses."

The remainder of *The Confidence-Man* fleshes out the manifesto implicit in its first parable/parabasis. Pitch, the Missourian who is the most sagacious of the confidence-man's interlocutors, reflects Melville's own resistance, and ultimate capitulation, to post-Romantic rhetoric. The confidence-man, in the guise of the P.I.O. man, proposes an "analogical theory" on the basis of which a boy who evinces "no noble quality" should be given "credit for his prospective one" (122). Analogy theory, which the novel associates with Romantic theories of symbolism that argue "from the physical to the moral" (121), functions similarly to proleptic memory in sustaining the freedom of confidence by denying the past. Pitch challenges the confidence-man's argument: "You pun with ideas as another man may with words" (124). His statement suggests the self-consciousness of Melville's rhetorical strategy in *The Confidence-Man;* syllepsis undercuts a logic of identity that depends on "confidence in human reason" represented by either "philosophical" (second teeth replacing first) or "natural" (butterfly replacing caterpillar) tropes. Yet even while rejecting the confidence-man's arguments, Pitch is willing to accept a boy "for the sake purely of a scientific experiment" (128). Syllepsis, by traducing redemptive relationships with the past, opens future possibility. The chapter ends with Pitch's grudging admission of confidence.

Pitch's sensitivity enables him to see repetitive elements in three separate guises of the confidence-man. As the first of the cosmopolitan's interlocutors, he exclaims, "You are another of them. Somehow I meet with the most extraordinary metaphysical scamps to-day" (136). His initial response to the cosmopolitan is "hands off!" (131). The cosmopolitan, failing to shake Pitch's distrust, departs after calling him an "Ishmael" (138). Pitch clings to a self-fetishizing role from Melville's earlier fiction, even though he is powerless before the endless textuality of confidence. He rejects the "metaphysical" pretensions of the trickster, yet all he can do is deny, not supplant or escape, them. Without genealogical time, the space between authorial priority and textual poetics fulfills a negative (ironic) function. The disabled trace of a previous textuality—the isolated, self-defining Ishmael of *Moby-Dick*—joins the chorus of phantoms which increasingly distresses the comedy of the novel. Just as one avatar of the confidence-man replaces another, Pitch's futile resistance leads into the tale's most extensive and bemusing parable, the "Metaphysics of Indian-Hating."

After several chapters dealing with John Moredock, Melville summarizes: "How evident that in strict speech there can be no biography of an Indian-hater *par excellence*, any more than one of a sword-fish, or other deep-sea denizen; or, which is still less imaginable, one of a dead man. The career of the Indian-hater *par excellence* has the impenetrability of the fate of a lost steamer" (150). As a "metaphysical," genealogical, or mythic concern, the "biography" which Indian-hating names cannot be represented in a poetic world. More important than the conclusions indicated by the passage, however, is its vertiginous richness of figurative echoes. The "sword-fish" recalls a central image of creative selfhood from *Mardi;* the "deep-sea denizen" invokes both *Moby-Dick* and Melville's statement to Hawthorne, on beginning *Pierre,* that "Leviathan is not the biggest fish;—I have heard of Krakens" (*Letters* 143); the missing biography picks up the lost stories of the emigrants in *Redburn,* as well as Ishmael's "old black-letter"; the "lost steamer" tropes the innumerable wrecks central to Melville's previous and subsequent works. To complicate matters, Moredock's story is a tale within a tale within a tale borrowed from a contemporary source. The effect of the passage, and increasingly of the entire novel, is of a textuality struggling to move forward against a spectacular clamor of feigned voices and ghostly echoes—a circumstance which *John Marr and Other Sailors* will associate with the sustaining power of the imagination (Short, "Memory's Mint").

To summarize, textual time in *The Confidence-Man* is rhythmic, repetitive, in-terminable, originary, unteleological, proleptic, noncausal, nonlinear, parabolic, imaginative, and invested in an unstable balance between polyvocal and univocal rhetorical structures. It is more than merely a "language machine" because of its sylleptic vulnerability to echoes and pre-texts. The ethos which it enables is disembodied from a Romantic genealogical standpoint and yet richly sensitive to the multitudinous silent memories—phantoms—of priority which haunt it. It constitutes itself as a "Voice out of Silence," but it does not speak that silence; its store of "more words than things" is not mere nominalization but echoes bygone things. Its irony keeps it from becoming self-fetishizing; it reflects the clinging "world-husk" of the "superabundance of materials" which is the inevitable background out of which modern literary art emerges. Its allusiveness implies an inevitable sense of loss for what is "past understanding," yet it knows no death. In sum, it is, in Melville's construal of the term, poetic.

An easy way to understand the accomplishment of *The Confidence-Man*'s rhetoric is to recognize that it completes a process of development which enables Melville to view writing as something other than self-definition. As the 1850s draw to a close, he becomes comfortable with an ethos which does not have to seek the "inmost leaf" in order to have authority. Because of the tropological shift from hyperbole to litotes, where Melville's early works give the impression of being ladled out of an ocean of expressive possibilities, his poetic art seems to push back a surrounding silence in order to make oblique, qualified, and highly specific statements. When his later work gets verbose, as in *Clarel* and parts of *Battle-Pieces*, it is ventriloquistic—it presents a variety of ethical stances other than Melville's own, and it disperses authority among a number of voices.

Because of its post-Romantic hard-mindedness and stylistic understatement, the rhetoric which Melville carries over from *The Confidence-Man* into his poetry reinforces the negative impression created by certain well-documented biographical circumstances which he faced in the late 1850s—increased isolation from literary friends, slackening production, loss of both popularity and the respect of even friendly reviewers, bouts of prostrating sciatica and physical exhaustion, financial concerns if not actual difficulties, marital tension, and nervous preoccupation. The period is a difficult one in his life, and his art loses some of its superficial buoyancy. Yet essentially the same rhetoric will stay with him, without loss of inventive power, throughout his career in the Customs Service (nicely summarized by Stanton Garner) and into an old age of relative stability and comfort. It takes on a wider than ever variety of tasks and subjects, but it changes far less in the thirty-four years between publication of *The Confidence-Man* and Melville's death in 1891 than in the thirteen years since he returned from the Pacific and began writing. Its basic shape and motivational structure continues to prove itself largely immune to external causes.

The rhetoric of *The Confidence-Man* announces Melville's mature voice and aesthetic thought. It culminates a process of development whose driving forces are self-consciousness, experimental zeal, and investment in a rhetorical view of literature. It reveals Melville, at the height of his powers, exerting an unprecedented degree of control over his expressive program, taking stock of the direction of his rhetorical development, making harder choices than ever, and sticking with them. Now that the literature and literary theory of our own time has moved closer to the aesthetic of *The Confidence-Man*, we are better equipped to appreciate, without condescension, its uncompromising penetration and muscularity and to give it its due as the climax to a tale of creative growth in which the highest order of energy, talent, sensitivity, and intelligence serves the highest courage. Through all its avatars, the stirring story of the development of Melville's ethos, as much as any literary-biographical narrative that I know, answers the call sounded in 1842 by one of his favored authors, Alfred Tennyson, "To strive, to seek, to find, and not to yield."[7]

12

"Such a cynosure": A Pisgah View of *Billy Budd*

Such a cynosure, at least in aspect, and something such too in nature,
though with important variations made apparent as the story proceeds,
was welkin-eyed Billy Budd.
—Melville, *Billy Budd*

*W*hen *Herman* Melville died in 1891, Elizabeth found a
"semi-final draft" of *Billy Budd, Sailor* among his papers, the result of work
most probably undertaken since 1885, the year he retired from two decades as
an inspector for the New York Custom House (*Billy Budd* 1). Since 1857, when
The Confidence-Man had appeared, he had published no fiction but four intense and difficult volumes of poetry.[1] Although the development of this work,
complex and compelling in its own right, lies beyond the scope of the present
study, a "Pisgah view" of *Billy Budd* (to borrow from the title of "The Encantadas," sketch 4) discloses its presentation, among many other things, of a
sharply drawn retrospective allegory of Melville's rhetorical career.[2] Both his
composing process, as outlined by Hayford and Sealts (*Billy Budd* 1–12), and
intertextual evidence suggest that the allegory is central to the developing shape
of the work. *Billy Budd* reflects, more thoroughly than ever, the impulse to
theoretical summary seen in *Moby-Dick* and *The Confidence-Man*. Although
there is no evidence that Melville saw it as his "final" statement on anything, it
thematizes and evaluates the central rhetorical movements of his literary life
with the clarity of focus often found in his art after *Pierre*.

In Melville's post-Romantic fiction—*Pierre*, the magazine stories, and *The
Confidence-Man*—a catachrestic tropological program undermines the principles of memory, redemption, and genealogical time essential to Romantic art,
to an ethos tied to the imaginative presence of the author. As a result, Melville
becomes interested, first, in the momentary, picturesque effects of sketch and
short story and, second, in poetics, the patterning surface movements of discourse. Although these interests lead naturally to the writing of verse, in *Battle-
Pieces* Melville is rescued from the radical textual experiments of *The Confidence-Man* by history, by the shaping memorial winds of the Civil War.

The aspects which the strife as a memory assumes are as manifold as are the
moods of involuntary meditation—moods variable, and at times widely at vari-

ance. Yielding instinctively, one after another, to feelings not inspired from any one source exclusively, and unmindful, without purposing to be, of consistency, I seem, in most of these verses, to have but placed a harp in a window, and noted the contrasted airs which wayward winds have played upon the strings. (*Poems* 33)

In *Battle-Pieces*, the memory of historical events reintroduces into Melville's voice sources of rhetorical authority and principles of ethical order central to the prescripts of Hugh Blair, discarded long since in the growing Romanticism of his early novels. Art bows to the writer's "knowledge of the subject, and profound meditation on it" (Blair II, 401) rather than measuring itself in terms of "that play of freedom & invention accorded only to the Romancer & poet" (*Letters* 70) or of "phantoms which flit along a page, like shadows along a wall" (*CM* 69). The bemusing aesthetics of Melville's subsequent verse result in large part from its interplay of neoclassic, Romantic, and post-Romantic rhetorical principles, an interplay which gives his ethos a wider variety of masks and gestures, some of them seemingly anachronistic, than ever. Empirically grounded and psychologically associated memories, the inventions of an imaginative subject, and the flitting phantoms of a disembodied textuality touch and interrelate to produce a rhetorical environment of unsurpassed richness. In *Clarel* and the late verse, Melville struggles to bend this unruly family of stances to his own ethical purposes, and in *Billy Budd* it is fully under control. Awareness of this control underlies his expansion of "Billy in the Darbies" into an allegory of literary rhetoric equal in retrospective fervor to *Moby-Dick* and *The Confidence-Man*, his two great, prior stock-taking efforts.

Billy Budd, Sailor begins in Melville's mind, as Hayford and Sealts demonstrate, with the poem "Billy in the Darbies" and Melville's subsequent attempt to flesh out Billy's tale. As the novel grows, Billy acquires the identifying marks of Melville's post-Romantic, *Pierre* rhetoric. Billy is picturesque, defined by his beauty. He has no past to redeem or be redeemed by. Like Isabel, Bartleby, Hunilla, and Don Benito, his meaningfulness to those around him, and to the narrator, is given by silence—by his inability to speak—and by death. Like the confidence-man, his presence is catachrestic, the essential nature of his being gives the lie to the assumptions on the basis of which an authoritative subjectivity is asserted first by Claggart and then by Vere. He undercuts the logic which they represent as Bartleby undercuts that of his would-be savior in "Bartleby, the Scrivener." Like many of Melville's post-Romantic protagonists, he replaces time and causality, the signposts of narrative progress, with fate. His story reaches the yardarm through a series of dramatic tableaux which fail to articulate a believable psychological or phenomenological substructure, an intentionality understandable in either neoclassic or Romantic terms.

In his status as "such a cynosure" (44), the "welkin-eyed" Billy achieves a phantasmic resonance common in Melville's *Pierre* rhetoric. Etymology reveals him for the "dog-star" crucial to navigation and links him not just to the handsome Jack Chase of *White-Jacket* but to Lem Hardy in *Omoo*, whose shocking tattooed face betokens escape from life as a "dog before the mast" (*O* 28). Billy's picturesqueness, the hapless timelessness of his nautical life, his silence, death, and catachrestic ethos combine to make him a "dream of the eye," a disturbing poetic presence in a world seeking to impose genealogical time on its actions. Although he dies, his story cannot. As Sealts reminds us, both Billy and his tale are slaves to the poetic death that begins Melville's process of composition ("Innocence and Infamy" 418). Lest we expect the circular resolution of the early novels, Melville warns us that "the story in which he [Billy] is the main figure is no romance" (53).

According to the generally accepted formulation of Hayford and Sealts, Claggart occupies the second stage of the novel's composition. In developing an antagonist for Billy, Melville produces one of his most exaggeratedly Romantic characters, and the contrasting rhetorical programs troped by the two deepen and square off. Claggart recalls Ahab, *Redburn*'s Jackson and Harry, Taji, and all the characters in Melville's fiction whose pasts hide iniquitous mysteries. His fascination with Billy is fetishistic in the manner of Ahab's for the white whale, and his single-minded initiative makes him prophetic in the sense which Melville borrowed from Hawthorne and put in play in *Moby-Dick*. He sins against nature, seeks revenge in the place of redemption, and provokes the narrator's Romantic mythologizing about primal depravity. By imposing his will upon those around him, he seeks to establish and justify a narcissistic subjectivity. Without his obsessive imaginative drive, nothing in the story would happen.

The balance between Billy and Claggart as allegorical loci of post-Romantic and Romantic principles of rhetorical authority is sustained by Melville's narrative voice, which takes a half-step back from the parabolic and manipulative intrusiveness of its earlier, post-Romantic avatars. Although all of Melville's characteristic tropes are repeated, the reader is no longer teased or preempted to the extent that Melville's *Pierre* rhetoric, in "Benito Cereno" and *The Confidence-Man*, permits. Language and world occupy distinct realms of fictional authority, but they do not bypass or throttle each other as they do in the magazine fiction. Melville has learned how to impose a powerful narrative voice without making that voice a cynosure in its own right, a "key to it all" that solipsistically appropriates plot and character.

The truly extraordinary accomplishment of *Billy Budd* lies in the addition of Captain Vere to the counterpoised meanings embodied in Billy and Claggart. Billy undermines causality, and Claggart fabricates it. Billy acts without rationale, and Claggart's reasons are deep and many-layered. The contradictory fictional worlds represented by them would be left to the narrator to juggle were it not for Vere, according to Hayford and Sealts, the product of Melville's third and final compositional stage. In Vere the novel both transcends and frames Melville's turn from Romantic to post-Romantic rhetoric.

Vere opens a synthetic umbrella over the dialectical opposition between Billy and Claggart, yet the shadow he casts raises questions of its own.[3] He stands for everything which Melville has found persuasive yet meretricious in the rhetoric of Hugh Blair, taught him in his youth. In rendering his verdict on Billy, Vere demands Blair's "perspicuity"—a clarity of gesture that the sailors on board cannot fail to understand. In tune with other central precepts of Blair, his ethos draws authority from both experience and reading, memory, "measured forms," an elite background and tastes, and critical sensitivity. He would impose on Billy's picturesque and feckless existence the rigorous, neoclassic teleology of the eighteenth-century Articles of War under which the *Bellipotent* sails. In the context of Melville's works—famous for nonexistent or dead fathers—his paternal responses to Billy are all the more chilling.[4]

Vere is one of Melville's most unique characters, among the very few who do not call to mind counterparts in the teeming populace of his fiction. Vere's uniqueness results from the fact that, in embodying the powerful but stifling forms of authority promulgated by Blair, he harks back not to Melville's earlier work but to the mute world of his preliterary youth. He frames the central dilemma of Melville's early literary upbringing: the rhetoric of Blair—the world of the Albany Philo Logos Society—fathers him as a writer, but only by imposing principles that would have doomed him to silence had he not set sail for the South Seas, a dog before the mast rather than a Chesterfieldian gentleman, and opened the floodgates of the wonder-world of Romance.

Each of Melville's allegorized stances has its moment in *Billy Budd, Sailor,* and each is undercut by the others. The daimonic Romanticism of Claggart initiates and drives the novel's plot forward, but toward his own destruction. Vere's neoclassic paternalism is permitted its judgment, but he is left with troubled deathbed memories of his victim. Billy's flitting picturesqueness kills him, but his death generates a textual "after-life" like that of Ishmael's "draughts," which extends the tale past its putative ending.[5] Rather than taking sides, the narrator permits Melville's allegory to flourish, as each stance in turn displays its rhetorical force. The "inside narratives" underlying the ethical authority of historical memory, Romantic invention, and poetic textuality balance and complement each other. Each in its own way leads to death, yet each gives death a voice, the purpose which unites them.

As Melville moves from stage to stage in composing *Billy Budd,* and the tale

becomes more and more intimately involved with its personal rhetorical allegory, it becomes increasingly difficult for him to end it in a conventional way. It
changes from fiction to intellectual autobiography, circling back on the various
stages of his creative life, not to resolve their dilemmas but to recast them in the
figures of his latest experiment. In exploring the possibility that the silence out
of which the voice of fiction comes is not for him given by the sea but by a prior
voice—the voice of Blair's rhetoric as it resonates in his education, youth, and
family's lost pretensions—Melville comes to entertain the corresponding idea
that the allegory which begins with Billy's death, insofar as it figures his career,
can end only with his own death, the inevitable silence which his works have,
over and over, beaten back. Rather than rush the novel to completion in characteristic fashion, Melville defers and delays, sharing his attention with the profound retrospective self-consciousness of his late verse.

What *Billy Budd, Sailor*, as an allegory of the terms of Melville's development,
testifies to is the rhetoric of fiction as he has conceived and practiced it. The
novel radiates his unshaken faith in his ability to speak not just with a variety of
momentarily persuasive voices but out of a deeply authoritative knowledge of
the underlying conditions of literary ethos. If the work engages rhetorical
conflicts central to the public discourse of his day, as Susan Mizruchi has
effectively argued, it does so in terms set by Melville's endless and endlessly
mutating literary self-awareness, his understanding that his fictional rhetoric
can regenerate itself, unto death, with unabated energy. When the narrator of
Billy Budd justifies the chapters following Billy's hanging, he echoes the final
line of *The Confidence-Man* in giving what can be taken as a motto for Melville's
literary career, unsurpassed in its commitment to change, experiment, and the
intertextual dialectics of its rhetorical development: "Something in way of
sequel will not be amiss" (128).

13

Coda: Tropics of Fiction

Tropes lie at the center of both Herman Melville's rhetorical thought and the ethos of his work. They give an intertextual focus to his novels, relating each to those which precede, and they determine the dialectical turns of his aesthetic development. In using them, he reaches beyond their individual effects to weave them into ordered webs, and he explores their theoretical bearing on the representation of selfhood central to the narrative art of his age. Although a study of one author cannot legitimate a rhetorical system, a review of the principles underlying the tropics of Melville's fiction reveals the relevance of his conceptions to Romantic and post-Romantic literary aesthetics.

Melville's use of tropes modifies current views of literary rhetoric because theories of figure have not, by and large, acknowledged the particular context of fiction. The rich linguistic world of the novel, eloquently described by M. M. Bakhtin, forces figure into roles implicit in classical rhetoric but submerged in contemporary theories. Literary criticism too often regards the Greek and Roman tropological traditions in the light of reductive generalizations like the following: "These devices were the classically defined tropes, regarded as useful decorations of linguistic utterances. They were deviations from a norm constituted by the structure of argument" (Adams and Searle 16). Melville's practice asks us to reread classical rhetoric in a way which rescues it from a desiccated, post-Enlightenment tradition in which trope is mere ornament, a system of "useful decorations of linguistic utterances."[1]

The mainstream Romantic literary view of trope, which runs from Vico through Diderot, Herder, Coleridge, Emerson, and many others, enthrones poetic figures as indices of the natural or primitive movements of the human soul. After Kant's *Critique of Judgment*, this notion becomes philosophically respectable, and tropes become windows on the rational order of the human spirit as well as on the passions unleashed by Storm and Stress. Hegel, according to such commentators as Walter Kaufmann and Donald Verene, draws heavily on Romantic literary theory, especially that of Goethe, in systematizing the figurative, rhetorical nature of the human mind. With changes in emphasis, the belief that tropes reveal important, perhaps hidden or subversive, structures of consciousness gets passed by way of Kierkegaard and Nietzsche to the phenomenology of Heidegger and on to de Man and Derrida. In Romantic and post-Romantic philosophy, trope is raised from the realm of stylistic ornaments to that of essential cognitive, phenomenological, or deconstructive functions.

The speculative philosophical tradition, sensitive though it is to figurative language, ends up by being as reductive to tropological thought as the school rhetorics of the past three centuries. Paul Ricoeur, in the most imposing modern study, illustrates the case. Reacting against the seemingly jejune proliferation of tropological ornaments in Hellenistic, Roman, Medieval, and Renaissance treatises, he privileges the scant definition of figurative language included by Aristotle in the *Poetics* and the *Rhetoric*. As a result, he treats all trope under the heading of metaphor, defined by Aristotle as a transference (*epiphora*) among words. He then turns around to blame Aristotle's provisional treatment of the topic for the imprisonment of later tropologies within the bounds of "semiotics"—lexical substitution—rather than the "semantics" of larger discourse units (66). He makes a lengthy case for metaphor as "semantic impertinence," a definition which permits it to contribute to the pure conceptual world of philosophy while defending the latter against I. A. Richards, Derrida, and other advocates of the ambiguity or essential figurality of language. "Metaphor" in his system functions to "bring an unknown referential field toward language" (*Rule* 299).

Ricoeur's case for the creativity of metaphor in opening up "unknown referential fields" to the denotative purview of language offers a model for the influence of "poetic" utterance on philosophy: metaphor, a propaedeutic to genuine speculation, permits intuitive expression of truths we have not yet learned to articulate. In opposition to Derrida's position in "White Mythology," Ricoeur sees dead metaphor as a sign of stabilized reference rather than the undecidability of ontological assertions. Nothing is gained, he points out, for "living metaphor" (the original title of his book) by theories which totalize its subversiveness. Ricoeur's case reaps the benefits of its underlying Aristotelianism, including the Thomistic analogy theory which answers Platonic (and Derridian) skepticism regarding the ability of "poetic" language to guide us toward the truths of "onto-theology" (272).

Ricoeur's argument opens the door to a rhetorical vision of tropes only to close it when the philosophical stakes get high enough to be interesting. Ultimately he reinforces Enlightenment notions responsible for the buckling of figure under the weight of metaphysics; not only does metaphor point outside language to its validating truths, it becomes a scapegoat to the univocality of words. The power of poetic figures rests in their reducibility to denotation. Ricoeur repeats the eighteenth-century replacement of classical rhetorical invention by scientific logic which characterizes the rhetorical world of Hugh Blair, against whom Melville struggles throughout his career.

If the modern rhetorical and philosophical traditions work in concert to disable the inventive power of tropes, twentieth-century linguistic theory in the wake of Ferdinand de Saussure, Roman Jakobson, and Emile Benveniste serves it little better. Structuralism and its bedfellow semiotics, as well as most other linguistically oriented theories, tend to reduce the distinction between literary and ordinary language. In some instances, as in Roland Barthes's *S/Z*, systems of "codes" as precious as medieval tropologies result; other instances, such as the famous reading of "Les Chats" by Jakobson and Claude Lévi-Strauss and Michael Riffaterre's early work, engender new forms of stylistic analysis; still others, as in Jakobson's influential discussion of metaphor and metonymy, Jean Cohen's "theory of the figure," and the work of Julien Greimas, grammaticalize figurative categories. What is lacking in such approaches is a method, in de Man's words, to "openly raise the question of the intentionality of rhetorical figures" (*Blindness and Insight* 187–88), another way of calling for a classical theory of invention. Rhetorical effect becomes a matter of manipulating the underlying logic of linguistic functions; it cannot account for the contextually defined distinctiveness essential to any ethical presentation.

Close in concept to Ricoeur are semantic theories of metaphor, notably those of George Lakoff and Mark Johnson and of Mark Turner. By showing how metaphors underlie the conceptual categories "we live by," they argue their importance to speculative language. The problem with Lakoff and Johnson's case, as Earl R. Mac Cormac argues, is that it transforms the distinction between metaphoric and nonmetaphoric utterance into one between "literal" and "figurative" metaphor (59). It is caught in Ricoeur's trap of defining figure as "semantic impertinence," when the semantic norm against which it should be measured is not clear. Yet to ground the notion of figure cognitively, as Mac Cormac attempts to do, moves even further away from the linguistic environment, outside of which the rhetorical impact (ethos or pathos) of tropes is undecidable.

Among the most promising modern tropologies are those of humanistic rhetoricians such as Ernst Cassirer, Kenneth Burke, and Hayden White. By accepting the given cultural value of classical figures without interrogating their underlying cognitive or grammatical grounds, they have been able to demonstrate the considerable structural force of these figures within various forms of discourse and, as a result, escape from constricted lexical or semantic categories. Although they fail, for reasons to which I will return, to achieve the richness either of classical tropologies or of Melville's fictional rhetoric, they give rise to true literary tropologies, notably those of Donald Rice and Peter Schofer and of James M. Mellard.

Both Rice and Schofer and Mellard base their analysis on key rhetorical concepts derived from the classical tradition: figure is an essential function of language; figure reflects but cannot be reduced to underlying cultural or psychological patterns (a point explored in detail by Umberto Eco); literature is distinguished from ordinary discourse by its degree of figurality and as a result by the type of attention (or interpretation) which it calls for from the reader. Melville would find these positions congenial; what he would disagree with is the manner in which both studies put them into effect. Because they accept the four-trope system (metaphor, metonymy, synecdoche, irony) which Hayden White derives from Vico, they cannot avoid treating the figures which they analyze as loci of unmediated (by ethos or pathos) rhetorical effect, as structures of cultural meaning rather than ways of constructing a meaningful voice in a specific situation. For Melville, tropes are contextual or intertextual; the minute, as he discovers in *Mardi,* that one treats a particular figure as transcendental, cognitively essential, or independent, it inflates (to use Hans Kellner's term), daimonizes the available rhetorical space, and shoulders other vocal registers aside.

Romantic and post-Romantic theories of poetic figure call on another long-standing notion acknowledged and modified by Melville. Poetry escapes crucifixion on the referentiality of language because of its darkness or iconicity; its job is not to mean but to be. The privilege of poetry as a figurally defined "message centered on itself" pervades Roman Jakobson's literary thinking, and Tzvetan Todorov asserts the effect of figure in rendering language opaque (102). Nicolas Abraham's interest in the psychic significance of poetic rhythm and Julia Kristeva's in poetic irruptions of the "semiotic" (about which more later) on the normal Oedipal face of language further exemplify the position. Such views revive a doctrine of *ut musica poesis* (Abrams 88) which accords the surface aspects of poetic form quasi-independent status as imaginative or emotional stimuli. In its least rhetorical avatars, the theory produces a cheap formulaic like that of Poe's "Philosophy of Composition" or else the willful vagueness of *symbolisme*. Melville flirts with the tradition in *The Confidence-Man,* but his concentration on the temporal implications of textual patterns continually reinscribes their effects within the intertextual field—determined by theories of memory—of his developing ethos.

The best cure for the reductive nature of modern tropological thinking—philosophical, linguistic, humanistic, or poetic—lies in the tradition which Ricoeur brackets, the post-Aristotelian rhetoric which dominated European thinking about figurative language from Hellenistic times through the Renaissance. The most comprehensive, intelligent, influential, and charming treatise is Quintilian's *Institutio Oratoria,* particularly book 9. Poised between Aristotle's minimal definition of metaphor and the helter-skelter enumeration of

figures common in contemporary and later school rhetorics, Quintilian's startling insights transcend both the rhapsodic plenitude and the technicality of his
discussion. Without Quintilian, the hegemony of tropical rhetorics from late
classical times to the Renaissance would be unthinkable.

Quintilian shows little discomfort in the face of the slipperiness of figurative
language. Although he distinguishes between trope (lexical substitution in the
manner of Aristotle) and figure (ordinary language given a new sense), he
points out that "the resemblance between the two is so close that it is not easy to
distinguish between them" (III, 349). Figure for Quintilian includes "schema"
and thus destroys the distinction between lexical and syntactic types lurking
behind views of metaphor as a substitution among words. Figure betokens both
the ordinary manner in which language gives "body" to ideas and extraordinary artistic departures. Furthermore, Quintilian gives equal weight to figures
of thought and figures of speech, and he again exemplifies the proximity of his
categories. Although metaphor is a trope, "*trope* and *figure* are often combined
in the expression of the same thought, since figures are introduced just as much
by the metaphorical as by the literal use of words" (III, 353). Irony "belongs to
figures of thought" (III, 349), yet "in some forms it is a *trope*" (III, 351); Quintilian concludes that "it makes no difference by which name either is called, so
long as its stylistic value is apparent, since the meaning of the things is not
altered by a change of name" (III, 353). The strategic power of nonliteral language transcends niceties of definition; more important, thought as well as
language contributes "stylistic value" to discourse.

A major result of Quintilian's categorical flexibility is to free trope from the
bonds of grammar. Ricoeur's recognition of the "word" as a category to be
affirmed and sublated opens his notion of speculative discourse, as Dominick
LaCapra has pointed out (18), to the charge of nominalization; modern linguistics, with its recognition of the grammatical primacy of verbs, has not put a stop
to the tendency of theorists like Ricoeur to imagine "unknown referential
fields" in substantive terms. Melville severely critiques the process of nominalization in "The Whiteness of the Whale" and the first half of *Pierre*. After all, he
reminds us in *Redburn*, there are "more names than things" in the world.
Furthermore, the logic of Ricoeur's semiotic and semantic distinction parallels
the Jakobsonian split between metaphor and metonymy, paradigm and syn-
tagm—a reduction of tropological to grammatical categories disastrous to the
polyvocality of fiction. Jacques Lacan follows suit (156–57), a move which
weakens his otherwise profound application of rhetorical theory to psychoanalysis.[2] Similar grammaticalizations underlie the hierarchical and opera-
tional discriminations of Benveniste and the Groupe μ.

Taking a cue from Quintilian, rhetorical figuration brings to discourse a set of ordering principles which extend beyond grammatical logic and which establish the context within which "semantic impertinence" can be judged. Eco stresses the latter point in his discussion of metaphor: "At any rate, for too long it has been thought that in order to understand metaphors it is necessary to know the code (or the encyclopedia): the truth is that the metaphor is the tool that permits us to understand the encyclopedia better. This is the type of knowledge that the metaphor stakes out for us" (129). Put another way, the relationships which figure establishes between elements (thoughts, images, habits, words) in a discourse—relationships at the heart of both Melville's exploration of "textual temporality" in *The Confidence-Man* and his overall intertextual ethical program—permit discourse to transcend the two-dimensional model established by Jakobson in responding to Saussure's even more constraining linearity. The notion of an extended syntagmatic chain holding together loci of paradigmatic substitution works fine in a discourse without memory, without the effects of echo put in play by Melville and feelingly described by John Hollander. Tropes give language not an opaque surface or cognitive substructure but a past, a voice, a theater for the sylleptic reverberations to which Riffaterre's intertextual theory continually returns ("The Intertextual Unconscious" 375). Paradigmatic substitution and syntagmatic association may relate words to each other logically; through tropes, figural units speak and refer to each other as aspects of a human voice.

Tropical reference or relationship undercuts the primarily spatial metaphors which have characterized much linguistic thought—a tendency especially strong in the otherwise important work of Gérard Genette. Genette understands both of Quintilian's senses of figure, yet he spatializes relationships of nonliteral embodiment (207). Quintilian points out that any linguistic habit can be spoken of as a figure insofar as it intrudes on one's style (III, 355). Trope operates doubly in relation to stylistic expectations; it creates and it disfigures, embodies and disembodies, the momentary determinants of voice.[3] In establishing contextual relationships, it shapes new contexts. Quintilian's sense of style has much to do with the oratorical situation which he takes for granted; orators do not simply declaim a text (although the practice was common enough in classical times to provoke Plato's mockery), they shape a changing, accumulating/discourse to the responses of their audience. Style unavoidably reflects back/on, echoes, and layers itself, and its semantic norms change as a speech goes on. Whatever language does, as rhetorical treatises continually avow, is in the interest of pathos, moving a listening audience. Late classical theory, like the "visionary" rhetoric which Harold Bloom finds in Romantic poetry, "might better be termed a making and a hearing, or a making heard" (*Ringers* 3–4); its figures establish "visions of relationship" (*Shelley's Mythmak-*

ing 115) which, because they annex both grammar and imagery to voice, "make the visible at least a little hard to see" (*Ringers* 37).

Quintilian's treatment of trope reflects the crucial ability of rhetoric to accommodate ineluctable slippages among thought, literal language, and figure. If criticism is to make heard the many and simultaneous whisperings of fiction, it will need to reoralize and retemporalize the brilliant but rhetorically reductive spatial figures spawned by both modern literature and, to extend Joseph Frank's argument, modern linguistic theory. Both classical rhetoric and Melville's fiction keep the mutable and inflatable power of trope in bounds by mediating its effects through the argumentative modes—ethos, pathos, and *logos*—which bear on discourse. Philosophical theories of figure, in their drive to logical purity, favor *logos* over the others and thus tend to forget that even it is rhetorically mediated. In contrast, the proliferation after Aristotle of endless lists of "ornaments" reflects an increasingly ethical focus. Rhetoric "degenerates" into style because style shapes ethos, the representation of selfhood which links Melville, and fiction in general, to the ancients.

In order to complete the picture of how tropes and *ethopoeia* interrelate and interdepend in classical rhetoric, one further notion—*kairos*—is needed. Plato's objections to Sophistic hark back to its insistence, outlined by Mario Untersteiner, on the Protagorean notion of *kairos*—immediacy, presence, the suitability of language to its occasion (197). Sophistic, in the hands of Gorgias and other powerful teachers of the day, gives precedence to the malleable, contentious, unavoidably linguistic reality which characterizes human argumentative situations (courtroom, senate, etc.).[4] Aristotle domesticates Sophistic by giving rhetoric its own form of proof—enthymeme—based on probability rather than the deduction from first causes of philosophical syllogism and the observations of scientific demonstration (*Rhetoric* 5). Among the arguments of rhetoric, ethos is "the most potent of all the means to persuasion" (9). Ethos "should be created by the speech itself, and not left to depend upon an antecedent impression" (8–9); it belongs not to the moral reputation of the rhetor but to the *kairos* of the rhetorical moment as enacted in its particular enthymematic argument, its *logos*.

The very notion of a primary rhetoric, of a discipline which enables ethical analysis of the human interactions which come before us in the form of discourse, depends on a sense of *kairos* disturbing to the philosophical tradition: from its perspective, language actually creates the ethics—the vocal and thus moral possibilities—of a situation. The combination of a theory of *kairos*, the flexibility obvious in oral language, and figurative (stylistic) *ethopoeia* produces a discipline unequaled in Western civilization in its influence, over many centuries, on the conduct of public business. It is no wonder that rhetoric, with its ability to transform desire into persuasion, comes to occupy the center of educational curricula, and that Augustine, trained in the tradition, defines Christian doctrine in comparable rhetorical terms.

With Augustine's *On Christian Doctrine,* classical rhetoric guarantees its transition from oral to written discourse. *Kairos* lies in God's written word, and a knowledge of figure aids in its interpretation and promulgation. The dark language of sacred texts adds to their authority: "The more these things seem to be obscured by figurative words, the sweeter they become when they are explained" (129). The grand style appeals because it is "forceful with emotions of the spirit," and its figures "are caught up by the force of the things discussed" (150). Tropological and ethical analysis hang on context and intention; we must try to understand why God speaks to us in the way he chooses, if we seek to understand his authority. For human rhetors, however, ethos comes from antecedent reputation rather than skill: "The life of the speaker has greater weight in determining whether he is obediently heard than any grandness of eloquence" (164). The truths which rhetoric expresses have stabilized; figure is a knot to be untied in seeking the transcendental locus of ethical force—in the terms of *Pierre,* "the Voice of our God." Not until the Reformation opens literary language to the dialectical self-fashioning of Herbert, Donne, and Edward Taylor will the power of trope recapture its classical, humanistic *kairos*—its freedom to determine the voice, and thus the truth, of the moment. At that point the Enlightenment translation of rhetorical invention into visual and logical terms signaled by "metaphysical" poetic imagery and the place-logic of Ramus (elucidated by Walter Ong) begins. Even Sir Philip Sidney, seeking a key to ethical authority at the beginning of *Astrophil and Stella,* looks in his heart rather than listening to his voice.

Fiction, from the Renaissance on, keeps open the space of what George Kennedy calls "primary rhetoric" by virtue of its structural licentiousness, its unsurpassed ability to represent the temporal and memorial grounds of selfhood, and a *kairos* enhanced by popularity and mechanical reproduction. As literature loses its courtly "aura" (to borrow Walter Benjamin's concept), fictional narrative absorbs and gives voice to the heteroglossia, the many-layered, shifty ethos, of an expanding, materialistic society. Narrative verse in the seventeenth and eighteenth centuries combines Augustinian and fictive values into a high-cultural rhetoric important as a background for the philosophical pretensions of Romantic poetic figuration; the novel, as Bakhtin and others have shown, sprawls and burgeons untrammeled by constraining idealisms.

The Augustinian rhetorical tradition culminates in Romantic and post-Romantic theories of myth. Writers of fiction like Melville struggle against the association of figure, and thus ethos, with supernal, autochthonous, or metaphysical truths rather than the rapidly mutating *kairos* or *Zeitgeist* of a muscular culture. The rhetoric of fiction demands a nonmythological temporality. Frank Kermode summarizes: "Fictions are for finding things out, and they change as the needs of sense-making change. Myths are the agents of stability, fictions the agents of change. Myths make sense in terms of a lost order of time, *illud tempus* as Eliade calls it; fictions, if successful, make sense of the here and now" (39).

Ernst Cassirer makes a comparable assertion: "What distinguishes mythical time from historical time is that for mythical time there is an absolute past, which neither requires nor is susceptible of any further explanation" (II, 105). Hans Blumenberg traces the dichotomy to the Greeks: "The Greek *mython mytheisthai* [to tell a 'myth'] means to tell a story that is not dated and not datable, so that it cannot be localized in any chronicle, but a story that compensates for this lack by being 'significant' [*bedeutsam*] in itself" (149). The confusion between a stable or originary, albeit unreachable, time and an undecidable time, exploited by Melville in *The Confidence-Man,* climaxes in Lévi-Strauss's previously quoted assertion that "since it has no interest in definite beginnings or endings, mythological thought never develops any theme to completion: there is always something left unfinished. Myths, like rites, are 'in-terminable' " (6).

Eliade, Kermode, and Cassirer reflect an essentially Augustinian view of myth which dovetails with Melville's sense of the past in his early, first-person novels. The job of tropes is to bridge the gap between mythical and human time. Lévi-Strauss's poetic or textual view brings myth, and the figurative processes on which it depends, closer to Quintilian's rhetoric, to an unstable, ongoing, temporalizing or oralizing (despatializing) linguistic environment much like that which Melville explores in the phantasmic, "poetic" world of *The Confidence-Man.* As Victorian doubt undermines the Augustinian worldview and demythologizing religious scholarship flowers, fiction becomes increasingly rhetorical in a classical sense: context-specific, politically and socially argumentative (after the classical modes of forensic, deliberative, or epideictic oratory), sensitive to an immediate *kairos,* ethical, fascinated (as in science fiction) by probabilistic speculation (enthymeme), and freely and highly figured; its forms proliferate like catalogs of tropes in late classical and medieval treatises.

Paul de Man writes in "Action and Identity in Nietzsche," "If the critique of metaphysics is structured as an aporia between performative and constative language, this is the same as saying that it is structured as rhetoric" (30). The distinction which speech-act theory makes between performative and constative parallels that between Lévi-Strauss's and traditional views of mythological time—between "rites" and "agents of stability"—as well as the common literary distinction between theme and form which Melville comes to question after *Moby-Dick*. What the correspondence to myth permits us to see in de Man's formula is an embedded confusion between what takes place within a representational system and how that system takes place, between time as understood in a myth and time as conveyed in the myth's enactment, between the act of critique and the experience of aporia. It is exactly this confusion which *The Confidence-Man* unpacks.

In the sets of dichotomous terms listed above, rhetoric can be called on in each case to express either term; de Man's point is that its true nature lies in holding them apart, in scandalizing metaphysical or technical ideologies which would reduce one set to the other. In so doing, rhetoric, for de Man, puts into play a variety of undervalued figures—allegory, irony, prosopopoeia—which discomfit traditional philosophical conceptions. Its deconstructive agenda frees it from the predictable cycle of metonymy, metaphor, irony, and synecdoche stressed by Hayden White and others. De Man glories in revealing the Augustinian—the ideologically reductive—rhetoric behind modern literary phenomenology. Melville evolves a comparable stance vis-à-vis the narrative conventions of his day when he destabilizes the relationship between authorial ethos and fictional event in *The Confidence-Man*—when he makes both equally phantasmic, ethical, and rhetorical.

In sum, both classical rhetoric and modern fiction reintegrate *logos* (constative language) with the specific circumstances of ethos (linguistic performance). Yet in so doing, they open the expressive act to construal on the basis of dislocating tropical structures—Melville's syllepsis, for example. This process defines the shadowy and always potentially intertextual presence of the author—the authoritative voice, in a fictional work. One can enjoy a novel in ignorance of the author defined by historical scholarship, or one can take theoretical exception to such scholarship, but as soon as the narrative voice of the novel solicits awareness of other possible voices, languages, or tropological environments, the author, like Mephistopheles, will appear as if by magic and refuse to go away. If one denies or deconstructs the author's presence, another author will leap out from behind like the next avatar of the confidence-man. If rhetoric scandalizes metaphysics, then rhetorical ethos scandalizes Augustinian or grammatical approaches to fiction which deny the re-membering of the author—the task of the present study in regard to Melville's development.

The characteristics of rhetorical ethos in fiction bring it as a discursive practice in line with psychoanalysis. Both disciplines rest on the construction of a narrative which shores up and gives a future to a nascent subjectivity. The stances (figures) of consciousness vis-à-vis the unconscious parallel those of fictive ethos vis-à-vis the silent or phantasmic past. In psychoanalysis, as Stanley Cavell asserts, "the idea that there is a life of the mind, hence a death, receives its proof" (390); similarly, fictional *ethopoeia* discloses authorship, the spirit moving on the face of textuality. In viewing literature as an arena of combat between poet and precursor, Harold Bloom's "psychomachia"—to use Peter Brooks's term (335)—fictionalizes it, gives it an ethos open to elaborate figures of memory, self-actualization, and death, Melville's key themes.

A tropics of fiction, if it is to "raise the question of the intentionality of rhetorical figures," finds itself cohabiting with psychoanalysis and catching its ailments to an extent uncomfortable to both. The histories of the two are inextricably intertwined (witness Freud's use of *Gradiva* and innumerable writers' use of Freud), and they both show a freely rhetorical face to the more lyrical, technical, or metaphysical discourses which surround them. In their attempt to give a memory to the present voice of human behavior, they face a host of similar and reciprocally illuminating problems.

Psychoanalysis displays the same division between the mythic (philosophic) and the poetic (textual) which Melville faces in attempting to rationalize his fiction. On the one hand, conservative Freudians treat the unconscious as a stable, denoted truth; on the other hand, Lacanians return all meaning to opaque expressive surfaces. A middle ground emerges in the tropologically oriented theory of Bloom and Kristeva. Their insights, along with those of Bakhtin and principles drawn from classical rhetoric, fit together to form a tropics of fiction made up of elements which suit the classical notion of "figures of thought." These elements enable "the crossover between psychic operations and tropes" (Brooks 340) essential to "the question of the intentionality of rhetorical figures." Taken as a system, they will permit us to describe and understand the broader implications of Melville's fictional program.

More programmatically and assiduously, indeed voluminously, than any other critic, Harold Bloom has explored "how to use the crossover between psychic operations and tropes" in order to "raise the question of the intentionality of rhetorical figures." Yet his contribution to a tropics of fiction lies less in his theory of the anxiety of influence and resulting "revisionary ratios" than in his ordering of tropes into a remarkably specific set of categories and relationships. Much resistance of Bloom stems from his incessant mix of sweeping oracle and dogmatically precise formula—in a word, from a cognitive and rhetorical style similar to that of Melville (and to Kristeva and Bakhtin as well). Over the course of numerous books, Bloom remains surprisingly true to the specific shape of his tropology—surprisingly because he admits early on, sounding like Quintilian, that "the six revisionary movements that I will trace in a strong poet's life-cycle could as well be more, and could take quite different names than those I have employed" (*Anxiety* 10).

Bloom's six key tropes—irony, synecdoche, metonymy, hyperbole (or litotes), metaphor, and metalepsis—divide up in two ways, as systematized in *A
Map of Misreading*. Irony, metonymy, and metaphor compose "figures of limitation," and synecdoche, hyperbole, and metalepsis are more potent "figures of
restitution" or "representation." Items in the two categories link dialectically by
way of "crossings" (best described in the final chapter of *Wallace Stevens*) and
thus constitute three hierarchical pairs. The "crossing of election" pairs irony
with synecdoche, the "crossing of solipsism" associates metonymy with hyperbole, and the "crossing of identification" moves from metaphor to metalepsis.
As arbitrary as this scheme may seem (perhaps as a result of Bloom's devotion
to a limited canon of "strong" poets), its structure proves extraordinarily helpful to the study of fiction.

First of all, Bloom's six tropes challenge the traditional (since Vico) limitation of "master tropes" to four. Hayden White's argument for the primacy of
four tropes, out of the hundreds available or the twelve emphasized by Quintilian, reproduces an essentially philosophical perspective. White associates figures with "the archetypal plot of discursive formations" (5). Bloom's modifica-
tion of White's system enables us to propose that fictional *ethopoeia,* in its
combined drive for freedom from cultural categories (obsessive in Melville's
case) and dialectical method, uses figures in a more open-ended, polyvocal,
nonlinear and even nonspatial (oral) manner than White's system admits. In so
doing, it need not give up the disciplined order which enables its ethical constructions to speak to and move (pathos) a contemporary reader. Melville
invests himself in tautology, repetition, syllepsis, parable, and nominalization,
which he puts into play as carefully defined aspects of a tropics calculated to
"depart" from the Romanticism associated with Bloom's metonymy, metaphor,
synecdoche, hyperbole, and metalepsis. If one wants to call Melville's movement from Romantic to post-Romantic rhetoric a "crossing," then one can
conclude that the link between the two tropological environments is provided
by the durable but deepening power of irony and the switch from hyperbole to
litotes notable in *The Confidence-Man*. Like all fiction, Melville's gives the lie to
a stable group of "master tropes," without in the least abandoning the necessity
of choosing the limited group that will be "the key to it all" in a given work.

Even Kenneth Burke admits that his favorite figures "do shade into one
another" (503); in fiction, no trope can be counted on to carry a predetermined, stable, and predictable "intentionality." As an age learns to read the
tropes which distinguish it from the previous one, those tropes become conventional rather than subversive. The history of tropological rhetoric mirrors
this flexibility: Aristotle's fourth definition of metaphor sounds like allegory;
the tremendously influential *Rhetorica ad Herennium* (long falsely attributed to
Cicero) lists metaphor under tropes and simile under figures of thought; me-

tonymy functions differently as a figure of contiguous association (Jakobson) than as a cause-effect substitution (Blair); metalepsis indicates either a "preposterous" antecedent-consequent substitution (Blair, Bloom) or a transition from one trope to another (Quintilian); hyperbole and litotes correspond in intentional effect for Bloom (and to a certain extent for Melville) and oppose for almost everyone else. Ideological possibilities—Eco's "encyclopedia" of a culture—constitute and are constituted by the changing dialectical interplay among tropes. It is a fundamental concern of both rhetorical theory and practice to interrogate the particular tropological web operating or anticipated in a specific context; what, for example are the implications (for literature, psychology, linguistics, other social sciences) of the widespread but spectacularly arbitrary willingness to treat metaphor and metonymy as a binary, dialectically related pair?

Recognizing the mutability of individual tropes, Bloom stresses that "what matters is not the exact order of the ratios, but the principle of substitution, in which representations and limitations perpetually answer one another" (*Map* 105). His division of tropes into two groups permits them to figure dialectical change and thus to embody the creative time without which no vision of authorial ethos is possible. To Bloom, trope addresses a writer's need for "self-recognition, or the apprehension of the Poetic Character in oneself," which is "a kind of divination because this self is in the future rushing toward us, and never in the present moment" (*Ringers* 7). In tropes, authors discover the shape of their potential, clear space for what they are about to write, and escape from the deadly weight of what has already been said: "A poem is written to escape dying" (*Map* 19). The "intentionality" of authorship and the tropes on which authorial voice depends occupy the moment between a burdensome past and a hazy future; the "unknown referential field" which figure brings "toward language" is the author's continuing ethical space, the possibility of further voicing.

Melville predicts Bloom's ideas in a number of ways. He uses tropes dialectically and self-reflexively. He seeks relationships with a past both necessary and threatening to his voice. He fears repetition. As he writes himself further and further away from the first-person, Romantic practice of his early novels, he becomes increasingly comfortable with the despatializing (parabolic rather than circular) "visions of relationship" established by his tropics. Melville's rhetorical intentionality is in many ways stronger than that of the poets whom Bloom prizes; he scandalizes almost every conventional principle of narrative self-representation, yet in so doing, he demonstrates over and over the power of a tropics of fiction to transmute abstract relational structures into art, to give them a *kairos* relevant to the literary history of his day.

Melville's practice also reflects, in modified form, Bloom's division of tropes into dialectically interrelated groups. In his early novels, irony, metonymy, and metaphor generally carry a sense of limitation, of the burdensome but enabling (once figured) circumstances which dog the expressive act. Irony figures Tommo's inauthentic relationship with the Typees; metonymy underlies the regressiveness of his wanderings; metaphor organizes the deadly world of *Redburn*. In each of these cases, tone and imagery reflect the bitterness of dreams shattered and creative blockages revealed, the irredeemability of a past to which one is chained. In contrast, high aspirations invoke synecdoche, hyperbole, and metalepsis; Melville's early works imagine success as the "restitution" of a lost or distanced past; such a restitution in turn promises the "representation" of an integrated selfhood.

Melville's rhetoric carnivalizes Bloom's system in a number of ways that indicate the difference between fiction and the poetry on which Bloom concentrates. The dialectical play of "crossings" which Bloom imagines taking place sequentially in works and careers simply refuses to progress cleanly. Individual novels jump around among Bloom's tropes, concatenate aspects of his different "crossings," layer conflicting tropological patterns, reuse abandoned tropes in unexpected ways, and add new ones. Fiction presents such a richly accumulating, extensive, and polyvocal verbal environment that potential tropes and crossings lurk behind every bush and tree; only on the basis of an external point of view can those which attain the true status of figures of thought be separated from those whose function, as in *The Confidence-Man*, is phantasmic. As in psychoanalysis, figurative interpretation demands a context, an intertextual ethos, which gives and receives, in a process of transference, the relevance of specific expressive patterns. Furthermore, the cumulative rhetoric of fiction preserves traces of earlier crossings and figurative systems; thus, a shift from one tropical focus to another has the potential to provoke a network of relational revisions that reach into the corners of a writer's art. Finally, the freedom of fiction from superficial patterns of imposed order (rhythm, stanza form, etc.) opens it to incessant echoes of languages other than its own; it is unavoidably ventriloquistic and sylleptic.

In order to create a counterpart to Bloom's system that stands up in the rhetorical world of Melville's fiction, a number of additional elements are needed. First and foremost, a third category of figures—figures of crisis—must be established. Melville often incites revolution in his fictional order by putting his figures in close and destructive proximity to each other and pressuring them into catachresis; at times he reexamines a tropical system through the lens of new figures so powerful as to put it under erasure—leave it standing but disabled. The tropes which he uses for this purpose—repetition, syllepsis, nominalization, tautology—make little sense in a traditional phenomenological or representational (intentional) environment, yet they serve a basic ethical function. Figures of crisis involve Melville, and fiction in general, in a rhetoric in which negative and dialectical tropical patterns gain new meaning. At this point, the position outlined by Kristeva in *Revolution in Poetic Language* proves helpful; Kristeva's notion of a "subject in process" answers key ways in which fictional ethos transgresses Bloom's bimodal tropological system.

Kristeva views "the subject in language as decentering the transcendental ego, cutting through it, and opening it up to a dialectic" (30). Her distinction between "the transcendental ego" and "the subject in language" corresponds to that between traditional notions of authorial intention, like E. D. Hirsch's, and fictional ethos. *Ethopoeia,* translated into Kristeva's terms, creates "a *subject in process/on trial,* as is the case in the practice of the *text,*" and because of its tropical nature, "deep structure or at least transformational rules are disturbed and, with them, the possibility of semantic and/or grammatical categorical interpretation" (37). Subjectivity, ethos, and the author in/of a fictional text explode grammatically based rhetorical conceptions. Art puts on trial—subjects to trial—the logical intentionality given by ideology just as rhetoric scandalizes metaphysics. It forces linguistic order, the ego, into dialectical interaction with irruptions of the disorderly, pre-Oedipal *chora* of processes out of which it has emerged. Calvin Bedient summarizes: "The semiotic *chora* is the spider of instinct at the bottom of poetry's cup" (809).

Figure, after Kristeva's model, has three distinct functions. It presents irruptions of the "semiotic" to consciousness, structures the Oedipal ego imposed by culture, and maps dialectical relationships between the two realms. The author (in a traditional sense) of a text lies in a heterogeneous past; fictional voice establishes tropical relationships with that "author" which figure its presence not within textuality but as textuality, as part of a dialectical movement which involves "both shattering and maintaining *position* within the heterogeneous *process*" (56). The shattering-maintaining patterns of fictional ethos continually promote "the passage from one sign system to another" (59), a process which parallels the working of figures of crisis. Bakhtin's sense of the many languages within the novel suggests a notion of "sign system" as a bolt of textual fabric woven from a set of reinforcing figural operations. Kristeva's process defines a dialectical intertextuality which she prefers to call "transposition." For her, "every signifying practice is a field of transpositions of various signifying systems (an inter-textuality)"; thus, "one then understands that its 'place' of enunciation and its denoted 'object' are never single, complete, and identical in themselves, but always plural, shattered. . . . In this way polysemy can also be seen as the result of a semiotic polyvalence—an adherence to different sign systems" (59–60).

Literature entails the unraveling and reweaving of sign systems in response to "semiotic" incursions—phantasmic evocations of the past in the manner of *The Confidence-Man*—on the dominant textile of the ego. Subjectivity, ethos, involves the constant interplay of cultural order and "semiotic" heterogeneity as they work themselves out in the process (trial) of art. The tropics of fiction defines a dialectic which neither returns meaning to the repressive order of Oedipal language nor dissolves it in untrammeled "polysemy"—that is, a dialectic occupying a middle ground between Ricoeur and Derrida.

Kristeva approvingly quotes Derrida's radical definition of dialectic as "the indefinite movement of finitude, of the unity of life and death, of difference, of original repetition, that is, of the origin of tragedy as the absence of simple origin" (140). However, she prevents "grammatology" from traducing "every thesis—material, natural, social, substantial, and logical" (143) by opening voice to the prelinguistic space of the "semiotic." Dialectic engages not Derrida's corrosive indefiniteness but instead the subconscious, prior heterogeneity out of which cultural identity emerges. Trope must hold in suspension and present to each other the conflicting yet interdependent claims of cultural and precultural (pre-Oedipal) meaning. In this way it weaves the dialectical fabric of textuality. Kristeva's totalizing treatment of dialectic recalls Bakhtin's "internal dialogism of the word" (282); both trope the essential relational—figurative—nature of all literary presentation, the space of rhetoric.

Kristeva's psychoaesthetics suggests that the true, creative (as opposed to mythologized or ideological) author "of" a text will find embodiment "in" it by way of the incursions of a heterogeneous preconscious (or otherness), rather than as a unified, institutionalized identity. Figures of crisis in Melville announce "authorial" intrusion as phantoms which haunt the smoothly running machinery of narrative; they overturn and deride whatever cultural authority a tropical fabric has put on and revise the context, and thus the mode of functioning, of trope itself. Under their influence, memory gets fragmented, recast in heterogeneous terms.[5] In *Pierre*, for example, nominalizations mock the hero's willingness to believe in Isabel as a representation of the father; the voice of the novel reconstitutes itself as a voice out of silence and invests itself in a new "sign system." In Melville's career, the insights of *Pierre* signal not a crossing but a trial or process which continues into *The Confidence-Man* and after; the old "sign system" is obviated but never forgotten. Romantic and even pre-Romantic structures of self-representation haunt Melville's works to the end and intrude in unpredictable ways (as in Vere's rationalizations in *Billy Budd*).

Kristeva's model of literary subjectivity reinforces Melville's complex sense of fictional (tropological) time. Narrative ethos displays a heterogeneous, sylleptic past which gives rise to an equally polyvalent future or sense of the possibilities of voice. The present exists as an unstable, context-determined point of apprehension of figural crisis and emerging dialectical movement. Time, as Melville realizes, frames the essential ground of a true rhetoric, of an art which organizes itself through relations among figures of thought. Bakhtin, ever alert to allegiances between fiction and culture, defines this sense of time in relation to social movement, tolling the knell of the Augustinian (mythopoeic) view of history: "The temporal model of the world changes radically: it becomes a world where there is no first word (no ideal word), and the final word has not yet been spoken. For the first time in artistic-ideological consciousness, time and the world become historical" (30). With Bakhtin, we emerge from literature into the rhetoric of history; the heterogeneity of historical causality tasks and enlivens public time by virtue of parallel tropological processes to those of fiction.

Bakhtin's work suggests the transportability of fictional *ethopoeia*, defined in tropological terms, to other forms of discourse. Both history and fiction would cease functioning, have no future, if rhetoric permitted stability in self-representation, the mythologization of voice. Through its tropical processes, fiction generates and regenerates; it permits the past to reemerge in new forms within the *kairos* of a culture's ongoing discourse without foreclosing change and possibility. The tropics of fiction spawns new patterns of creative address which populate, expand, and reform existing genres and offer models to other forms of cultural activity. As long as they continue to find a path between the Scylla of myth and the Charybdis of grammar, fictional figurative processes will continue to recuperate and exemplify the classical rhetorical tradition around which so much of Western thought took its shape.

If this coda to *Cast by Means of Figures* remakes literary rhetoric in the image of Herman Melville, the intent is ethical. Without ethos and the tropes, self-representations, dialectical departures, phantoms, crises, temporal manipulations, and other flights of "metaphysics and conic-sections" on which ethos depends in Melville's developing art, the full power of his rhetoric to shape and convey human subjectivity and its story would remain an "unknown referential field." The "question of the intentionality of rhetorical figures" raised by rhetorical biography receives its most compelling answer in the image of an art, like that of Melville, courageously devoted to its own future. In Melville's faith in his creative future lies keys to our faith in our own. If those futures are "cast by means of figures, in some perplexed and difficult way"—if they are born out of the freedom of rhetoric rather than the stability of myth—that makes them no less worthy of our trust.

Notes

1. Manifest: "Cast by Means of Figures"

1. I use "rhetoric" in the traditional sense of a system of persuasive discourse. Rhetoric, in classical treatises, includes means of inventing and organizing ideas as well as techniques for their expression. Aristotle and his followers take for granted the unavoidable overlap between rhetoric and forms of analysis which we think of today as belonging to sociology, psychology, or political science. The degeneration of classical rhetoric from a general theory for the formulation of arguments (*logoi*) into catalogs of stylistic devices has been amply documented by Brian Vickers, George Kennedy, and others. Because of this decline, the term "rhetoric" in literary criticism today often implies technical or stylistic analysis. *Cast by Means of Figures* seconds Paul de Man's assertion that the "traditional forms of rhetoric" have suffered only a "temporary eclipse" and that it is now possible to "more or less openly raise the question of the intentionality of rhetorical figures" (*Blindness and Insight* 187–88). In bridging the gap between the "intentionality of rhetorical figures" and their persuasiveness, the present study bridges the gap between literary theory and classical rhetoric.

2. The notion of a "descriptive" study confronts a common dubiety summarized by Susan Stewart, writing in *Profession 89*. Description in literary study equals "prescription bereft of the temporal consciousness that transforms it from the perfunctory to the ethical" (11). Such a view underlies a distrust of objective representation which, although theoretically justified, has the unfortunate side effect of keeping theory and scholarship from working comfortably together. From a rhetorical perspective, however, description, among persuasive modes, carries no special metaphysical baggage. In its claim to "describe" the development of Melville's rhetoric, *Cast by Means of Figures* differs significantly in method from the "hermeneutic" rhetorical analysis espoused by Steven Mailloux.

3. I have used the following abbreviations for the Northwestern/Newberry editions of Melville's works: *T, Typee; O, Omoo; M, Mardi; R, Redburn; WJ, White-Jacket; MD, Moby-Dick; P, Pierre; PT, Piazza Tales; CM, The Confidence-Man.*

4. Dan McCall discusses this point in asserting that "throughout Melville's work one finds him deeply interested in rhetorical performance" (114).

5. Kenneth Dauber in *The Idea of Authorship in America* outlines the literary-historical context of Melville's authorial self-creation by arguing that the need to negotiate rather than assume authority for the act of writing was typical of early American literary life. Jonathan Arac makes a parallel point in discussing *Moby-Dick* as "aspiring to the new, 'literary' way of writing" characteristic of Poe and Hawthorne (42).

6. The evidence of Melville's failing popularity, ill health, financial problems, expressions of family concern, the apocalyptic tenor of his fiction, and his abandonment of

prose entirely paints a picture of increasing depression during the late 1850s. In its strongest versions (Marvin Fisher, Alan Lebowitz), this view credits his woes with the pessimism of his mature fiction—a judgment which leads to misreading of or conde-scension toward the verse works which he labored zealously over and published in 1866, 1876, 1888, and 1891. The efforts of such commentators on Melville's poetry as Walter Bezanson, William B. Stein, Vincent Kenny, and Stan Goldman suggest that his per-spicuity and experimental vigor remain unabated, a view which I argue elsewhere (1979, 1986) and which I maintain here.

7. I use "trope" synonymously with "figure," and I do not distinguish, as classical rhetoric does, between figures of speech and figures of thought. Chapter 1 outlines the definition of tropes available to Melville in the rhetorical theory current in his day, and subsequent chapters detail the manner in which specific tropes—metaphor, metonymy, metalepsis, syllepsis, etc.—gain additional meaning for him as his career develops. The exact nature of this meaning is explained along the way, and the Coda spells out the implications of the resulting general theory of tropes. Where I do not stipulate other-wise, I intend a common-sense notion of a trope as a figurative device which establishes some sort of relationship between two terms. A trope differs from a symbol in that in the latter the second term, or "tenor," is vague, ambiguous, or intended to be ineffable. Thus, as Umberto Eco concludes, "A trope cannot be taken 'literally' without violating a pragmatic maxim according to which a discourse is supposed to tell the truth; it must be interpreted as a figure of speech, since otherwise it would appear senseless or blatantly false. On the contrary, the instances of the symbolic mode do suggest a second sense, but could also be taken literally without jeopardizing the communicational intercourse" (141).

8. The two places where the present study most clearly addresses a theoretical rather than a Melvillean audience are in its notes and in the Coda, "The Tropics of Fiction." The latter expands Melville's tropological practice into a general theory of literary rhetoric. Students wishing to read *Cast by Means of Figures* primarily as an example of the application of theoretical rhetorical criticism may find it helpful to read the Coda first.

9. Foucault's formulation has become popular partly because it addresses the impor-tant belief that literature is or should be freer from social determination than other forms of discourse, that it has a unique capacity for ideological subversion, unauthor-ized forms of cognition, or pleasure (Julia Kristeva, Gilles Deleuze and Félix Guattari, Roland Barthes). Through analysis of the author-function, literature can be freed from appropriation by hegemonic institutions. Because of this underlying value, Foucault criticizes the poststructuralist denial of the author on the basis that its clouding of issues leaves repressive patterns intact: "The themes destined to replace the privileged position accorded the author [the notion of the "work" and of *écriture*] have merely served to arrest the possibility of genuine change" (118). For a comparable argument in a feminist context, see Cheryl Walker, "Feminist Literary Criticism and the Author."

10. An essential discussion of this question is Hershel Parker's *Flawed Texts and Verbal Icons: Literary Authority in American Fiction*. Melville's *Pierre* represents a prime case of the interplay between ambiguous literary and ambiguous biographical data. It is worth asking whether Parker's immense knowledge and scrupulous respect for biographical and textual detail does not, in its own way, replicate the charge which he and Brian Higgins, in a later essay, level against "Post-New-Critical" approaches: "Such formula-tions, however 'precisely' edged they are, probably leave most readers, whether sophisti-cated young enthusiasts to theory or simplistic old biographers and bibliographers,

stranded, farther remote from *Pierre* than ever" ("Reading *Pierre*" 220). Whatever side one takes on the issues which Parker raises, his critique of the New-Critical imposition of an arbitrary, intrinsic coherence on literary texts and his acknowledgment in "Reading *Pierre*" that "the authors of this chapter are now, for better or worse, part of the literary history of *Pierre*" (220) do more to open the door to a Foucauldian perspective than the vast majority of current readings of Melville.

11. John Carlos Rowe finds "among a broad variety of formal and historical approaches" to nineteenth-century American literature "a persistent reliance on a familiar romantic paradigm of *Bildung* as the dialectical unfolding of oppositions that ultimately intends and is governed by a unifying *telos*" (7). In literary biography, telos—Melville's progress toward greatness, unpopularity, silence, depression, etc.—has the effect of occulting the radically negative and synthetic movements essential to the unpredictable "unfolding" and incessant "changing" which Melville felt himself to be undergoing as an author (*Letters* 130, 143, 147).

12. Rhetorical biography makes its own methodological choices. In describing internally conditioned rhetorical departures, the present study turns attention away from relationships between Melville's writings and larger cultural issues such as gender, politics, and empire, successfully explored by Neal Tolchin, Michael Paul Rogin, Wai-chee Dimock, and T. Walter Herbert. Its rhetorical or tropological armature, however, stands in contrast to the freer structural and thematic phenomenology practiced by Edgar Dryden, John Seelye, Brodtkorb, and others.

13. Warwick Wadlington states: "In classical rhetorical terms, the principal basis of Melville's appeal here and in all the early books is that of ethos. His narrative presence, relatively unobtrusive but strongly inflected, wins a jeopardized confidence as the encompassing voucher for truth" (52).

14. "The Temporality of Rhetoric" argues that rhetoric, literary criticism, and psychoanalysis are sister arts. They are "practical" in that they are situated between the "productive" arts and the "theoretical." A practical, or rhetorical, art cannot adhere to purely theoretical formulas. For this reason, the relationship between theory and practice in literary criticism is discomfited by the importation of philosophical concepts, such as those of deconstruction, until it sorts them out on the basis of rhetorical, or ethical, impact.

2. "Dumb and Deaf": Melville's Youth

1. James A. Berlin notes that Blair's *Lectures on Rhetoric and Belles Lettres* went through 130 British and American editions between 1783 and 1911 (25). John Michael Wozniak outlines the dominance of Blair, along with George Campbell's *Philosophy of Rhetoric* and Richard Whately's *Elements of Rhetoric,* in Eastern colleges during the first half of the nineteenth century (11–30). Blair's rhetoric was the most prevalent until 1828, when Whately's, closely allied in theory, overtook it. Campbell was commonly used as a more advanced text. James L. Golden and Edward P. J. Corbett conclude that "there is no question that of the three texts published by these men, Blair's enjoyed the widest sale and was written in the most lucid and charming style" (25). All three remained popular throughout the century.

2. My discussion of Melville's education follows William H. Gilman's ground-breaking discussion in *Melville's Early Life and Redburn,* as modified and amplified by John P.

Runden, David K. Titus, Merton M. Sealts, Jr., and the editors of the Northwestern-Newberry *Piazza Tales*.

3. Theoretically oriented rhetorics such as those of Blair, Campbell, Whately, and their American imitators were, from the late eighteenth century on, increasingly standard texts in American college curricula. Although secondary curricula were less philosophical and more oriented toward recitation and the parsing of sentences, principles and practices drawn from the British rhetoricians filtered down and exercised tremendous authority in American education throughout the period of Melville's life. On the popularity of British rhetoric in America, and American rhetorical education in the nineteenth century, see Crowley, Berlin, Golden and Corbett, Wozniak, Robert J. Connors, and Warren Guthrie.

4. A specific instance which Melville is likely to have encountered is Alexander Jamieson's 1818 *Grammar of Rhetoric and Polite Literature*, which was in its twenty-fourth American edition by 1844. Jamieson, adopted by a number of Eastern colleges from 1822 on, "was studied mostly by freshmen" and "usually supplemented by one or more of the weightier English works" (Wozniak 12). Jamieson overtly acknowledges his debt to Blair (vi). After its 1827 publication, Bowdoin College professor Samuel P. Newman's *Practical System of Rhetoric* rapidly became popular as an introductory text, again heavily indebted to its more elaborate eighteenth-century British precursors. Newman is listed in the Albany Academy curriculum (a fact pointed out to me by James Oldham), although it is not certain that Melville encountered it when he was there.

5. My historical argument derives from Crowley, who holds the developments leading up to Blair responsible for the stilted nature of twentieth-century rhetorical theory and writing instruction. Crowley differs from Berlin, whose historical argument covers similar ground, in discounting the influence of Romantic literary theory on rhetoric after midcentury. Crowley's discussion of the development of rhetorical education in America permits us to see rhetorical and literary theory—two extremely powerful traditions in nineteenth-century American culture—as existing side by side in almost schizophrenic isolation from each other: American writers followed the lead of Emerson and the British Romantics, while American students and orators continued to study Blair, Campbell, Whately, and their native offspring. Sensitivity to both traditions underlies Melville's struggle to define the sources and nature of authority in literary discourse. I contend that this struggle, with its footing in contending theories of discourse, has more to do with the developing shape of Melville's works than religious or psychological conflict.

6. Blair's treatment of tropes follows Campbell, first published in 1776, in its foregrounding of metaphor, synecdoche, and metonymy; but its inclusion of metalepsis, so important to *Typee*, is highly idiosyncratic, as is the prominent place which it gives to its discussion of hyperbole and apostrophe. Campbell also stresses the value of figurative language in appealing to the passions and the imagination. All three major British rhetoricians—Blair, Campbell, and Whately—discuss style in terms of the property of perspicuity.

7. Gilman (90ff.) summarizes the controversy: on returning from teaching school near Pittsfield for a term, Melville found the Philo Logos Society moribund. He revived it by getting his uncle Peter Gansevoort to loan the club a room in Stanwix Hall, and when it began to meet, it immediately elected him president. His election was contested by Charles Van Loon, and the two published a series of seven letters arguing the matter back and forth in the scandal-happy pages of the *Microscope*. Gilman's conclusion that

"the warriors were equally matched" is borne out by comparable, and comparably neoclassic, rhetoric. Gilman publishes the complete text of Melville's letters and some of Van Loon's.

8. I use the term "departure" to describe the movement of Melville's dialectic in order to emphasize the negative or differential nature which it shares with Hegelian *aufhebung*. For Melville's rhetoric, as for Hegel, the terms of a thesis-antithesis opposition are not simply combined but radically transformed. The *aufgehoben*, sublated, or synthesized terms take on an oppositional relationship to their earlier forms. Melville's rhetoric develops not merely by the accumulation of figurative devices but by opening possibilities inimical to its previous rhetorical environments. It is not known whether Melville had been introduced to Hegel in 1839, but his 1849 journal reports the German philosopher to be among those discussed in the many serious conversations with George Adler undertaken during his voyage of that year (*Journals* 8). For an analysis of Hegel's dialectic in terms close to those of Melville's, see Donald Philip Verene, who asserts: "My point is that dialectic is really a logical way of describing what are essentially rhetorical processes or rhetorical powers of the mind. Their form is essentially tropic and this form is evident in the metaphors and ironies through which Hegel has spirit or *Geist* move" (23).

3. "The author at the time": *Typee*

1. This chapter first appeared, in considerably different form, in *Texas Studies in Literature and Language* 31 (1989): 386–405. It is reprinted by permission of the University of Texas Press.

2. The early success of *Typee* owed much to its style. Both its publisher, John Murray, and a reviewer for the London *John Bull* wondered that a sailor could write so well (*T* 286). Other reviewers praised the work in terms such as "so graceful, so graphic," "brilliantly colored," and "lightly but vigorously written" (Hetherington 24, 25, 33).

3. Both Hugh W. Hetherington (20–65) and Leon Howard's "Historical Note" in *T* (286ff.) summarize the contemporary public controversy over the novel's veracity, a controversy put to rest by the unheralded resurfacing of Toby—Richard Tobias Greene— a house and sign painter in Buffalo. Melville visited his old shipmate and got from him the statement which appears as a sequel in later editions of *Typee*. The most authoritative modern treatment of the issue, Charles R. Anderson's *Melville in the South Seas*, compares the novel with the narratives that Melville read while writing *Typee*. Anderson finds Melville's borrowings extensive enough to warrant the conclusion that he could have written *Typee* without having visited the Marquesas at all (191).

4. Conservative reviewers were outraged by Melville's negative view of missionaries and the effect of their efforts on the islanders. Serious modern treatments of the cultural thematics of *Typee* include those of T. Walter Herbert, Jr. (149–91), James Duban (3–11), John Wenke, A. N. Kaul, and Anderson (69–195).

5. See Tolchin, Rogin, Thompson (43–55), and Edwin Haviland Miller (118–35).

6. William B. Dillingham (24) discusses the theme of the "irrecoverable" past in *Typee;* Warwick Wadlington (46–68) describes the contradictory, or "dialectical," nature of the book's narrative point of view; Rowland A. Sherrill (7–32) discusses the "retrospective narrator" of the work.

7. In answering de Man's call for a rhetoric which "raises the question of the intentionality of rhetorical figures" (see note 1 in chapter 1), the analysis conducted through-

out the present study describes not simply the devices which Melville uses, irony for example, but the way in which those devices both shape the underlying conceptual structure—the thematics—of a work and manifest the author's personal investment (intentionality). "Rhetorical biography" in this way goes beyond technical tropological analysis.

8. On Poe's potential influence on Melville, see Mary K. Bercaw (110) and Perry Miller (21). Melville's relationship with Poe remains shadowy. Although both were known in the Duyckinck literary circle in New York during the late 1840s, they may never have met. No record exists of Melville's ownership of Poe's works before 1860, yet he thought well enough of them to give an edition to his wife. In 1847 Melville purchased an 1832 sea narrative by Benjamin Morrell, which is a probable source for *Pym*, and he also bought J. N. Reynolds's 1835 *Voyage of the United States Frigate Potomac*, following up an interest leading back to Reynolds's 1839 *Knickerbocker* article on Mocha Dick. Reynolds was acquainted with Poe, and his passion for Antarctic exploration and for J. C. Symmes's theory that the earth contained concentric spheres open at the poles links him to *Pym* as well. It is likely that common interests and sources would have led Melville to Poe's work, even if his reputation and presence in New York did not.

9. Milton R. Stern (61) makes this point.

10. Irony carries two traditional senses: an ironic statement expresses a contradictory double meaning; an ironic statement intends derision (Puttenham's "drie mock"). For the Romantics, best represented by the German critic Karl Solger, irony comes to be associated with the self-consciousness of art, a view which combines the idea of doubleness in the first sense of the figure with the idea of rhetorical intention in the second: modern art cannot escape awareness of its own secondariness vis-à-vis both nature and its great classical precursors; its belatedness and artificiality doom it to irony; it cannot speak directly, naively, in the way that myth does. Romantic irony heightens awareness of the essential figurative nature of language. *Typee* demonstrates Melville's increasingly Romantic view of irony and other tropes—his tendency to see them as underlying structural principles rather than as discrete stylistic devices. For an extensive discussion of Romantic irony, see Anne K. Mellor, *English Romantic Irony*, and the essays in *Romantic Irony*, ed. Frederick Garber.

11. See Stern (40) and Dryden (45) on Tommo's corrupting influence on the Typees.

12. John Samson, in *White Lies*, asserts that "Melville re-presents through Tommo the narratives of white encounters with natives in a way that exposes their absurdity, their contradictions, their lack of meaning. He begins with the word 'savage,' juxtaposes it with its opposite, 'civilized,' and shows that they are basically the same. Then he shows that both are meaningless and that this self-contradictory meaninglessness extends to 'progress,' 'primitive,' and even 'truth' itself" (53). Samson's treatment of Melville's sources is extremely helpful.

13. See Stern's "Typee" in *Critical Essays on Herman Melville's "Typee"* and Dryden, *Melville's Thematics* (37), on Tommo's self-consciousness and growth.

14. Samson in *White Lies* agrees that the excisions result in "a more carefully controlled narrative voice" (39n).

15. All four earlier accounts were referred to by Melville during the writing of *Typee* (Bercaw 19). Herbert discusses Stewart, Porter, and Ellis at some length; Anderson details Melville's borrowings from all sources. What is worth emphasis is how extensive existing commentary on Marquesas Island native life was and how ethnocentric and rhetorically neoclassic it tended, without exception, to be.

16. In *The Widening Gyre,* Frank summarizes the effects of spatialization on narrative: "For the duration of the scene, at least, the time-flow of the narrative is halted; attention is fixed on the interplay of relationships within the immobilized time-area" (15); "past and present are apprehended spatially, locked in a timeless unity that, while it may accentuate surface differences, eliminates any feeling of sequence by the very act of juxtaposition" (59).

17. Feidelson sees the "topography" of *Typee* as "metaphoric" (165). Insistence on the metonymic nature of Tommo's valley experiences has the effect of replacing Feidelson's programmatically symbolic perspective with a view of the figurative processes in the novel that corresponds more closely to de Man's notion of "allegory"—an approach more in tune with the ethos-defining, vocal rather than metaphysical, functions of rhetoric. I deal with this distinction in the Coda and at length in "Literary Ethos: Dispersion, Resistance, Mystification."

18. Metonymy traditionally (in Blair and previously) indicates conventional, associated, rather than logical, relationships—a term substituted for one which is contiguous, cause substituted for effect, etc. This tradition carries over into Jakobson's famous use of metonymy to name the "syntagmatic" function of language—the way in which one word in a sentence relates to that which is next to it—as opposed to the metaphoric or "paradigmatic" function, which establishes categories of elements (nouns, etc.) sharing similarities that allow them to be substituted for each other. In post-Freudian theory, metonymy becomes attached to the psychic mechanism of "displacement," by which emotional loading gets transferred from one thing to another. Since metonymy operates in this context unconsciously, metonymic chains—free associations—can reveal the buried levels of the psyche; to give oneself over to them becomes a regressive act. Bloom overtly associates metonymy with regression, an association which makes sense in Melville's works. The metonymic tenor of Typee valley, for example, goes along with Tommo's regressive status as "child in cannibal land," to use E. H. Miller's phrase (118).

19. John Samson, in "The Dynamics of History and Fiction in Melville's *Typee*" (289), sees in this passage a "Wordsworthian" temporal motif. He argues that "Tommo's intimations of immortality can at this point come only through recollection of his 'childhood' in Typee." Samson relates the combined retrospective and proleptic temporality of the scene to the "transcendent, spiritual meaning" which Tommo gives to events rather than to the rhetoric of Melville's voice.

20. *A Map of Misreading* (102–3). Bloom points out the traditional "preposterous" nature of metalepsis in conflating what comes "pre," or before (Blair's antecedent), with what comes "post," or after (Blair's consequent). For another discussion of metalepsis, see Gérard Genette (234–37).

21. Paul Witherington in "The Art of Melville's *Typee*" (144) points out that Tommo's real name is not even "Tom," since that one was picked on the basis of its supposed ease of pronunciation. Tommo's "real" name, like his past and his future, exists outside the limits of the narrative.

4. "No further connection": *Omoo*

1. Gansevoort Melville died unexpectedly in May of 1846, just two months after the American publication of *Typee. Omoo* was finished seven months later, at the end of the year. Gansevoort's death freed Melville from whatever inferiority he felt vis-à-vis an

older, ostensibly more brilliant, and more successful brother. Since the death of Melville's father in 1832, the family's genteel social pretensions, when they were not sustained by the generosity of Herman's wealthy maternal uncle Peter Gansevoort, were heavily invested, financially and psychologically, in Gansevoort's roller-coaster business and legal career. Gansevoort's early rhetorical interests, his introduction of his brother into the Albany debating societies, and his success as a political orator would naturally have been associated, for Herman, with the social standing of Blair's rhetoric, as reflected in the first of his "Fragments from a Writing Desk." To find his own voice was for Melville to find a selfhood defined in terms other than those, inherited by both brothers from a distinguished lineage, which Gansevoort exemplified; yet Gansevoort's death made it inevitable that Herman accrue, in his family's eye, a measure of his older brother's authority. Thus, the dialectic of Melville's rhetorical responses to Blair was mirrored in, and reinforced by, the events defining his personal situation during 1846.

2. Melville's shift from irony to synecdoche corresponds to Harold Bloom's "crossing of election," discussed in the Coda below. Bloom's formulation accounts well for the rush of confident energy that accompanies a strong poet's movement from reliance on a figure of "limitation" to a figure of "restitution" or "representation." In this instance, however, although the psychic defense mechanism of "reaction formation" which Bloom associates with irony fits the uneasy narrative self-consciousness which complicates *Typee,* the masochistic "turning against the self" which Bloom pins to synecdoche does not appear in *Omoo.* Bloom's figures define the dominant ethos of high Romanticism with startling insight, but Melville's rhetoric, which reaches backward to Blair and forward to structures which are either modern or idiosyncratic, is not easily contained within Bloom's envelope. Rather than exemplifying Bloom's three "crossings," Melville puts into play a series of dialectical departures which appear and overlap in a complex manner and involve more tropes than Bloom's privileged six.

3. Bloom describes synecdoche as the trope which "represents macrocosm through microcosm" (*Map* 98). Synecdoche is easily confused with symbolism, especially in Romantic and post-Romantic literary theory and literature of a transcendental cast. The differences are two: First, as explained above in note 7 in chapter 1, synecdoche, a trope, must be read figuratively if the intended act of communication is to take place; a symbol, however, does not necessarily establish a locus of meaning or referent outside itself. Second, the larger reality signified by a synecdoche is specified or potentially specifiable, whereas symbolism invokes multiple and indeterminate referents. On the implications of symbolism as opposed to figuration (trope), see chapter 7 of the present study, as well as my "Literary Ethos: Dispersion, Resistance, Mystification."

4. Samson, in an excellent treatment of the novel's religious theme, points out that "the structure of *Omoo* also reinforces this comic reduction of the sacred to the profane" (*White Lies* 66).

5. "The drawn soul of genius": *Mardi*

1. Watson Branch, in his summary essay "The Quest for *Mardi,*" in *A Companion to Melville Studies,* ed. John Bryant, concludes, "Despite its apologists' efforts to explain away its artistic failings, *Mardi* must finally stand or fall on its own, and fall it does" (140).

2. Elizabeth S. Foster, *M* 679. Among critics who treat *Mardi* as a prefiguration of Melville's later, greater novels are Richard Brodhead in "*Mardi*: Creating the Creative," Barbara Blansett, Stuart Levine, and Mildred Travis.

3. Merrell Davis's classic study *Melville's Mardi: A Chartless Voyage* breaks the work into three disjointed parts: "narrative beginning," "Romantic interlude," and "travelogue-satire," presided over by a narrative "voice" which, in John Seelye's words, begins as "a strong first-person presence reminiscent of Tommo" but later becomes "disembodied, disinterested" (30). Brodhead calls the book "the loosest and baggiest of prose monsters" ("Creating the Creative" 29). Branch lists five stages in the composition of *Mardi* (129).

4. Bloom, in his famous 1969 essay "The Internalization of Quest-Romance," summarizes: "The movement of quest-romance, before its internalization by the High Romantics, was from nature to redeemed nature, the sanction of redemption being the gift of some external spiritual authority, sometimes magical. The Romantic movement is from nature to the imagination's freedom (sometimes a reluctant freedom), and the imagination's freedom is frequently purgatorial, redemptive in direction but destructive of the social self. The high cost of Romantic internalization, that is, of finding paradises within a renovated man, shows itself in the arena of self-consciousness. The quest is to widen consciousness as well as to intensify it, but the quest is shadowed by a spirit that tends to narrow consciousness to an acute preoccupation with self" (6).

5. Melville heard Emerson lecture in Boston on Feb. 5, 1849 (Sealts, *Pursuing Melville* 255). In a March 3 letter to Duyckinck, he claims previously to have "glanced at a book of his once in Putnam's store" (*Letters* 79). Of course Melville would have heard aspects of Emersonian transcendentalism discussed in the New York and Boston literary society to which he had access. The proofs of *Mardi* were completed (according to Augusta's letter) on Jan. 27 (Leyda, *Log* I, 287). Rather than argue the influence of Emerson on *Mardi*, a case summarized and largely rejected by Sealts, I will trace the importance of Emerson as a way for Melville to understand and articulate implications which the rhetoric of his third novel has for his ethos, his authority as a writer.

6. Tyrus Hillway, in an influential 1944 article "Taji's Abdication in Herman Melville's *Mardi*," argues that the end of the novel amounts to a "suicide" on Taji's part.

7. Sealts (*Pursuing Melville* 252) points out that both Melville's relationship to Emerson and the ostensible "transcendentalism" of some of his ideas were mentioned by a number of *Mardi*'s reviewers. The letter to Duyckinck follows by a week an earlier letter in which Melville mentions having heard the Concord sage lecture. It is likely that the second letter is Melville's response to uneasy queries by his devoutly Episcopalian friend as to the Emersonian tendencies of his thought. The case of the relationship between *Mardi* and the letter to Duyckinck exemplifies numerous instances throughout Melville's career in which a line of rhetorical thought or a figurative pattern overflows the work in which it originates.

8. Because Aristotle discusses figurative language under the general heading of "metaphor," it has often been treated as a more embracing category than the other tropes (Ricoeur, *Rule*), or even as a special function of language (Jakobson). Blair shows metaphor no such favoritism in describing it as that figure based on "the relation of Similitude and Resemblance" (I, 370). My discussion follows Blair. As the trope of comparison, metaphor stands in logical opposition to irony. This opposition, accepted by Melville, is clouded by radical generalizations of the figurative nature of language

such as those common in both phenomenology and deconstruction (e.g. Ricoeur, *Interpretation Theory* 46–53; Derrida, "White Mythology") which stress "the tension between two terms in a metaphorical utterance" (*Interpretation Theory* 50).

9. The liveliest account of Melville's New York literary milieu is still Perry Miller's *Raven and the Whale*. For an updated treatment (oriented to the 1850s), see Donald Yannella, "Writing the '*Other* Way': Melville, the Duyckinck Crowd, and Literature for the Masses," in *A Companion to Melville Studies*, ed. John Bryant. Yannella's bibliography lists others of his important studies of the literary circumstances in which Melville found himself during this period.

6. "More names, than things": *Redburn*

1. Rogin, Duban, and Samson's *White Lies* offer the best discussions of the political worldliness of *Redburn*. Dimock's argument is illuminating but narrower. Biographically oriented studies, such as those of E. H. Miller and Tolchin, follow in the footsteps of Gilman's elegant and still invaluable 1951 work *Melville's Early Life and Redburn*. On Melville's peripheral involvement in the Astor Place riots, see Leyda, *Log* I, 302–3.

2. The theme of "paternity" in the novel is central to Tolchin's reading of *Redburn* as a "mourning pilgrimage" (85–105). Tolchin's biographically oriented case is offset by Régis Durand's interesting Lacanian treatment of the "absent father" as a dominant and more structurally than personally telling theme in Melville: " 'The Captive King': The Absent Father in Melville's Text," in *The Fictional Father*, ed. Robert Con Davis, 48–72.

3. Gilman (208–9) discusses the boy-man split in the novel's narrative perspective and judges the work to fail at resolving it. Critical commentary on the issue, reaching back to F. O. Matthiessen, is summarized in Hershel Parker's fine "Historical Note" to *R* (348–49) and Wilson Heflin's "*Redburn* and *White-Jacket*" in *A Companion to Melville Studies* (152–53). Samson summarizes opinion on the related issue of Redburn's maturation in *White Lies* 88.

4. Dryden (*Melville's Thematics*) sees the lack of resolution caused by the fragmented point of view in the novel as indicative of its "ironic vision" (60); Kaul associates it with the "grim" tone of the work; for Sherrill it relates to Melville's disabusing of "dear delusions" (33); for Durand it leads to the "unheimlichkeit" of *Redburn* (54).

5. By specifying the "first voyage" nature of Redburn's tale, Melville places it in the genre of the "boy at sea" *Bildungsroman* made very popular by Frederick Marryat. In Marryat's most successful works, especially *Peter Simple* (1834), the hero is a midshipman—an inexperienced boy sent to sea on a military vessel to become trained as an officer. Marryat's novels do not just offer sentimental adventure but serve as a moral and social conduct book for an aspiring middle-class; as such, they can be seen as a male equivalent to popular domestic novels like Susan Warner's *Wide, Wide World*. In all three cases, there is an emerging, modern sense of adolescence as a stage which must be traversed, and during which hard lessons are likely to be learned, on the way to adult responsibility.

6. Smith lectured on rhetoric at Edinburgh early in his career. His thinking, particularly on the nature of scientific discourse, significantly influenced the rhetorical theory of his friend Blair, who may have attended his lectures. Smith did not publish on rhetoric during his lifetime, and his notes were burned, by instruction, at his death. His lectures, reconstructed from student notes, have been published in the twentieth cen-

tury. Melville would have known Smith as a member of the same circle that Blair belonged to and might have known about Smith's rhetorical training, but he would not have had available Smith's rhetorical theory. For a brief discussion of Smith's rhetorical contributions, see Crowley 46–49.

7. In associating metaphor with sublimation, Bloom notes the "incoherence" of the Freudian concept (*Map* 101). For rhetorical purposes, metaphor suggests a similarity—logical, sensuous, or emotional—between two distinct objects. It is the trope by which values associated with one term become transferred to another that shares some distinguishing characteristic. In psychoanalysis, the point of comparison between the two terms is unconscious; yet when that unconscious link becomes articulated in the analytic discourse, its unconscious nature—and resulting force—loses rhetorical significance. For this reason, sublimation as a psychoanalytic concept falls short of the explanatory or figurative vigor of other defense mechanisms—repression, introjection, etc.

8. Melville refers to himself as a "woodsawyer" again in a May 1850 letter to Dana (*Letters* 106). Willard Thorp, in the "Historical Note" to *WJ*, summarizes Melville's commercial expectations for his two "jobs" (408–9).

7. "The strong shunning of death": *White-Jacket*

1. Any apocalyptic vision requires a combination of synecdochic and metaleptic figures—a microcosmic representation of achieved or achievable temporal redemption. Apocalypse also requires a vision of death which may or may not call upon the type of metaphoric logic central to *Redburn*. Samson, in *White Lies* 128–72, elaborates the related theme of millennialism in *White-Jacket*.

2. Dryden in *Melville's Thematics of Form* voices the strongest suspicions concerning White-Jacket's truthfulness (70–71). Samson reiterates the view (134).

3. Melville's condescending comments about his fourth and fifth novels make it clear that, in spite of his having "spoken pretty much as I feel," he does not identify them with either the "higher purpose" of *Mardi* or the "unknown worlds of knowledge" which he, like the "truck-horse" in *Redburn,* hides inside himself. In evaluating his comments, it helps to recognize that they exactly reflect the rhetoric of "bottomless" but "secret" selfhood central to the two works. Rhetorically, his comments indicate his participation in and identification with the voice of the novels rather than a distanced, objective judgment on them. Both novels and letters reveal satisfaction with the honest accomplishments of his ethos in *Redburn* and *White-Jacket* and dissatisfaction with the limits of its rhetoric. As with all of Melville's letters, it is misleading to treat them as the locus of some sort of emotional standpoint external to the works; they are, for the most part, every bit as rhetorical (sometimes more so) as his fiction, and every bit as complex, self-aware, and cagey when it comes to self-revelation.

8. "So as to Kill Time": *Moby-Dick*

1. The key statements of this case, sympathetically summarized in the "Historical Note" to *MD* (581–85), are Howard Vincent's pioneering book and Harrison Hayford's updated version in "Unnecessary Duplicates: A Key to the Writing of *Moby-Dick*." Other instances are cited by Bezanson in reviewing the argument in "*Moby-Dick*: Document,

Drama, Dream" (176). Robert Zoellner makes the parallel assertion that "Melville really wrote two novels in a single creative act" (239). James Guetti charges Melville with "failure to compose experience in any way or create coherent rhetorical structures of any sort" (1).

2. Eco points out that symbolism, as opposed to allegory, relates the signifier not to a chain of referents but to a "pragmatics of interpretation" always validated by a "legit-imating theology" (163). I discuss this notion at length in "Literary Ethos: Dispersion, Resistance, Mystification." The figural nature which Melville attributes to Moby-Dick in "Loomings" has much to do with readings of the novel, following that of D. H. Law-rence's *Studies in Classic American Literature,* which emphasize its seemingly transcen-dental reach.

3. Sharon Cameron discusses the relationship between exterior and interior in this passage and throughout *Moby-Dick* as signaling the thematics of body and soul, literal and allegorical expression, central to the "primative issues of identity" to which the novel's "hermeneutic issues" are "forced to cede" (19). From the perspective of *Cast by Means of Figures,* Cameron's account of the "fall to selfhood" through "disembodiment" (66) tropes the rhetoricity which makes the book look outside itself and link up to those that precede and follow in grounding Melville's ethical authority.

4. See P. Adams Sitney for a discussion of Ahab's question.

5. For a discussion of the prominence of the circle motif in a later Melville work, see Richard Kopley, "The Circle and Its Center in 'Bartleby the Scrivener.' "

6. It is not clear whether Melville's discussions with Adler touched on the subject of memory, or what other treatments he may have extrapolated from in revisiting a topic common in both neoclassic and Romantic rhetorical theory. For a discussion of Hege-lian memory, see Jacques Derrida's "Art of *Mémoires.*" I use the specific Hegelian terms, as explicated by Derrida, for their convenience in representing a line of thought available to Melville and in order to insist on their distinctness. On the Melville-Adler relation-ship, see Sanford E. Marovitz.

9. "Nimble center, circumference elastic": *Pierre*

1. See my "Memory's Mint" and "Like Bed of Asparagus" for instances.

2. Priscilla Wald makes a similar point in asserting that "silence (and its counterpart, meaningless noise) emerges in resistance to narrative and meaningful language, not as an absence but as an alternate presence, the *embodiment,* perhaps, of possibility" (120). Wald reads the silence which broods over *Pierre* as contributing to "Melville's de-construction of the national script of identity" (132). My argument is not intended to contradict the historicist readings of Wald, Arac, Dimock, Tolchin, Rogin, Simon, and others of Melville's most penetrating critics but to focus attention on aspects of authorial ethos which give Melville's career its powerful rhetorical drive into, through, and beyond the critical or apocalyptic gestures which characterize *Pierre* as a "moment" in the logic of his development.

3. Melville's tombs come uncannily close to the psychic "crypts" which Abraham describes in "The Shell and the Kernel" and *The Wolf-Man's Magic Word.* Peggy Kamuf summarizes: "The crypt, produced by a series of fantasmic incorporations, operates on the order of a fake Unconscious" (36). Pierre's unconscious remains centered in repeated

incest, which images of "deep-diving" or vacancy dissemble. Melville's image of the self becomes "cryptic" in the context of the novel.

10. "A dream of the eye": Magazine Fiction

1. For a helpful chronology of Melville's works during the years between *Pierre* and *The Confidence-Man*, see Sealts's "Historical Note" to *PT* 492–96. For publication and reprint histories of the individual works, see Newman, *Reader's Guide*.

2. The case for Melville's later works as a deliberate affront to his audience is made most strongly by Ann Douglas.

3. As Jaffe points out, Melville competed not just with other American authors but with British writers like Dickens, whose *Bleak House* was serialized in *Harper's* in 1852 and 1853. Sealts in the "Historical Note" to *PT* details the case for the success of Melville's magazine fiction: he was paid five dollars per page rather than the usual three dollars; his works were taken and quickly published by two of the most prestigious magazines of the day, *Harper's* and *Putnam's*; they were rapidly reprinted; and reviews were generally quite positive (484–508). See Inge (23–53) for reprinted reviews of *The Piazza Tales*.

4. Dan McCall summarizes: "Melville—the artist, was going on radiantly. It's a pity that scholars have to put so much effort into asking us to choose between Melville sick and Melville sound; everything we know about him compels us to conclude that both stories—and only both of them together—are true" (39). In respect to Melville's developing voice, it is his soundness that we encounter in the magazine fiction.

5. Kingsley Widmer discusses this point at length from a philosophical perspective.

6. Hershel Parker in *Reading Billy Budd* discusses Melville's indebtedness to the British poets of the day (27). McCall, in arguing that the narrator of "Bartleby, the Scrivener" is indeed "reliable," cites and discusses in detail the arguments on both sides of the issue (99–154). From a rhetorical perspective, however, the narrator's manner of speaking— his ethos—raises serious questions whether or not one ends by crediting his character and testimony.

7. On the tale's entropic nature, see Peter A. Smith, "Entropy in Melville's 'Bartleby the Scrivener.' "

8. Melville's image here reverses his earlier tattooing motif: the "strange cyphers" engraved on the lid of Hunilla's soul obscure rather than fix her essential ethical identity.

9. Darryl Hattenhauer discusses the "ambiguities of time" in "The Encantadas" as a deconstruction of the notion of historical progress which foregrounds "our eternal connection with sin" (8); in the work "there is one form of timelessness: death" (11), an argument that seconds H. Bruce Franklin's contention that "in 'The Encantadas' life is a form of death" (quoted in Hattenhauer 13). I argue that Melville brackets the compelling but reductive opposition between change and death, as he does other important philosophical issues, in order to explore its rhetorical underpinnings. With the common sense of the experienced writer, he seeks ways of embodying death and silence in words without stopping language altogether.

10. Double negatives in *Moby-Dick* are discussed in Gayle L. Smith, "The Word and the Thing: *Moby-Dick* and the Limits of Language." The same device is analyzed in detail by Paola Cabibbo and Paola Ludovici in " 'Bartleby': Il sistema semantico della doppia negazione." The function of *copertura* (coverage, whitewashing) which Cabibbo and Ludovici (45) attribute to the grammatical figure in "Bartleby" is similar in "Benito Cereno."

11. "Mysterious touches": *The Confidence-Man*

1. The distinction between voice and voiced corresponds on a rhetorical level to that between signifier and signified in semiotics. The difference between the two sets of relationships is that voice is a higher-order linguistic phenomenon, composed of chains of grammatically or figuratively related signifiers. As a result, to stress the incongruence between voice and voiced may highlight an instability in a culture's ideology regarding speech acts, but it does not "deconstruct" sense-making in a radical or totalizing fashion. Indeed, from a rhetorical point of view, the latter act is impossible, since language speaks with a voice that moves its audience whether one wants it to or not. Voice operates economically within the envelope of culture as signification does within the structure of language, but the decline of the discipline of rhetoric treated by Vickers, Ginette, Kennedy, and others has impoverished our sense of the possibility of describing and categorizing vocal modes, and Romanticism has mystified or theologized the notion of voice in ways which still impinge on our concepts.

2. In this context, the history of rhetoric revises literary history: what appears postmodern in *Pierre* and *The Confidence-Man* is really post-Romantic—Melville's escape from a view of ethos dominated by phenomenological representationality and its corresponding sense of time. In turn it can be argued that post-Romanticism boils down to a postneoclassic attack on the canon of memory as central to rhetorical invention. Crowley argues the hegemony of neoclassic concepts in what becomes the "current-traditional rhetoric" of the nineteenth and twentieth centuries.

3. This issue is discussed in detail in the Coda below.

4. The phantasmic echoes which the lamblike man ushers into *The Confidence-Man* inhabit the novel in a manner similar to that which Dryden discusses in respect to Melville's magazine fiction: "For almost every statement is qualified, twisted, or redirected by the other voices that speak through it, with the result that the present seems troubled by a past that can only manifest itself as a disturbing ghostlike presence" ("From the Piazza" 48).

5. See William Ramsey, " 'Touching' Scenes in *The Confidence-Man*," for a discussion of this theme.

6. On syllepsis, see John Hollander's superb study *The Figure of Echo* and also the essays in *On Puns*, ed. Jonathan Culler; on puns in *The Confidence-Man*, see John G. Blair, "Puns and Equivocations in Melville's *The Confidence-Man*." Writing about "Benito Cereno," Louise K. Barnett points out that "in its successive interpretations of a single structure of events the narrative form is similar to the rhetorical figure of syllepsis" (62).

7. "Ulysses" (90). Melville read Tennyson and bought copies of his works to present to others at a number of points throughout his life (Sealts, *Melville's Reading* 219–20).

12. "Such a cynosure": A Pisgah View of *Billy Budd*

1. Melville's published poetic works were *Battle-Pieces,* a collection of Civil War poems published in 1866; *Clarel,* a narrative poem of 14,000 lines, 1876; and two thematically organized collections: *John Marr and Other Sailors,* 1888, and *Timoleon,* 1891. Among his papers when he died were the manuscript of *Billy Budd* and a draft of an additional collection of poems, "Weeds and Wildings, with a Rose or Two." See Stanton Garner on

Melville's life in the Customs Service. On critical and textual issues central to *Billy Budd*, see *Critical Essays on Melville's Billy Budd, Sailor,* ed. Robert Milder, and Hershel Parker, *Reading Billy Budd,* as well as the Hayford and Sealts edition.

2. Merton M. Sealts in "Innocence and Infamy: *Billy Budd, Sailor*" suggests that "scholars and critics wishing to minimize the subjective element in their approach to *Billy Budd, Sailor* will need to devote more attention than their predecessors to the story as the work of an older Melville" (424). Such a project would require situating Melville in relation to contemporary poetic theory, a task too complex in its own right to be undertaken here.

3. Hershel Parker in *Reading Billy Budd* points out that "when he died on 28 September 1891, Melville was still revising the manuscript of *Billy Budd, Sailor,* not having resolved the direction in which Vere's characterization was to go" (40). One way of assessing Vere's possible "directions" would be to relate him to the extraordinary combination of sentiment, irreverence, and caginess, discussed in detail by William Bysshe Stein, central to "Weeds and Wildings, with a Rose or Two."

4. In "Innocence and Infamy" Sealts summarizes the critical attention, much of it biographically oriented, which Vere's fatherliness has received. Melville's first son, Malcolm, had died of a self-inflicted pistol shot in 1867, and his second, Stanwix, died a thirty-five-year-old wanderer in San Francisco in 1886, "when Melville was presumably at work on the poem and headnote that evolved into *Billy Budd*" (416). Melville's grief and guilt, perhaps renewed by the death of his older sister Helen in 1888, could have been a motive for the retrospective allegory, and Vere's role in it, that the novel became as he continued to revise it.

5. See Barbara Johnson (80–81) on the several endings of *Billy Budd.*

13. Coda: Tropics of Fiction

1. This topic is amply covered in previously cited studies by Berlin, Crowley, Genette, Kennedy, and Vickers, among others.

2. On Lacan's use of metaphor and metonymy, see Jane Gallop (114–31), also Juliet Flower MacCannell (90–117).

3. On rhetorical (tropological) "disfigurement," see Cynthia Chase.

4. Untersteiner's classical account of the Sophists is qualified and updated by Susan C. Jarratt's *Rereading the Sophists: Classical Rhetoric Refigured.*

5. From this perspective, rhetorical memory shows a strong parallel to the disconnected body-parts or "desiring machines" postulated by Gilles Deleuze and Félix Guattari in *Anti-Oedipus,* another study, like Kristeva's, which puts in play a radically rhetorical approach to discourse without fully recognizing its underlying classical roots.

Works Cited

Abraham, Nicolas. "Notes on the Phantom: A Complement to Freud's Metapsychology."
Trans. Nicholas Rand. *Critical Inquiry* 13 (Winter 1987): 287–92.

——. "Psychoanalytic Esthetics: Time, Rhythm, and the Unconscious." Trans. Nicholas
Rand. *Diacritics* 16 (Fall 1986): 3–14.

——. "The Shell and the Kernel." Trans. Nicholas Rand. *Diacritics* 9 (Spring 1979): 16–31.

Abraham, Nicolas, and Maria Torok. *The Wolf Man's Magic Word: A Cryptonymy.* Trans.
Nicholas Rand. Minneapolis: University of Minnesota Press, 1986.

Abrams, M. H. *The Mirror and the Lamp: Romantic Theory and the Critical Tradition.*
New York: Norton, 1958.

Adams, Hazard, and Leroy Searle, eds. *Critical Theory since 1965.* Tallahassee: Florida
State University Press, 1986.

Anderson, Charles R. *Melville in the South Seas.* New York: Columbia University Press,
1939.

Arac, Jonathan. "'A Romantic Book': *Moby-Dick* and Novel Agency." *Boundary 2* 17
(Summer 1990): 40–59.

Aristotle. *Poetics.* Trans. Leon Golden. Englewood Cliffs, N.J.: Prentice-Hall, 1968.

——. *Rhetoric.* Trans. W. Rhys Roberts. New York: Modern Library, 1954.

Augustine. *On Christian Doctrine.* Trans. D. W. Robertson, Jr. Indianapolis: Bobbs-
Merrill, 1958.

Bakhtin, M. M. *The Dialogic Imagination.* Ed. Michael Holquist. Austin: University of
Texas Press, 1981.

Barnett, Louise K. "'Truth Is Voiceless': Speech and Silence in Melville's *Piazza Tales.*"
Papers on Language and Literature 25 (Winter 1989): 59–66.

Barrett, Laurence. "The Differences in Melville's Poetry." *PMLA* 70 (September 1955):
606–23.

Barthes, Roland. *The Pleasure of the Text.* Trans. Richard Miller. New York: Hill and
Wang, 1975.

——. *S/Z.* Trans. Richard Miller. New York: Hill and Wang, 1974.

Baumlin, James S., and Tita French Baumlin. "Psyche/Logos: Mapping the Terrains of
Mind and Rhetoric." *College English* 51 (March 1989): 245–61.

Bedient, Calvin. "Kristeva and Poetry as Shattered Signification." *Critical Inquiry* 16
(Summer 1990): 807–29.

Bell, Michael Davitt. *The Development of American Romance.* Chicago: University of
Chicago Press, 1980.

Benjamin, Walter. "The Work of Art in the Age of Mechanical Reproduction." In *Il-
luminations,* ed. Hannah Arendt, 217–42. New York: Schocken, 1969.

Benveniste, Emile. *Problems in General Linguistics.* Trans. Mary Elizabeth Meek. Coral Gables, Fla.: University of Miami Press, 1971.

Bercaw, Mary K. *Melville's Sources.* Evanston, Ill.: Northwestern University Press, 1987.

Berlin, James A. *Writing Instruction in Nineteenth-Century American Colleges.* Carbondale: Southern Illinois University Press, 1984.

Berthoff, Warner. *The Example of Melville.* Princeton: Princeton University Press, 1962.

Bezanson, Walter E. "*Moby-Dick:* Document, Drama, Dream." In *A Companion to Melville Studies,* ed. John Bryant, 169–210. New York: Greenwood Press, 1986.

Bickley, R. Bruce, Jr. *The Method of Melville's Short Fiction.* Durham, N.C.: Duke University Press, 1975.

Blair, Hugh. *Lectures on Rhetoric and Belles Lettres.* 1785 ed. 3 vols. New York: Garland, 1970.

Blair, John G. "Puns and Equivocations in Melville's *The Confidence-Man.*" *American Transcendental Quarterly* 22 (Spring 1974): 91–95.

Blansett, Barbara Ruth Nieweg. "From Dark to Dark: *Mardi,* a Foreshadowing of *Pierre.*" *Southern Quarterly* 1 (April 1963): 213–27.

Bloom, Harold. *The Anxiety of Influence.* New York: Oxford University Press, 1973.

———. "The Internalization of Quest-Romance." In *Romanticism and Consciousness,* ed. Harold Bloom, 3–23. New York: Norton, 1970.

———. *A Map of Misreading.* New York: Oxford University Press, 1975.

———. *Ringers in the Tower.* Chicago: University of Chicago Press, 1971.

———. *Shelley's Mythmaking.* Ithaca: Cornell University Press, 1969.

———. *Wallace Stevens: The Poems of Our Climate.* Ithaca: Cornell University Press, 1977.

Blumenberg, Hans. *Work on Myth.* Trans. Robert M. Wallace. Cambridge: MIT Press, 1985.

Branch, Watson. "The Quest for *Mardi.*" In *A Companion to Melville Studies,* ed. John Bryant, 123–43. New York: Greenwood Press, 1986.

Braswell, William. "The Early Love Scenes in Melville's *Pierre.*" In *Critical Essays on Herman Melville's Pierre,* ed. Brian Higgins and Hershel Parker, 210–16. Boston: G. K. Hall, 1983.

Brodhead, Richard H. *Hawthorne, Melville, and the Novel.* Chicago: University of Chicago Press, 1976.

———. "*Mardi:* Creating the Creative." In *New Perspectives on Melville,* ed. Faith Pullin, 29–53. Kent, Ohio: Kent State University Press, 1978.

———. *The School of Hawthorne.* New York: Oxford University Press, 1986.

Brodtkorb, Paul, Jr. *Ishmael's White World.* New Haven: Yale University Press, 1965.

Brooks, Peter. "The Idea of a Psychoanalytic Literary Criticism." *Critical Inquiry* 13 (Winter 1987): 334–48.

Bryant, John, ed. *A Companion to Melville Studies.* New York: Greenwood Press, 1986.

———. "*The Confidence-Man:* Melville's Problem Novel." In *A Companion to Melville Studies,* ed. John Bryant, 315–50. New York: Greenwood Press, 1986.

Buell, Lawrence. "The Last Word on *The Confidence-Man?*" *Illinois Quarterly* 35 (November 1957): 15–29.

Burke, Kenneth. *A Grammar of Motives.* New York: Braziller, 1955.

Cabibbo, Paola, and Paola Ludovici. "'Bartleby': Il sistema semantico della doppia negazione." In *Melvilliana,* ed. Paola Cabibbo, 43–59. Rome: Bulzoni Editore, 1983.

Cameron, Sharon. *The Corporeal Self: Allegories of the Body in Melville and Hawthorne.* Baltimore: Johns Hopkins University Press, 1981.

Campbell, George. *The Philosophy of Rhetoric.* Ed. Lloyd F. Bitzer. Carbondale: Southern Illinois University Press, 1963.

Cassirer, Ernst. *The Philosophy of Symbolic Forms.* 2 vols. Trans. Ralph Mannheim. New Haven: Yale University Press, 1953.

Cavell, Stanley. "Freud and Philosophy: A Fragment." *Critical Inquiry* 13 (Winter 1987): 386–93.

Chase, Cynthia. *Decomposing Figures: Rhetorical Readings in the Romantic Tradition.* Baltimore: Johns Hopkins University Press, 1986.

Clark, Michael. "Melville's *Typee:* Fact, Fiction, and Esthetics." In *Critical Essays on Herman Melville's Typee,* ed. Milton R. Stern, 211–25. Boston: G. K. Hall, 1982.

Cohen, Jean. "A Theory of the Figure." In *French Literary Theory Today: A Reader,* ed. Tzvetan Todorov, 65–91. Cambridge: Cambridge University Press, 1982.

Coleridge, Samuel Taylor. *Biographia Literaria.* Ed. George Watson. London: Dent, 1956.

Connors, Robert J. "The Rhetoric of Explanation: Explanatory Rhetoric from Aristotle to 1850." *Written Communication* 1 (1984): 189–210.

Cowan, Bainard. *Exiled Waters: Moby-Dick and the Crisis of Allegory.* Baton Rouge: Louisiana State University Press, 1982.

Crowley, Sharon. *The Methodical Memory: Invention in Current-Traditional Rhetoric.* Carbondale: Southern Illinois University Press, 1991.

Culler, Jonathan, ed. *On Puns: The Foundation of Letters.* New York: Basil Blackwell, 1988.

Dana, Richard Henry, Jr. *Two Years before the Mast.* 1912. Reprint. London: Dent, 1972.

Dauber, Kenneth. *The Idea of Authorship in America: Democratic Poetics from Franklin to Melville.* Madison: University of Wisconsin Press, 1990.

Davis, Merrell R. *Melville's Mardi: A Chartless Voyage.* New Haven: Yale University Press, 1952.

Davis, Robert Con, ed. *The Fictional Father: Lacanian Readings of the Text.* Amherst: University of Massachusetts Press, 1981.

Deleuze, Gilles, and Félix Guattari. *Anti-Oedipus.* Trans. Helen R. Lane, Robert Hurley, and Mark Seem. New York: Viking, 1977.

Derrida, Jacques. "The Art of *Mémoires.*" Trans. Jonathan Culler. In *Memoires for Paul De Man,* 45–88. New York: Columbia University Press, 1986.

———. "White Mythology." Trans. Barbara Johnson. In *Dissemination,* 230–45. Chicago: University of Chicago Press, 1983.

Diderot, Denis. *Rameau's Nephew and Other Works.* Trans. Jacques Barzun and Ralph H. Bowen. New York: Doubleday, 1956.

Dillingham, William B. *An Artist in the Rigging: The Early Works of Herman Melville.* Athens: University of Georgia Press, 1972.

———. *Melville's Short Fiction, 1853–1856.* Athens: University of Georgia Press, 1977.

Dimock, Wai-chee. *Empire for Liberty: Melville and the Poetics of Individualism.* Princeton: Princeton University Press, 1989.

Douglas, Ann. *The Feminization of American Culture.* New York: Alfred A. Knopf, 1977.

Dryden, Edgar A. "From the Piazza to the Enchanted Isles: Melville's Textual Rovings." In *After Strange Texts: The Role of Theory in the Study of Literature,* ed. Gregory S. Jay and David L. Miller, 47–69. Tuscaloosa: University of Alabama Press, 1985.

———. *Melville's Thematics of Form: The Great Art of Telling the Truth.* Baltimore: Johns Hopkins University Press, 1968.

Duban, James. *Melville's Major Fiction: Politics, Theology, and Imagination.* DeKalb: Northern Illinois University Press, 1983.

Dubois, Jacques, et al. (Groupe μ). *A General Rhetoric.* Trans. Paul B. Burrell and Edgar M. Slotkin. Baltimore: Johns Hopkins University Press, 1981.

Durand, Régis. " 'The Captive King': The Absent Father in Melville's Text." In *The Fictional Father,* ed. Robert Con Davis, 48–72. Amherst: University of Massachusetts Press, 1981.

Eco, Umberto. *Semiotics and the Philosophy of Language.* Bloomington: Indiana University Press, 1984.

Emerson, Ralph Waldo. *Essays: First Series.* Ed. Joseph Slater. Cambridge: Harvard University Press, 1979.

Feidelson, Charles, Jr. *Symbolism and American Literature.* Chicago: University of Chicago Press, 1953.

Fisher, Marvin. *Going Under: Melville's Short Fiction and the American 1850's.* Baton Rouge: Louisiana State University Press, 1977.

Foucault, Michel. "What Is an Author?" Trans. Donald F. Bouchard and Sherry Simon. In *Language, Counter-Memory, Practice,* ed. Donald F. Bouchard, 113–38. Ithaca: Cornell University Press, 1977.

Frank, Joseph. *The Widening Gyre.* New Brunswick, N.J.: Rutgers University Press, 1963.

Franklin, H. Bruce. *The Wake of the Gods: Melville's Mythology.* Stanford, Calif.: Stanford University Press, 1963.

Fussell, Edwin. *Frontier: American Literature and the American West.* Princeton: Princeton University Press, 1965.

Gallop, Jane. *Reading Lacan.* Ithaca: Cornell University Press, 1985.

Garber, Frederick, ed. *Romantic Irony.* Budapest: Akadémiai Kiadó, 1988.

Garner, Stanton. "Surviving in the Gilded Age: Herman Melville in the Customs Service." *Essays in Arts and Sciences* 15 (June 1986): 1–14.

Genette, Gérard. *Figures of Literary Discourse.* Trans. Alan Sheridan. New York: Columbia University Press, 1982.

Gilman, William H. *Melville's Early Life and Redburn.* New York: New York University Press, 1951.

Golden, James L., and Edward P. J. Corbett. *The Rhetoric of Blair, Campbell, and Whately.* New York: Holt, Rinehart and Winston, 1968.

Goldman, Stan. "The Small Voice of Silence: Melville's Narrative Voices in *Clarel.*" *Texas Studies in Literature and Language* 31 (Fall 1989): 451–73.

Greimas, A.-J. *Structural Semantics: An Attempt at a Method.* Trans. Daniele McDowell, Ronald Schleifer, and Alan Velie. Lincoln: University of Nebraska Press, 1983.

Guetti, James. *The Limits of Metaphor.* Ithaca: Cornell University Press, 1967.

Guthrie, Warren. "The Development of Rhetorical Theory in America, 1635–1850." *Speech Monographs* 13 (1946): 14–22; 14 (1947): 38–54; 15 (1948): 61–71; 16 (1949): 98–113; 18 (1951): 17–30.

Hattenhauer, Darryl. "Ambiguities of Time in Melville's 'The Encantadas.' " *American Transcendental Quarterly* 56 (March 1985): 5–17.

Hauss, Jon. "Masquerades of Language in Melville's *Benito Cereno.*" *Arizona Quarterly* 44 (Summer 1988): 5–21.

Hayford, Harrison. "Unnecessary Duplicates: A Key to the Writing of *Moby-Dick.*" In *New Perspectives on Melville,* ed. Faith Pullin, 128–61. Kent, Ohio: Kent State University Press, 1978.

Heidegger, Martin. *Poetry, Language, Thought*. Trans. Peter D. Hertz. New York: Harper and Row, 1971.

Herbert, T. Walter, Jr. *Marquesan Encounters: Melville and the Meaning of Civilization*. Cambridge: Harvard University Press, 1980.

Herder, Johann Gottfried. *On the Origin of Language*. Trans. John H. Moran and Alexander Gode. Chicago: University of Chicago Press, 1966.

Hetherington, Hugh W. *Melville's Reviewers: British and American, 1846–1891*. Chapel Hill: University of North Carolina Press, 1961.

Higgins, Brian, and Hershel Parker, eds. *Critical Essays on Herman Melville's "Pierre; or, The Ambiguities."* Boston: G. K. Hall, 1983.

———. "The Flawed Grandeur of Melville's *Pierre*." In *New Perspectives on Melville*, ed. Faith Pullin, 240–66. Kent, Ohio: Kent State University Press, 1978.

———. "Reading *Pierre*." In *A Companion to Melville Studies*, ed. John Bryant, 211–40. New York: Greenwood Press, 1986.

Hillway, Tyrus. "Taji's Abdication in Herman Melville's *Mardi*." *American Literature* 16 (November 1944): 204–7.

Hirsch, E. D., Jr. *Validity in Interpretation*. New Haven: Yale University Press, 1973.

Hollander, John. *The Figure of Echo*. Berkeley: University of California Press, 1981.

Howard, Leon. *Herman Melville*. Berkeley: University of California Press, 1951.

Inge, M. Thomas. *Bartleby the Inscrutable: A Collection of Commentary on Herman Melville's Tale "Bartleby the Scrivener."* Hamden, Conn.: Archon Books, 1979.

Jaffe, David. *"Bartleby the Scrivener" and Bleak House: Melville's Debt to Dickens*. Arlington, Va.: Mardi Press, 1981.

Jakobson, Roman. *Selected Writings II: Word and Language*. Paris and The Hague: Mouton, 1971.

Jakobson, Roman, and Morris Halle. *The Fundamentals of Language*. The Hague: Mouton, 1956.

Jakobson, Roman, and Claude Lévi-Strauss. "Les Chats de Charles Baudelaire." *L'Homme* 2 (1962): 5–21.

Jamieson, Alexander. *A Grammar of Rhetoric and Polite Literature, Comprehending the Principles of Language and Style, the Elements of Taste and Criticism, with Rules for the Study of Composition and Eloquence, Illustrated by Appropriate Examples Selected Chiefly from the British Classics, for the Use of Schools or Private Instruction*. 24th ed. New Haven: Maltby, 1844.

Jarratt, Susan C. *Rereading the Sophists: Classical Rhetoric Refigured*. Carbondale: Southern Illinois University Press, 1991.

Jay, Gregory S. *America the Scrivener: Deconstruction and the Subject of Literary History*. Ithaca: Cornell University Press, 1990.

Johnson, Barbara. "Melville's Fist: The Execution of *Billy Budd*." In *The Critical Difference: Essays in the Contemporary Rhetoric of Reading*, 79–109. Baltimore: Johns Hopkins University Press, 1980.

Kamuf, Peggy. "Abraham's Wake." *Diacritics* 9 (Spring 1979): 32–43.

Kant, Immanuel. *Critique of the Faculty of Judgment*. Trans. James Creed Meredith. Oxford: Oxford University Press, 1952.

Karcher, Carolyn L. *Shadow over the Promised Land: Slavery, Race, and Violence in Melville's America*. Baton Rouge: Louisiana State University Press, 1980.

Kaufmann, Walter. *Discovering the Mind*. Vol. 1. New York: McGraw-Hill, 1980.

Kaul, A. N. "Herman Melville: The New-World Voyageur." In *The American Vision:*

Actual and Ideal Society in Nineteenth-Century Fiction, 222–35. New Haven: Yale University Press, 1963.

Kellner, Hans. "The Inflatable Trope as Narrative Theory: Structure or Allegory?" *Diacritics* 11 (March 1981): 14–28.

Kennedy, George A. *Classical Rhetoric and Its Christian and Secular Tradition from Ancient to Modern Times.* Chapel Hill: University of North Carolina Press, 1980.

Kenny, Vincent. *Herman Melville's Clarel: A Spiritual Autobiography.* Hamden: Shoe String Press, 1973.

Kermode, Frank. *The Sense of an Ending.* New York: Oxford University Press, 1967.

Kierkegaard, Søren. *The Concept of Irony.* Trans. L. M. Capel. Bloomington: Indiana University Press, 1968.

Kopley, Richard. "The Circle and Its Center in 'Bartleby the Scrivener.'" *ATQ [American Transcendental Quarterly]* 2 (September 1988): 191–206.

Kristeva, Julia. *Revolution in Poetic Language.* Trans. Margaret Waller. New York: Columbia University Press, 1984.

Lacan, Jacques. *Écrits: A Selection.* Trans. Alan Sheridan. New York: Norton, 1977.

LaCapra, Dominick. "Who Rules Metaphor?" *Diacritics* 10 (Winter 1980): 15–28.

Lakoff, George, and Mark Johnson. *Metaphors We Live By.* Chicago: University of Chicago Press, 1980.

Langbaum, Robert. *The Poetry of Experience.* New York: Norton, 1963.

Lawrence, D. H. *Studies in Classic American Literature.* New York: Thomas Seltzer, 1923.

Lebowitz, Alan. *Progress into Silence: A Study of Melville's Heroes.* Bloomington: Indiana University Press, 1970.

Lee, A. Robert. "Voices Off, On and Without: Ventriloquy in *The Confidence-Man.*" In *Herman Melville: Reassessments,* ed. A. Robert Lee, 157–75. Totowa, N.J.: Barnes and Noble, 1984.

Levine, Stuart. "Melville's 'Voyage Thither.'" *Midwest Quarterly* 3 (Summer 1962): 341–53.

Lévi-Strauss, Claude. *The Raw and the Cooked.* Trans. John Weightman and Doreen Weightman. New York: Harper and Row, 1969.

Leyda, Jay. *The Melville Log.* 2 vols. New York: Harcourt, Brace, 1951.

McCall, Dan. *The Silence of Bartleby.* Ithaca: Cornell University Press, 1989.

MacCannell, Juliet Flower. *Figuring Lacan: Criticism and the Cultural Unconscious.* London: Croom Helm, 1986.

Mac Cormac, Earl R. *A Cognitive Theory of Metaphor.* Cambridge: MIT Press, 1985.

Mailloux, Steven. *Rhetorical Power.* Ithaca: Cornell University Press, 1989.

Man, Paul de. "Action and Identity in Nietzsche." *Yale French Studies* 52 (1975): 16–30.

———. "The Rhetoric of Temporality." In *Blindness and Insight,* 2d rev. ed., 187–228. Minneapolis: University of Minnesota Press, 1983.

Marovitz, Sanford E. "More Chartless Voyaging: Melville and Adler at Sea." In *Studies in the American Renaissance, 1986,* ed. Joel Myerson, 373–84. Charlottesville: University Press of Virginia, 1986.

Marryat, Frederic. *Peter Simple.* London: Victor Gallencz, 1969.

Matthiessen, F. O. *American Renaissance: Art and Expression in the Age of Emerson and Whitman.* New York: Oxford University Press, 1941.

Mellard, James M. *Doing Tropology: Analysis of Narrative Discourse.* Urbana: University of Illinois Press, 1987.

Mellor, Anne K. *English Romantic Irony.* Cambridge: Harvard University Press, 1980.

Melville, Herman. *Billy Budd, Sailor.* Ed. Harrison Hayford and Merton M. Sealts, Jr. Chicago: University of Chicago Press, 1962.

——. *Clarel: A Poem and a Pilgrimage in the Holy Land.* Ed. Walter Bezanson. New York: Hendricks House, 1960.

——. *Collected Poems of Herman Melville.* Ed. Howard P. Vincent. Chicago: Hendricks House, 1947.

——. *The Confidence-Man: His Masquerade.* Ed. Harrison Hayford et al. Historical Note by Watson Branch, Hershel Parker, and Harrison Hayford with Alma A. MacDougall. Evanston, Ill.: Northwestern University Press and Newberry Library, 1984.

——. *Journals.* Ed. Harrison Hayford et al. Historical Note by Howard C. Horsford with Lynn Horth. Evanston, Ill.: Northwestern University Press and Newberry Library, 1989.

——. *The Letters of Herman Melville.* Ed. Merrell R. Davis and William H. Gilman. New Haven: Yale University Press, 1960.

——. *Mardi, and a Voyage Thither.* Ed. Harrison Hayford et al. Historical Note by Elizabeth S. Foster. Evanston, Ill.: Northwestern University Press and Newberry Library, 1970.

——. *Moby-Dick.* Ed. Harrison Hayford et al. Historical Note by Harrison Hayford, Hershel Parker, and G. Thomas Tanselle. Evanston, Ill.: Northwestern University Press and Newberry Library, 1988.

——. *Omoo: A Narrative of Adventures in the South Seas.* Ed. Harrison Hayford et al. Historical Note by Gordon Roper. Evanston, Ill.: Northwestern University Press and Newberry Library, 1968.

——. *The Piazza Tales, and Other Prose Pieces, 1839–1860.* Ed. Harrison Hayford et al. Historical Note by Merton M. Sealts, Jr. Evanston, Ill.: Northwestern University Press and Newberry Library, 1987.

——. *Pierre.* Ed. Henry A. Murray. New York: Hendricks House, 1962.

——. *Pierre; or, The Ambiguities.* Ed. Harrison Hayford et al. Historical Note by Leon Howard and Hershel Parker. Evanston, Ill.: Northwestern University Press and Newberry Library, 1971.

——. *Poems of Herman Melville.* Ed. Douglas Robillard. New Haven: College and University Press, 1976.

——. *Redburn: His First Voyage.* Ed. Harrison Hayford et al. Historical Note by Hershel Parker. Evanston, Ill.: Northwestern University Press and Newberry Library, 1969.

——. *Typee; or, A Peep at Polynesian Life.* Ed. Harrison Hayford et al. Historical Note by Leon Howard. Evanston, Ill.: Northwestern University Press and Newberry Library, 1968.

——. *White Jacket; or, The World in a Man-of-War.* Ed. Harrison Hayford et al. Historical Note by Willard Thorp. Evanston, Ill.: Northwestern University Press and Newberry Library, 1970.

Milder, Robert. *Critical Essays on Melville's Billy Budd, Sailor.* Boston: G. K. Hall, 1989.

——. " '*Nemo Contra Deum . . .*': Melville and Goethe's 'Demonic.' " In *Ruined Eden of the Present: Hawthorne, Melville, and Poe,* ed. G. R. Thompson and Virgil Lokke, 205–44. West Lafayette, Ind.: Purdue University Press, 1981.

Miller, Edwin Haviland. *Melville.* New York: Braziller, 1975.

Miller, J. Hillis. *The Ethics of Reading.* New York: Columbia University Press, 1986.

Miller, Perry. *The Raven and the Whale: The War of Words and Wits in the Era of Poe and Melville.* New York: Harcourt, Brace, 1956.

Mizruchi, Susan. "Cataloging the Creatures of the Deep: 'Billy Budd, Sailor' and the Rise of Sociology." *Boundary 2* 17 (Spring 1990): 272–304.

Newman, Lea Bertani Vozar. *A Reader's Guide to the Short Stories of Herman Melville.* Boston: G. K. Hall, 1986.

Newman, Samuel. *A Practical System of Rhetoric of the Principles and Rule of Style Inferred from Examples of Writing, to Which Is Added a Historical Dissertation on English Style.* 7th ed. Boston: Newman, 1838.

Ong, Walter. *Ramus, Method, and the Decay of Dialogue.* Cambridge: Harvard University Press, 1958.

Parker, Hershel. *Flawed Texts and Verbal Icons: Literary Authority in American Fiction.* Evanston, Ill.: Northwestern University Press, 1984.

——. *Reading Billy Budd.* Evanston, Ill.: Northwestern University Press, 1990.

Poe, Edgar Allan. *Poetry and Tales.* New York: Library of America, 1984.

Poulet, Georges. "Phenomenology of Reading." In *Critical Theory since Plato,* ed. Hazard Adams, 1213–22. New York: Harcourt Brace, 1971.

Quintilian, Marcus Fabius. *Institutio Oratoria.* 4 vols. Rpt. 1976. Trans. H. E. Butler. Cambridge: Harvard University Press, 1921.

Ramsey, William M. " 'Touching' Scenes in *The Confidence-Man.*" *ESQ* 25 (First Quarter 1979): 37–62.

Rhetorica ad Herennium. Trans. H. Caplan. London: Loeb Classical Library, 1954.

Rice, Donald, and Peter Schofer. *Rhetorical Poetics: Theory and Practice of Figural and Symbolic Reading in Modern French Literature.* Madison: University of Wisconsin Press, 1983.

Richards, I. A. *The Philosophy of Rhetoric.* London: Oxford University Press, 1971.

Ricoeur, Paul. *Interpretation Theory: Discourse and the Surplus of Meaning.* Fort Worth: Texas Christian University Press, 1976.

——. *The Rule of Metaphor.* Trans. Robert Czerny. Toronto: University of Toronto Press, 1977.

Riffaterre, Michael. "The Intertextual Unconscious." *Critical Inquiry* 13 (Winter 1987): 371–85.

——. *Text Production.* Trans. Terese Lyons. New York: Columbia University Press, 1983.

Rogin, Michael Paul. *Subversive Genealogy: The Politics and Art of Herman Melville.* New York: Alfred A. Knopf, 1983.

Rowe, John Carlos. *Through the Custom-House: Nineteenth-Century American Fiction and Modern Theory.* Baltimore: Johns Hopkins University Press, 1982.

Runden, John P. "Columbia Grammar School: An Overlooked Year in the Lives of Gansevoort and Herman Melville." *Melville Society Extracts* 46 (May 1981): 1–3.

Samson, John. "The Dynamics of History and Fiction in Melville's *Typee.*" *American Quarterly* 36 (1984): 276–90.

——. *White Lies: Melville's Narratives of Facts.* Ithaca: Cornell University Press, 1989.

Saussure, Ferdinand de. *Course in General Linguistics.* Trans. Wade Baskin. New York: McGraw-Hill, 1966.

Sealts, Merton M., Jr. "Innocence and Infamy: *Billy Budd, Sailor.*" In *A Companion to Melville Studies,* ed. John Bryant, 407–30. New York: Greenwood Press, 1986.

——. *Melville's Reading.* Rev. ed. Columbia: University of South Carolina Press, 1988.

———. *Pursuing Melville, 1940–1980.* Madison: University of Wisconsin Press, 1982.

Seelye, John. *Melville: The Ironic Diagram.* Evanston, Ill.: Northwestern University Press, 1970.

Sherrill, Rowland A. *The Prophetic Melville: Experience, Transcendence, and Tragedy.* Athens: University of Georgia Press, 1979.

Short, Bryan C. "'The Author at the Time': Tommo and Melville's Self-Discovery in *Typee.*" *Texas Studies in Literature and Language* 31 (Fall 1989): 386–405.

———. "Form as Vision in Herman Melville's *Clarel.*" *American Literature* 50 (January 1979): 553–69.

———. "'Like bed of asparagus': Melville and Architecture." In *Savage Eye: Melville and the Visual Arts,* ed. Christopher Sten. Kent: Kent State University Press, 1992.

———. "Literary Ethos: Dispersion, Resistance, Mystification." In *Ethos: New Essays in Rhetorical and Critical Theory,* ed. James S. and Tita French Baumlin. Dallas: Southern Methodist University Press, 1992.

———. "'Memory's Mint': Melville's Parable of the Imagination in *John Marr and Other Sailors.*" *Essays in Arts and Sciences* 15 (June 1986): 31–42.

———. "'The Redness of the Rose': The *Mardi* Poems and Melville's Artistic Compromise." *Essays in Arts and Sciences* 5 (July 1976): 100–112.

———. "The Temporality of Rhetoric." *Rhetoric Review* 7 (Spring 1989): 367–79.

Simpson, David. *Fetishism and Imagination.* Baltimore: Johns Hopkins University Press, 1982.

Sitney, P. Adams. "Ahab's Name: A Reading of 'The Symphony.'" In *Modern Critical Views: Herman Melville,* ed. Harold Bloom, 223–38. New York: Chelsea House, 1986.

Smith, Adam. *Lectures on Rhetoric and Belles Lettres.* Ed. John M. Lothian. Carbondale: Southern Illinois University Press, 1971.

Smith, Gayle L. "The Word and the Thing: *Moby-Dick* and the Limits of Language." *ESQ* 31 (1985): 260–71.

Smith, Peter A. "Entropy in Melville's 'Bartleby the Scrivener.'" *Centennial Review* 32 (Spring 1988): 155–62.

Stein, William Bysshe. *The Poetry of Melville's Late Years.* Albany: State University of New York Press, 1970.

Stern, Milton R. *The Fine-Hammered Steel of Herman Melville.* Urbana: University of Illinois Press, 1957.

Stewart, Susan. "The Interdiction." *Profession 89:* 10–14.

Sundquist, Eric J. *Home as Found: Authority and Genealogy in Nineteenth-Century American Literature.* Baltimore: Johns Hopkins University Press, 1979.

———. "Suspense and Tautology in *Benito Cereno.*" *Glyph* 8 (1981): 103–26.

Sussman, Henry. "The Deconstructor as Politician: Melville's *Confidence-Man.*" *Glyph* 4 (1978): 32–56.

Tennyson, Alfred. *Poetical Works.* Rpt. 1962. London: Oxford University Press, 1953.

Thompson, Lawrence. *Melville's Quarrel with God.* Princeton: Princeton University Press, 1952.

Tichi, Cecelia. "Melville's Craft and the Theme of Language Debased in *The Confidence-Man.*" *ELH: A Journal of English Literary History* 39 (December 1972): 639–58.

Titus, David K. "Herman Melville at the Albany Academy." *Melville Society Extracts* 42 (May 1980): 1, 4–10.

Todorov, Tzvetan. *Littérature et Signification.* Paris: Larousse, 1967.

Tolchin, Neal L. *Mourning, Gender, and Creativity in the Art of Herman Melville*. New Haven: Yale University Press, 1988.

Travis, Mildred K. "Melville's Furies: Technique in *Mardi* and *Moby-Dick*." *ESQ* 47 (Second Quarter 1967): 71–73.

Trimpi, Helen P. *Melville's Confidence Men and American Politics in the 1850's*. Hamden: Connecticut Academy of Arts and Sciences, 1987.

Turner, Mark. *Death Is the Mother of Beauty*. Chicago: University of Chicago Press, 1987.

Untersteiner, Mario. *The Sophists*. Trans. Kathleen Freeman. New York: Philosophical Library, 1954.

Verene, Donald Philip. *Hegel's Recollection: A Study of Images in the Phenomenology of Spirit*. Albany: State University of New York Press, 1985.

Vickers, Brian. *In Defense of Rhetoric*. Oxford: Clarendon Press, 1988.

Vico, Giambattista. *The New Science*. Trans. T. G. Bergin and M. H. Fisch. Ithaca: Cornell University Press, 1971.

Vincent, Howard P. *The Trying-Out of Moby-Dick*. Carbondale: Southern Illinois University Press, 1949.

Wadlington, Warwick. *The Confidence Game in American Literature*. Princeton: Princeton University Press, 1975.

Wald, Priscilla. "Hearing Narrative Voices in Melville's *Pierre*." *Boundary 2* 71 (Spring 1990): 100–132.

Walker, Cheryl. "Feminist Literary Criticism and the Author." *Critical Inquiry* 16 (Spring 1990): 551–71.

Warner, Susan [pseud. Elizabeth Wetherell]. *The Wide, Wide World*. New York: G. P. Putnam, 1856.

Wenke, John. "Melville's *Typee*: A Tale of Two Worlds." In *Critical Essays on Herman Melville's Typee*, ed. Milton R. Stern, 250–58. Boston: G. K. Hall, 1982.

Whately, Richard. *The Elements of Rhetoric*. Ed. Douglas Ehninger. Carbondale: Southern Illinois University Press, 1963.

White, Hayden. *Tropics of Discourse*. Baltimore: Johns Hopkins University Press, 1978.

Widmer, Kingsley. *The Ways of Nihilism: A Study of Herman Melville's Short Novels*. Los Angeles: Anderson, Ritchie and Simon (for the California State Colleges), 1970.

Witherington, Paul. "The Art of Melville's *Typee*." *Arizona Quarterly* 26 (1970): 136–50.

Wozniak, John Michael. *English Composition in Eastern Colleges, 1850–1940*. Washington, D.C.: University Press of America, 1978.

Yannella, Donald. "Writing the '*Other* Way': Melville, the Duyckinck Crowd, and Literature for the Masses." In *A Companion to Melville Studies*, ed. John Bryant, 63–81. New York: Greenwood Press, 1986.

Zoellner, Robert. *The Salt-Sea Mastodon*. Berkeley: University of California Press, 1973.

Index